Infertility
and the
Creative Spirit

Roxane Head Dinkin
and
Robert J. Dinkin

iUniverse, Inc.
Bloomington

Infertility and the Creative Spirit

iUniverse books may be ordered through booksellers or by contacting:

iUniverse
1663 Liberty Drive
Bloomington, IN 47403
www.iuniverse.com
1-800-Authors (1-800-288-4677)

ISBN: 978-0-5955-1731-2 (pbk)
ISBN: 978-0-5956-2009-8 (ebk)
ISBN: 978-0-5955-0585-2 (hbk)

Printed in the United States of America

iUniverse rev. date: 3/15/2011

ACKNOWLEDGMENTS

We would like to express our deep appreciation to the many people who helped us over the years in bringing this project to its completion, starting with Jean O'Barr, Professor Emeritus of Women's Studies at Duke University, whose invitation to join the department in 1998-99 as visiting scholars and whose ongoing interest in our research helped our book to be conceptualized and drafted. Our gratitude also goes to Ellen Gruenbaum, former Dean of the School of Social Sciences at California State University, Fresno, whose administrative support allowed us to take a sabbatical leave to conduct the research. We would also like to thank members of Roxane's writing group at Duke, Katherine Carter, Canadian literature scholar, and Monica Russell y Rodriguez, anthropologist and Chicano/a studies scholar, without whose encouragement and feedback this project would have taken a different form. We are grateful to the many librarians who guided our research at Duke, UNC Chapel Hill, Vassar College, the Georgia Historical Society, the St. Augustine Historical Society, the Library of Congress, California State University, Fresno, and New College, Sarasota, Florida, and especially to Elizabeth Dunn of Duke University's Special Collections, who introduced us to the Campbell Family Archives. Many thanks as well to our readers: Teresa Bailey, Judy Diamond, Marilyn Gelber, Gail Goodwin Gomez, Karen Johnson, Pamela Lackie, Melody Lowman, Justine Strand, Norma Whitfield, and Anita Wilkerson, whose thoughtful comments and suggestions helped shape the book's final form. We also appreciate the technical assistance provided by Ron Ullman, Ethan Hertz, and Dan Able and photographic assistance from Clarence Jones. Thanks too to our family, friends, and colleagues for listening patiently to our stories about infertile women, wondering if the project would ever be completed. Finally, this book is dedicated to our students and clients, from whom we learned a great deal and whom we hope to give back.

CONTENTS

Photo courtesy of Thinkstock.

Chapter 1
Introduction

This book is about women in the past who wanted to have children and could not. It has its origins more than fifteen years ago in our own experiences as an infertile couple. When we were unable to have a child, we asked ourselves what we could create together. Robert was teaching and researching American women's history at California State University, Fresno. Roxane was working as a clinical psychologist in San Francisco counseling women and couples facing infertility, and had written a workbook to help people prepare emotionally to undertake IVF (in vitro fertilization). Focusing on the intersection of reproductive psychology and women's history, we wondered how involuntarily childless women in previous generations had dealt with infertility and pregnancy loss. Prior to the past four decades, women who had such difficulties did not have the options of advanced reproductive technology, and could not expect much medical assistance as they struggled to have children. Adding to the already isolating experience of infertility, reproduction was long viewed as a private matter not to be spoken about openly. Motherhood was considered central to women's identity, and those unable to produce children were frequently scorned and looked down upon. Mary Chesnut, an accomplished woman who gained posthumous fame for a book based on her detailed diaries of the Civil War era, nevertheless referred to herself as "a childless wretch," after listening to her relatives' implicit criticism of her reproductive failures. She once recorded a family discussion where her mother-in-law boasted of her offspring, including twenty-seven grandchildren, to which her father-in-law, turning to his wife, added: "*You* have not been a *useless* woman in this world."[1] Given such attitudes, how did women in the past, like Mary Chesnut, cope with feelings of uselessness and respond to the social ostracism they often endured?

To answer these questions, we began to identify women in history who were involuntarily childless, searching through various biographical and autobiographical accounts of past prominent women that might contain relevant information. But because most people remained silent regarding reproductive matters, this task was not easy. Even if a woman was known not to have born children, it often proved difficult to ascertain whether her childlessness was voluntary, situational, or involuntary. In the absence of contradictory evidence, we tended to exclude from our study those women who appeared to be childless by choice or circumstance, such as a brief marriage or being initially wed at an age—in their late thirties and beyond—where childbearing was unlikely. (Before recent reproductive breakthroughs and increasing social options, age and length of marriage were the main factors in determining the possibility of childbearing.) We also tried to eliminate those couples where male factor infertility may have been responsible for lack of conception. Still, we ultimately uncovered close to a hundred notable women from the past two centuries about whom some evidence of infertility exists, and we studied their lives to understand how they were affected by reproductive trauma and the inability to have a child. Infertility, we noticed, was often a major defining event for such women and profoundly influenced their subsequent life course. As we will see, in most instances the lives they led were far from "useless."

Our book began to take its present shape a decade ago when we had the privilege of spending a sabbatical year at Duke University in the Women's Studies Department. As we researched the subject and talked with colleagues, our study evolved from the general to the specific, from analyzing various coping patterns among infertile women to focused biographies of seven highly creative individuals. With the focused biography format, the story of each person centers on a basic question: how did each respond to the trauma of infertility and seek to rebuild meaning and identity in her life? Personal relationships and career achievements are not neglected but are viewed with an eye toward their connection with infertility. Using a feminist approach to biography, we look especially at biological issues and attitudes toward motherhood, and how a woman's failure to produce offspring affected her life choices in her time. While two fairly recent scholarly books address the medical and social implications of infertility in American history,[2] and brief studies of certain aspects of the subject exist for a few other countries, the impact of infertility on the lives of individual women of the past has been relatively neglected. Until very recently, terms such as infertility, childlessness, and pregnancy loss were not even indexed in the biographies of most childless women. The authors of many biographical accounts when broaching the topic simply remarked, "she had no children," or ignored mentioning it entirely.[3] We hope that our study opens new avenues for research, bringing attention to the complexities and ambiguity of infertility and reproductive loss in women's lives. We aspire to the active voice described by the editors of *The Challenge of Feminist Biography*: "Inherent in that voice is the willingness to learn from the specificity of a subject's life, to acknowledge and express her complexities, contradictions, and tensions."[4]

Infertility constitutes a profound loss for those women who hold the expectation that they will reproduce. They anticipate bringing new life into the world, nurturing and teaching their offspring, and passing along their genetic and material heritage. Infertility and reproductive loss, however, can disrupt or limit the expression of generativity, or how an individual contributes to and cares for the next generation. The life of an infertile woman, past or present, is atypical regarding expected transitions, as she becomes both excluded and exempt from the demands of childbirth and childrearing. Not being able to bear and raise children can interfere with a woman's projected life path, raising questions about her identity, altering her primary relationships, and moving her toward a more marginal position in society. Just as many women today experience reproductive failure as a traumatic event on a par with divorce or death, such feelings were as strong if not stronger long ago when motherhood was a more universal female norm. Whether due to the lack of conception or to pregnancy loss, a woman's inability to reproduce has traditionally been associated with images of abject failure. The Hebrew Talmud, in fact, specifically referred to barrenness as "living death."[5]

On the other hand, the absence of genetic offspring allowed some women the chance to disengage from their investment in the status quo. In the process of adapting to personal loss and marginalized status, certain childless women began to perceive relationships in the world quite differently, a process we have labeled a "perceptual shift." Our use of the term perceptual shift refers to new ways of looking at relationships: the connection between women and work, women and creativity, and women and their bodies, as well as the links between people and animals, human beings and culture, and among racial and religious groups. This shift in perception is something like the switch from a standard camera lens to a telephoto lens, as the distance increases between an infertile woman and the life and culture she has previously assumed for herself. The time and energy that a woman expected to go into childrearing now became available for other kinds of thought and activity. As we will see, how each individual went about redefining identity and engaging in the world depended on her talents and interests, and the historical and situational opportunities available to her.

Our goal is to explore this perceptual shift by means of focused biographies of seven women who struggled in one way or another with infertility, and, as it turns out, accomplished most of their creative work during the first three-quarters of the twentieth century:

Juliette Low, founder of the Girl Scouts of America

Josephine Baker, entertainer and adoptive mother of twelve

Joy Adamson, wildlife conservationist and author of *Born Free*

Frida Kahlo, innovative Mexican artist

Emma Goldman, leading anarchist and social reformer

Ruth Benedict, acclaimed anthropologist and author

Marilyn Monroe, movie star and sexual icon

We selected these particular women to study for a number of reasons. They were among the few who left some record of their thoughts and feelings about their inability to bring children into the world. Several of them produced an autobiography; others wrote letters, gave interviews, passed on information to friends and relatives, or in a variety of ways made reference to their childless state. In addition, the degree of fame each one achieved has encouraged in-depth research into their private lives and yielded further details about their reproductive efforts. Our choice of biographical figures was necessarily narrowed by the limitations of our own historical expertise and knowledge of foreign languages; thus the persons selected are primarily associated with the Western world in modern times. Still, they reflect considerable diversity in regard to ethnicity, religion, culture, language, and socioeconomic background. In terms of geography, these seven women lived for lengthy periods on three continents (North America, Europe, and Africa) and in nine countries (the United States, Mexico, Canada, England, Scotland, France, Austria, Russia, and Kenya).[6] These women also reflect a range of variability in their responses to reproductive failure. Their choices span a continuum from aggressive attempts to overcome infertility (Joy Adamson, Josephine Baker, and Marilyn Monroe) to ambivalence and limited action (Frida Kahlo and Ruth Benedict) to relative acceptance of childlessness (Juliette Low and Emma Goldman). Rather than generalizing about women who experienced infertility from the life stories of these seven highly creative individuals, we hope to explore the complexity of adaptation by each of them to reproductive loss and childlessness.

Definitions and Boundaries of Infertility

While we initially sought a clear-cut definition for infertile women in history (either someone was able to have children or not), we came to appreciate the ambiguity and fluidity in the boundaries between infertility and childlessness by choice or circumstance. In present-day medical terms, infertility is generally defined as the lack of conception after twelve months of unprotected sexual intercourse. Infertility implies that conception has been attempted but without success, whereas involuntary childlessness is a broader term that encompasses all unsuccessful efforts to have children, including pregnancy loss. In reality, many women experience both infertility and reproductive loss, and the rates of miscarriage and premature labor today are actually higher among infertile women attempting to conceive with the help of reproductive technology. In addition, some underlying conditions, such as tubal scarring, are related both to a decreased likelihood of conception as well as to increased incidence of pregnancy loss. Many current writers use the term infertility to include all unsuccessful efforts to have children, including reproductive loss, and we will also be using the term infertility in its broadest meaning. Another term that encompasses both infertility and pregnancy loss is reproductive trauma, a phrase that captures the life-and-death struggles involved in becoming pregnant, carrying a pregnancy to term, and giving birth to a living child. Sometimes we will employ the term "infertile woman," just as we referred to ourselves as an infertile couple, without implying that one's infertile status necessarily defines an individual.

In addition to infertility, childless women can also be childless by situation, or childless by choice, or both, though these categories are not as distinct as they might appear. Many well-known women writers of the nineteenth century, for example, such as Emily Bronte and George Eliot (Mary Ann Evans), never married; they were childless by situation and not necessarily infertile. On the other hand, Margaret Mitchell, writer of *Gone with the Wind* in the 1930s, was childless by choice; she married twice in her twenties but deliberately chose not to attempt conception.[7] Women who are childless by choice today are sometimes referred to as "childfree," an attempt to create a more positive descriptor. Other infertility-related terms include sterility, which implies the permanent inability to conceive, whereas infertility refers to a more ambiguous state. What constituted sterility in the past may be diagnosed as infertility today because many more related physical problems can either be treated or bypassed with the aid of recent reproductive technology. Sterility has been a word that could also be applied to men, but barrenness, an older and more stigmatizing label for those unable to reproduce, was given only to women.

The issue of whether or not a woman in the past was infertile is also complicated by what she said or believed about her condition. Knowingly or unknowingly, individuals sometimes made statements on the subject that have proven to be inaccurate. In our research we found a number of women who altered the facts about their gynecological history in order to put a better light on their situation, i.e., to avoid the stigma of reproductive failure, or perhaps, to ease their own pain. Some women invented pregnancies or miscarriages in an attempt to show that they were once capable of conception, or, like Marilyn Monroe, told stories of having born a child in adolescence and given it away. Certain women who were actually infertile have claimed to be childless by choice, possibly including Lila Wallace, co-founder with her husband Dewitt Wallace, of the *Reader's*

Digest. Wallace stated on numerous occasions that "we have no children quite deliberately," yet a recent biographer argues that her husband may have been infertile, and the fact that she herself was close to thirty-four at the time of their marriage raises the question whether she was still capable of childbearing.[8] (Women who came of age more than a half century ago and married in their mid-thirties appear to have been less likely to bear children than comparable women today.) There are also cases like that of writer Anaïs Nin, who in her published diary and subsequent interviews insisted that "nature" denied her the opportunity to attain motherhood, but whose biographer claims that a flawed late-term abortion procedure was the real cause of her inability to have a child.[9]

Although the medical definition of infertility is straightforward for a particular individual during a given period of time, the boundaries of infertility over a person's life span are much less clear. Infertility can be construed as a continuum, and whether or not someone is viewed as infertile can shift with changing life circumstances. One of our subjects, Marilyn Monroe, tried again and again to bring a pregnancy to term, and underwent surgery to increase the possibility of success, whereas others like Ruth Benedict and Emma Goldman did not, rejecting any risky interventions that might have improved their chances of having children. Some women, like the writer Dorothy Parker, tried to have children in their forties and then suffered recurrent miscarriages;[10] meanwhile, others in that age range, regardless of what they did, were unable to conceive at all. There are also women who produced a child early in life but not again, a condition known as secondary infertility. Among the most famous women to suffer from this misfortune were actress Vivien Leigh and writer Pearl Buck. For Leigh, a miscarriage at age thirty-two during her second marriage (to actor Laurence Olivier) not only brought an end to the possibility of childbearing but seems to have contributed to the development of emotional problems that she experienced in the years to come. Buck, on the other hand, went on to adopt several children and was very active in the international adoption movement, besides writing a huge number of popular novels and nonfiction works.[11]

Another highly neglected aspect of the infertility experience, and one that blurs the lines between voluntary and involuntary childlessness, is ambivalence over whether or not to have a child. Ambivalence is a natural aspect of becoming pregnant, giving birth, and raising children, as these events transform both a woman's biology and her social role. Just as women without fertility problems may have mixed feelings about the physical changes, medical risks, and role implications associated with motherhood, infertile women can similarly experience ambivalence. In our reading, biographers of women have generally categorized their subjects as holding clear-cut positions—either longing intensely for children, or not wanting them at all. In fact, uncertainty regarding the pursuit of motherhood or changing one's mind about it over the course of time has not been unusual; it is as much a part of the complexity of the lives of infertile women as it is in the lives of women who are able to bear children. A good example of such a shift in attitude can be seen in the statements of famed athlete Mildred "Babe" Didrikson. During her thirties when married to wrestler and sports promoter George Zaharias, Didrikson had at least one miscarriage, and was quoted by one of her golfing associates as saying "I'd give up every trophy I ever won if I could have a baby." Yet golfer Betty Dodd, who later became Babe's partner and a kind of surrogate daughter, declared: "She never did say she wished she had a child . . . It didn't sound to me like she was very upset about it. Ever."[12] Perhaps in her situation, as in many others, attitudes toward having children can shift with age and outlook at a particular time and with the quality of a marriage, which in Didrikson's case deteriorated after the first few years.

British feminist sociologists, Gayle Letherby and Catherine Williams, have recently addressed the issue of boundaries between infertility and childlessness by choice. They described non-motherhood, whether voluntary or involuntary, as a "lost discourse in feminism." Bringing their own personal perspectives to bear on the categories of "childless" and "childfree" women, they challenged the stereotypes of women as either pitiable or enviable depending on their assignment to one narrow group or the other. Letherby and Williams commented that the "detailed discussion that validates the experiences of women who don't mother is still lacking."[13] Researching the lives of our historical subjects frequently validated Roxane's own personal observations over the years as an infertile woman and a professional working in the infertility field regarding the boundaries of being fertile or infertile. She found that these exclusive categories of motherhood, infertility, and voluntary childlessness defy the real-life experiences of hope, sorrow, and ambivalence found among all women trying to have children. We hope that our discussion of the seven women we have chosen to study in depth honors the complexity of their personal encounters with infertility, as well as challenging the boundaries of exclusion that women have faced in not having children.

Historical Background: 1860s to 1960s

In looking at the life span of our seven main subjects, we find that their lives collectively cover a chronological period from roughly the 1860s through the 1960s.[14] While we identified a few remarkable childless women from earlier centuries, frequently little or no information about their experience of infertility was available. For example, a notable late-eighteenth-century Floridian, Maria Evans, resident of the "Oldest House" in St. Augustine, was married and widowed three times yet remained childless. She was well known locally through her career as a midwife and also assisted her second husband in running an inn. As she became older, Evans hired a sixteen-year-old male as an apprentice, whom she may have viewed in part as a surrogate child since she left him her entire estate. Her life story, with particular attention to the ways she adapted to her childless condition, was popularized in the historical novel *Maria*, by Eugenia Price,[15] who concluded that Evans might have felt "haunted" by her childlessness. The story of Maria Evans is very interesting in terms of her achievements, which can be documented from the census records[16] and her will.[17] But like virtually all others of her time, she left no statement of her thoughts or feelings about her childlessness, so that anything said about it, like the comment of the author quoted above, is purely conjectural.

The roughly one-hundred-year period from the 1860s to the 1960s saw considerable expansion of freedom and opportunities for women, including access to higher education. In conjunction with educational advances was a growing acceptance of women having careers, though not until recent decades has this been true for married women, and especially for those with children. In the past employers were reluctant to hire young married women, fearing that they would soon become pregnant and leave the job market and were therefore not worth training. The (mostly single) women who sought professional careers during the early twentieth century found that the areas available for employment and the possibilities for advancement were few. Professional women were generally restricted to fields associated with "women's work" such as teaching, nursing, librarianship, and social work. Women involved in these pursuits could be accepted and even admired for what they accomplished. But upper-level positions in business, law, and politics were usually off limits to a woman as they were considered part of a man's world. Women who entered such fields could operate only as men's subordinates or on the fringes, in jobs where they catered mainly to the needs of women. Even in academia, except at women's colleges, female professors were normally confined to teaching in just a few subject areas such as literature, home economics, and physical education. In the realm of entertainment, a number of women were able to achieve considerable renown by the early twentieth century, but stage and screen performers were generally regarded as less than reputable and often had trouble maintaining their popularity as they aged.

The time span of the 1860s to the 1960s also encompassed the rise of modern gynecology, as substantial progress occurred in many aspects of the field and early attempts at infertility treatment took place. Among the major developments were identification and treatment of sexually transmitted diseases, treatment of endometriosis, understanding of male factor infertility and introduction of semen analysis, treatment of tubal factor infertility, and the beginning of safe gynecological surgery. In the late nineteenth century, infertility was as common as it is today, primarily due to the incidence of sexually transmitted diseases such as syphilis and gonorrhea for which there were no cures. While about seven percent of ever-married white women in the United States were childless in 1835, that proportion had climbed to sixteen percent by 1870, and the pattern among African-American women was similar. The availability of sulfa drugs in the 1930s and 1940s improved the chances for successful childbearing, but in recent decades, as people have tended to have more sexual partners and to marry later, the proportion of women who become infertile has increased to about one in eight.

Infertility and Health Status

The biological substrate of infertility not only affected a woman's ability to conceive but had broad health consequences. With many of the more common causes of infertility, including sexually transmitted diseases, the accompanying pelvic pain sometimes limited a woman's overall capacity to function in other spheres. Gonorrhea, for example, in many cases produced pelvic inflammation and acute pain, and syphilis could bring on not only severe discomfort but compromised functioning in a number of organ systems. Endometriosis for some women was also seriously disabling. Whatever the underlying factor, chronic pain in turn could lead to decreased activity, a diminished sense of well-being, and dependence on analgesic medication. One famous infertile woman whose documented syphilis affected her health and influenced her creative focus was the Danish writer Isak Dinesen, best known for her book *Out of Africa*. Dinesen contracted syphilis from her husband Baron Bror Blixen when the couple moved to Kenya around the time of the First World War, rendering her both unhealthy and childless. She was treated for the disease intermittently but unsuccessfully over the rest of her life. As she aged, she suffered increasingly from severe pain and reduced mobility associated with syphilitic spinal degeneration. In referring to her condition, Dinesen regarded syphilis as the price she had paid for her title of Baroness (obtained through marrying Blixen) and for her success as an author. Her writing often reflected themes of illness, infertility, and dead or deformed children. According to her biographer Judith Thurman, Dinesen claimed that "she had promised the Devil her soul, in exchange for the power of telling tales."[18]

In contrast, infertility has affected the health status of some women in a positive direction by enabling them to avoid the hazards associated with giving birth. Pregnancy and childbirth carry the inherent risk of maternal mortality, though it decreased by a factor of fifty over the hundred-year time span from 1860 to 1960. A 1998 study in the journal *Nature* compared records for 13,667 women aristocrats born in Britain between the years 740 and 1875, and found that long-lived married women tended to have later first births and fewer children than other women. Half of the women who lived past eighty-one had no children, compared to less than one-third who died before that age.[19] The authors of this study have even argued that reduced fertility is linked to longer life spans and that there may be a genetic tradeoff between fertility and longevity in women.

The Range of Adaptation to Infertility

Energy for Career and Creativity

Besides eliminating the risk of maternal mortality and perhaps increasing one's life span, infertility for many women ended the choice to have children and allowed a freeing up of time and energy for other pursuits. Unlike those who kept on searching for ways to overcome their childlessness, some women accepted their situation and took advantage of the alternatives that became available. The eminent psychologist Anne Anastasi, for example, became infertile in the 1930s due to the side effects of radiation treatment for cervical cancer diagnosed a year after her marriage. Later in life she reflected on the outcome, stating, "An inevitable side effect, however, was complete reproductive sterility. Having accepted this fact as given, I simply concentrated with renewed vigor on my work. The possible role conflict was obviously resolved, and the decision was taken out of my hands."[20] At the time of the radiation treatment Anastasi was employed in her first full-time teaching position in the Psychology Department of Barnard College. While not having children may have been painful, she was able to shift her focus to the expanded opportunities in her chosen field of endeavor. Similarly, Julia Child, who wanted to devote her time to the nursery, wound up focused on the kitchen. Child had married at age thirty-four in 1946, after having served in the Office of Strategic Services (OSS) during World War II. She fully expected to start a family when her husband, an official in the American diplomatic corps, was posted to France the following year. However, as no children were forthcoming during her sojourn in Paris, she started taking cooking classes on a serious basis and then writing books about French cuisine. Child later stated that if she had born any offspring she would have wanted to be a full-time mother and would not have pursued a career as a chef, author, and TV personality.[21]

Fantasy/Fiction Children

In the absence of their own children, some individuals felt the need to create children, either through fantasy or fiction. When playwright Edward Albee in his highly acclaimed drama, *Who's Afraid of Virginia Woolf?* (1962), had the main characters George and Martha talking about an imaginary son, some critics and playgoers questioned the authenticity of such an invention. Yet envisioning a fantasy child is not as unusual as one might think, and fantasy children appear not only in fictional works but in the lives of actual people. The late nineteenth-century poet Ella Wheeler Wilcox, who reached a broad audience with lines like, "Laugh, and the whole world laughs with you; /Weep, and you weep alone," provides an interesting example. She and her husband Robert talked throughout her first and only pregnancy about an anticipated daughter whom they named Winifred: "She became a real personality to us; and we thought of her as if she had lived many years under our roof." In reality Wilcox gave birth to a son, Robert, Jr., who survived for only twelve hours. Naturally, both she and her husband were devastated by the sudden loss, after having been so excited about the prospect of becoming parents. Later, in her autobiography, Wilcox explained why the image of Winifred remained deeply in their consciousness for years whereas the real child, Robert, Jr., did not. She wrote, "So brief was the life of this son, and so unprepared were we to think of him as a son, that, as time passed he became like the memory of a dream to us, while the thought of Winifred has always lingered, as of one we had known and loved and dwelt with."[22] Others who have dwelled upon imaginary children include the early twentieth-century British writer of poetry and prose Katherine Mansfield, who with her husband-to-be John Middleton Murray, fantasized about a baby boy "Dicky," and Theodore Geisel, author of the popular Dr. Seuss books, who with his infertile wife Helen invented a young girl they named "Chrysanthemum-Pearl."[23]

Theodore Geisel was hardly alone as a childless author of books for children, as many of the best-known writers of such works have been childless. A number of them never married, including Louisa May Alcott, Lewis Carroll, Hans Christian Andersen, and J. M. Barrie, or like Beatrix Potter, the Englishwoman who wrote *Peter Rabbit*, married beyond the average childbearing age. Some authors of popular children's books, however, were involuntarily childless, such as Eleanor Porter, author of *Pollyanna*, and Kate Wiggin, who wrote *Rebecca of Sunnybrook Farm*. Interestingly, both Porter and Wiggin in their major works devoted considerable space to the subject of childless women or orphaned and abandoned children. In fact, in the two books noted above, the main protagonists, Pollyanna and Rebecca, are both adopted. Even more focused on the themes of infant loss and maternal longing was Marjorie Kinnan Rawlings, best remembered for her Pulitzer Prize-winning novel of a young boy coming of age, *The Yearling* (1938). Rawlings was married for many years but never had a child. After moving to Florida and divorcing her husband, she began writing short stories and then novels about primitive life in the backwoods areas of the state. In many cases the main character was a young boy, and her letters suggest that these literary creations represented the child she always wanted but couldn't have. The boys in the stories were usually based on actual youths, whom she befriended and who often did household chores for her. As she once stated, wherever she lived there was always "some damn little boy to break your heart."[24]

For one husband-wife book-writing team, Hans and Margret Rey, a literary child became a fantasy child as well: "Curious George." The Reys were a childless couple who probably delayed trying to conceive until they felt physically and financially secure, which for Margret, then in her mid-thirties, was too late. They had immigrated to the United States from Europe on the eve of World War II, and in 1941 published the first book in what became a popular children's series about a monkey-like character with human qualities. There were seven volumes in the Curious George series, and the creation of each one was very hard work for them. Margret Rey later told an interviewer that they often waited for years between books, "until the pain was forgotten, like a mother in childbirth." To help her husband conceptualize the illustrations for the next project, the diminutive Margret would move around their living room monkey-style. Over the years, in the absence of actual children, Curious George began to acquire more and more reality in the authors' lives. According to their friend, giftedness educator Annemarie Roeper, when the couple was working on their last book, *Curious George Goes to the Hospital* (1966), they became very distressed at the notion that George might actually be ill enough to require hospitalization, leading to their revising the manuscript several times and ultimately having him swallow a puzzle piece rather than suffer from a serious injury or illness.[25]

Relationships with the Children of Relatives and Friends

Faced with the absence of offspring, many women in history, like childless women today, developed strong attachments to the children of others, most commonly their own nieces and nephews. The twentieth-century American writer Katherine Anne Porter, author of *Ship of Fools*, who suffered several reproductive failures and had a hysterectomy in her mid-thirties, became very close to the children of her sister Gay, sometimes pretending that she, not Gay, was the mother of her niece Mary Alice.[26] She also became a dear friend to the daughter of prominent southern writers Allen Tate and Caroline Gordon. Later on, as she and they grew older, she became more of a mentor and aide to these individuals, not just a smiling aunt or friend. Among them, she perhaps had the most lasting and positive impact on her nephew, Paul Porter, who eventually became a writer and served as the executor of her estate. Paul's statement below describes her influence upon his intellectual growth:

> I can't say exactly when I wrote her a long letter telling her
> all that I had been reading, thinking, and doing. She wrote back
> at once an even longer letter telling me what I should have been
> reading, thinking, and doing. That pretty much set the tone
> for the next forty years. She began to send me lists of books to
> read and music to listen to. Boxes of books began to arrive by
> parcel post. I was snatched a light year's distance further along in
> my education and taste. A whole new world was illumined and

revealed. It was my by-then-favorite aunt who did that for me, and I have never forgotten it.[27]

Adoption

In the absence of offspring, some infertile women, in the past as well as the present, have sought children through adoption, both formally and informally. Until the middle of the nineteenth century most adoption in the U.S. and elsewhere was informal. Even with the passage of the first adoption law in this country in 1851 by the state of Massachusetts, much adoption continued to be handled informally among family members. As many parents died young (life expectancy for both women and men in the decades prior to 1900 was less than sixty), it was common for relatives, especially childless ones, to simply take over the responsibility of child-raising. Adoption became more formal in the twentieth century, and most western countries set up stringent laws regarding adoption and qualifications for those seeking to become adoptive parents. In societies like the United States where non-parenthood was somewhat stigmatized and the desire for children was strong, there was often competition for "adoptable" children. During the past half century, applicants have outnumbered available children by as much as seven to one. Yet many childless women and their spouses have not sought adoption, seeing it as a less desirable alternative. (Only one of our seven main subjects, Josephine Baker, seriously pursued adoption.) Especially in more recent decades, many couples have been put off by the complexity and cost of the adoption process, as well as issues regarding the child's background and contact with the birth mother.[28] However, many infertile women who wanted children have found adoption a viable path for creating families, such as the former Hollywood movie star Jane Russell, who both adopted children of her own and became active in facilitating international adoption in the 1950s.[29] Of course, wanting children does not necessarily make an adoptive mother a good parent, as illustrated by the behavior of the late actress Joan Crawford. In recent decades Crawford has become infamous for having abused her adopted children, particularly her eldest daughter Christina, who described many of the unpleasant details in her book *Mommy Dearest.*[30]

Social Welfare of Children

Some infertile women have worked to benefit the next generation, either through promoting the welfare of children, generating knowledge about child development, or donating money to support child-related charitable organizations. One notable figure who took part in such activity around the turn of the twentieth century was Madeline McDowell Breckinridge, a well-educated woman from a distinguished family in Lexington, Kentucky, who engaged in many civic causes and helped raise funds for the creation of schools and playgrounds. Another was Marie Selby of Sarasota, Florida, a philanthropist and co-creator of Selby Gardens, who left a considerable amount of money to promote several child-related endeavors. Famed chocolate maker Milton Hershey and his wife Catherine, unable to have children due to her long-term struggle with syphilis, established a school for orphans near their home in Pennsylvania, the Hershey Industrial School, which became the largest institution of its kind and still exists today.[31] On the international level, the one-time first lady of Argentina, Eva Perón, for a brief time attracted considerable attention by devoting enormous energy to charitable works for children. In her role as wife and close confidant of Juan Perón, the nation's president, Eva Perón initially spent most of her time in public simply appearing at ceremonial events. But in a country that offered limited social services, Mrs. Perón soon became involved in dispensing aid to the poor, especially to women and children. Eventually her work became institutionalized through what became known as the Eva Perón Foundation, which in addition to donating food and clothing to the less fortunate, built many schools and hospitals, and sponsored a national soccer tournament for young boys. Perhaps the most unique youth-related project Mrs. Perón initiated was the creation of a "Children's City" on the outskirts of Buenos Aires. Located on a four-block site, it was built like a real city with a church, a school, a bank, several stores, and a town hall. Four to five hundred youths, ages two to seven, from the poorest and most troubled families were brought to the new facility, housed in dormitories, and cared for by social workers and educators. The settlement, part of the plan for a "New Argentina," had as its goal helping these youngsters develop the habits and skills they would need to function in school and later in the real world. It was said that Mrs. Perón sometimes visited the dormitories in the evening to see whether or not things were running smoothly, though her untimely death from uterine cancer subsequently put an end to the visits and then the entire project.[32]

Reproductive Trauma and Grief Resolution

Grief is a complex cognitive, emotional, and physiological response to loss. In general, grieving occurs with the loss of a relationship, role, or material possessions that are important to a person's sense of self. Individuals experiencing infertility today frequently become increasingly depressed and anxious as time goes by without a successful pregnancy. They begin to feel set apart and different from the mainstream world of people with children. Women often feel the emotional consequences of infertility more profoundly than men and can become deeply depressed. The centrality of motherhood in women's identity, the bodily longing for pregnancy, and the let down that occurs when conception does not take place are aspects of women's experience of infertility that make grieving more complex and prolonged. Women who experience recurrent miscarriages or stillbirth feel very deeply affected by the loss of life within their bodies. Some aspects of the losses associated with reproductive trauma are not permanent in an absolute sense, in that one can acquire the role of mother through adoption, for example, or nurture future generations through teaching or social change. The original loss, however, lasts forever, alters identity, and changes life course. The depth of that alteration of identity and life course is not universal; it varies from individual to individual depending on the meaning and context of the loss. When motherhood is a fundamental life goal, then infertility produces a deeper and more enduring life crisis than for the woman who does not perceive it as essential to her sense of self.

One can see evidence of the lingering sadness of infertility in the comments of women writers such as Susan Glaspell who, reflecting on life with her husband and fellow author George Cram Cook, said, "There were other disappointments . . . Jig and I did not have children. Perhaps it is true there was a greater intensity between us because of this. Even that, we would have foregone."[33] Letting go of a longing for children, even while finding satisfaction in other life paths, may be less likely than accepting other kinds of more finite losses. The childless Australian-born author, educator, and former Smith College president Jill Ker Conway declared that when in her thirties she chose to marry fellow scholar John Conway, she "began dreaming of the son who would have his father's merry eyes and mischievous humor. That child, and his sister, a less determinate figure, but real nonetheless, lived so profoundly in my imagination that it took a long time for it to sink in that I would not give birth to them."[34] Writer Anne Taylor Fleming mentioned a similar response in her book, *Motherhood Deferred: A Woman's Journey*:

> As to my other journey, it, too, was done, but I did not heal
> as fast as I had hoped. As the months went by and became years,
> I began to understand that I would not ever completely heal, that
> I would carry with me always the child I had never had—in times
> of sorrow, in times of exuberance, in new and foreign places when
> I wanted that specific someone to show things to. . . .[35]

The best-known model of grieving, popularized by psychiatrist Elizabeth Kübler-Ross in the 1960s, focuses on the bereaved individual moving through the emotional stages of denial, anger, bargaining, and depression toward an acceptance of loss. This stage-model of grieving was based on the transitions experienced by terminal patients facing their own deaths; it was generalized to include anyone who had experienced a loss. This traditional view of grieving implies that an infertile woman might similarly experience the various phases of grief, ending in resolution and acceptance of infertility. Newer conceptualizations, such as that of researcher Robert A. Neimeyer,[36] focus more on the positive role of continued attachment to the lost person, or as applied to reproductive difficulties, to the lost potential child or children. The work of Neimeyer and others allows the continuing attachment of infertile women to the children of others and to future generations to be seen as an index of psychological health. This newer model of grief emphasizes a more active and self-directed process involving creativity, a search for meaning, and the courage to disengage from previously held beliefs. Mardy Ireland, herself an infertile psychologist, has described the mourning process in the context of infertility as a transformation in identity that allows a shift from a focus on loss to the realization of creative potential.[37]

Related to changing models of grieving is the shift within the field of trauma psychology to a focus on the degree of positive change that can occur after loss or trauma. Researchers in this area have focused their attention on what is referred to as posttraumatic growth, meaning both the individual growth and societal change that can occur in response to trauma.[38] Trauma expert Judith Herman described the transformation of personal trauma into a broader mission in this way: "The trauma is redeemed only when it becomes the source of a survivor mission. . . . the survivor gains the sense of connection with the best in other people. In this reciprocal connection, the survivor can transcend the boundaries of her particular time and place."[39] Posttraumatic growth often involves a heightened awareness of how fragile life can be, leading to an increased appreciation for life and a shift in life priorities.

Grief resolution for infertile women has sometimes been conceptualized and simplified as a matter of developing child-substitutes in the form of creative products. Regardless of their fertility status or gender, however, people frequently adopt a birthing analogy to describe the creative process. Both men and women may refer to their creative products as their children and to the creative process as giving birth. Pablo Picasso, for example, a male artist with a number of his own biological offspring, called his paintings his children. We can also examine the writings of individual childless women who specifically objected to the notion of creative work as a potential child-substitute. The British writer Virginia Woolf, who wanted children and anticipated having them when she married, wrote, "Never pretend that children, for instance, can be replaced by other things." Woolf's husband Leonard made the decision for her in 1913, after consulting a number of physicians, that childbearing would pose too great a threat to her emotional stability. While she apparently chose to accept her husband's and doctors' wishes, she later deeply regretted this course and blamed herself, writing in her diary in 1926: "my own fault too—a little more self control on my part, & we might have had a boy of 12, a girl of 10: This always makes me wretched in the early hours." When Woolf felt depressed, the issue of childlessness contributed to intense feelings of failure. One of her recent biographers succinctly described Woolf's experience as follows:

> Though she knew that childlessness left her open to, or
> helped create, other kinds of relationships and other sorts of work
> ("These efforts of mine to communicate with people are partly
> childlessness"), that perception did not lessen the "horror that
> sometimes overcomes me."[40]

Woolf acknowledged that being childless influenced her creative work, but she rejected the notion that children were replaceable with writing. Writer Susan Glaspell made similar comments in reaction to visiting neighbors and hearing them talk about her books as being equivalent to children: "Women say to one: 'You have your work. Your books are your children, aren't they?' And you look at diapers airing by the fire, and wonder if they really think you are like that. . . ."[41]

Viewing the creative work of infertile women as child-substitutes may reflect a use of language in the early twentieth century that made certain types of work by women more acceptable by framing them within a mothering role. The founding of the Girl Scouts by Juliette Low in 1912, for example, was frequently viewed as an activity stemming from unsatisfied maternal love, making her organizational work and ideas an extension of mothering. And women themselves may have defined their creative output in the language of maternal longing, as Joy Adamson frequently did, to render their innovative life paths more acceptable to themselves or to others. A dramatic example of the use of maternal language is that of the legendary labor organizer Mary Jones, who lost her husband and all four of her children to yellow fever. After becoming a full-time activist, she referred to herself only as "Mother" and to the workers she sought to help as her "boys."[42] Conceptualizing forms of work within the language of mothering may also have provided ways for women to develop a coherent life story and identity that challenged the cultural stigma of childlessness.

Marginality and Generativity

While all losses and traumatic events have the potential to lead to social isolation, infertility for women in past times has had an additional dimension. By virtue of exclusion from an expected life role, infertile women became further marginalized.[43] Historically, infertility placed an individual outside the norm with regard to nearly universal expectations for adult women. One potential consequence of marginality is an enhanced ability to step outside of normal conventions and to see things differently from others, providing a potential link between marginality and creativity or innovation. Letty Pogrebin, in *Deborah, Golda, and Me,* described the benefits of marginality in the development of an increased capacity to see things differently from, or more clearly than, those situated within the cultural norm. She said, "One advantage of living in the margins is that it allows a person to see the center more closely than those who are in it. Because we must monitor at least two realities at once, marginalized people develop the survival skill I've called double vision."[44] While Pogrebin was referring to the two major aspects of her identity—being feminist and Jewish—that she explored in her memoir, the clarity of seeing things from outside the cultural norm often provided the opportunity for infertile women to distance themselves from the status quo.

The "double vision" that arises from marginality can contribute to broader expressions of generativity, or forms of caring for the next generation. Generativity is a term that encompasses biological parenting, social parenting, and the creation of material or cultural products that "outlive the self."[45] Psychologist Erik Erikson conceived of generativity as a developmental stage of adulthood, following identity and intimacy and roughly corresponding to middle-adult years. He wrote that generativity encompasses activities that guide the next generation and that there are individuals who "through misfortune or because of special and genuine gifted in other directions" do not focus on their own offspring.[46] Erikson's developmental framework continues to stimulate considerable study by contemporary researchers in psychology, such as Dan P. McAdams and feminist psychologist Abigail J. Stewart.[47] Infertility is an obvious disruption of biological generativity and the opportunity to pass on one's genes and culture to genetic offspring, and there is some evidence that threats to generativity (called "generativity chill") are associated with a subsequent increase in generative behavior. High levels of generativity among adults are also associated with well being, providing a way of looking at active concern for the next generation as an important feature of psychological health, rather than as pathological grieving, child-substitutes, or mere sublimation of instincts.

A historical example of the potential impact of infertility on generativity is found in the lives of David and Mary Campbell, plantation owners in pre-Civil War southwestern Virginia. The Campbells, who were first cousins, had longed for children of their own but Mary Campbell was never able to conceive.[48] As an alternative, they developed a strong attachment to the five children of Mary's impoverished brother who resided in Tennessee. First bringing their eighteen-year-old nephew, William Bowen Campbell, to attend the Abingdon Academy for two years and then paying for his legal education, they subsequently brought his youngest sister, Virginia Tabitha Jane Campbell, to live with them and be educated.

In addition to their deep commitment to their nieces and nephews, the Campbells then developed an attachment to their slaves and the slaves' children, referring to them as "the negro family" or "our negro family." Their letters brag about the special gifts of the slaves' children much in the same way some parents carry on about the talents of their genetic children. More importantly, the Campbells allowed their niece Virginia, assisted by a literate slave, to violate state laws by teaching their slaves to read. Several of the slaves joined Mary Campbell and her niece as members of the Methodist church, and some slave weddings were conducted by a white Methodist minister at the church. In an essay based on the archival material, Norma Taylor Mitchell makes the point that "life within Mary and David Campbell's household had offered them [the slaves] an unusually high degree of individual and group autonomy before emancipation."[49] In the absence of genetic heirs, the Campbells contributed to future generations by defying state law and undermining the conventions that had long maintained the degradation of slavery. Their generativity moved from caring for their own potential children to broader arenas, first to the children of relatives and then toward education and increased autonomy for slaves and their children. As suggested by the story of the Campbells, generativity can involve positive efforts like caring and education, and it can also aid in putting an end to a negative legacy such as racism. As generativity moves from genetically related children to society at large, it can become more universal and may require courage to challenge the status quo.

In the past two decades the role of life stories told by individuals has been studied by psychologists and sociologists. McAdams and others have developed a life-story theory of identity that focuses on the construction of life narratives as a way of developing an integrated and meaningful sense of self. The development of a generative narrative can provide a way to judge one's life as worthwhile. Interestingly, McAdams and his research team found through the use of life-story interviews that highly generative adults describe themselves as both more likely to be "singled out in childhood with a special advantage" and "more sensitive to the suffering of others at an early age."[50] Their work suggests that generative adults both experience the self as special and are unusually attuned to the needs of others. As we turn to the lives of the seven creative women we have chosen to write about at length, the theme of life narratives in relationship to identity will be present throughout their stories. Within the historical context of a woman's life, we will look at the role of involuntary childlessness in relationship to the experiences of grief, marginality, and generativity. We hope to explore how these women created new meaning in their lives following the experience of reproductive trauma, and how infertility affected their engagement in the wider world. In the language of Judith Herman, we seek to explain how loss and trauma were transformed into "gifts for others."[51]

NOTES

[1] C. Vann Woodward and Elisabeth Muhlenfeld, *The Private Mary Chesnut* (New York: Oxford University Press, 1984), 41, 44-45.

[2] Two scholarly books published during the time we were researching this subject provided very helpful background information for an exploration of the lives of individual infertile women. Elaine Tyler May, *Barren in the Promised Land* (Cambridge, MA: Harvard University Press, 1995), discusses the social and cultural history of infertility in America. Margaret Marsh and Wanda Ronner, *The Empty Cradle: Infertility in America from Colonial Times to the Present* (Baltimore: Johns Hopkins University Press, 1996), presents an analysis of infertility in American history focusing on the development of medical treatment. Marsh, a historian, and Ronner, a physician, are sisters who are both infertile themselves.

[3] See, for example, the entries in Edward T. James et al., eds., *Notable American Women, 1607-1950*, 3 vols. (Cambridge, MA: Harvard University Press, 1971). Douglas G. Brinkley, *Rosa Parks: A Life* (New York: Viking Penguin, 2000), is a recent example of a biographical work that ignores the subject of childlessness.

[4] Sara Alpern, Joyce Antler, Elisabeth I. Perry, and Ingrid W. Scobie, eds., *The Challenge of Feminist Biography: Writing the Lives of Modern American Women* (Chicago: University of Chicago Press, 1992), 11. See also Carolyn G. Heilbrun, *Writing a Woman's Life* (New York: W.W. Norton, 1988).

[5] Judah Goldin (trans.), *The Living Talmud: The Wisdom of the Fathers and Its Classical Commentaries* (New York: New American Library, 1957).

[6] Some feminist scholars have recently begun to study cross-cultural issues in infertility. See, for example, Marcia C. Inhorn, *Infertility and*

Patriarchy: The Cultural Politics of Gender and Family Life in Egypt (Philadelphia: University of Pennsylvania Press, 1996).

[7] For Margaret Mitchell's attitude toward motherhood, see Darden A. Pyron, *Southern Daughter: The Life of Margaret Mitchell* (New York: Oxford University Press, 1991), 205-7, 210.

[8] Peter Canning, *American Dreamers: The Wallaces and READER'S DIGEST, An Insider's Story* (New York: Simon and Schuster, 1996), 38, 74.

[9] Deidre Bair, *Anaïs Nin: A Biography* (New York: G.P. Putnam's Sons, 1995), 198-203; Anaïs Nin, *A Woman Speaks* (Chicago: Swallow Press, 1975), 258.

[10] Marion Meade, *Dorothy Parker: What Fresh Hell is This?* (New York: Villard Books, 1988), 263-65, 293-95.

[11] Peter Conn, *Pearl S. Buck: A Cultural Biography* (New York: Cambridge University Press, 1996), 71; Anne Edwards, *Vivien Leigh* (New York: Simon and Schuster, 1977), esp. 139-40.

[12] Susan E. Cayleff, *Babe: The Life and Legend of Babe Didrikson Zaharias* (Urbana, IL: University of Illinois Press, 1995), 215.

[13] Gayle Letherby and Catherine Williams, "Non-motherhood: Ambivalent Autobiographies," *Feminist Studies* 25 (1999): 719-28.

[14] Two of the women, Josephine Baker and Joy Adamson, actually lived beyond the 1960s, though most of their creative work occurred before the end of that decade.

[15] Eugenia Price, *Maria* (New York: Bantam Books, 1977).

[16] Donna Rachal Mills, *Florida's First Families: Translated Abstracts of Pre-1821 Spanish Censuses* (Tuscaloosa, AL: Mills Historical Press), 4, 60.

[17] Maria Evans Testamentary Proceedings, 1792, St. Augustine Historical Society Research Library, St. Augustine, Florida.

[18] Judith Thurman, *Isak Dinesen: The Life of a Storyteller* (New York: St. Martin's Press, 1982), esp. 136-40. The quotation is on page 337.

[19] Rudi G. J. Westendorp and Thomas B. L. Kirkwood, "Human Longevity at the Cost of Reproductive Success," *Nature* 396 (1998): 743-46.

[20] Agnes N. O'Connell and Nancy Felipe Russo, eds., *Models of Achievement: Reflections of Eminent Women in Psychology*, vol. 2 (New York: Columbia University Press, 1983), 83.

[21] Noel Riley Fitch, *Appetite for Life: The Biography of Julia Child* (New York: Doubleday, 1997), 169.

[22] Ella Wheeler Wilcox, *The Worlds and I* (New York: George H. Doran Co., 1918), 124.

[23] On Mansfield, see *The Autobiography of John Middleton Murray* (New York: Julian Messner, 1936), 232-33; Claire Tomalin, *Katherine Mansfield: A Secret Life* (New York: Alfred Knopf, 1998); on Geisel, see Judith and Neil Morgan, *Dr. Seuss and Mr. Geisel: A Biography* (New York: Random House, 1995), 90-91.

[24] On Rawlings, see Elizabeth Silverthorne, *Marjorie Kinnan Rawlings* (Woodstock, NY: The Overlook Press, 1988).

[25] Personal communication from Annemarie Roeper. On Hans and Margret Rey, see Anne Commire, ed., *Something About the Author*, vol. 26 (Detroit: Gale Research Co., 1982), 165-67.

[26] Joan Givner, *Katherine Anne Porter: A Life* (New York: Simon and Schuster, 1982), 96.

[27] On Porter's relationship with her nephew, see Paul Porter, "Remembering Aunt Katherine," in Clinton Machann and William B. Clark, eds., *Katherine Anne Porter and Texas* (College Station, TX: Texas A. & M. Press, 1990), 25-37. The quotation is on page 27.

[28] On the history of adoption, see Julie Berebitsky, *Like Our Very Own: Adoption and the Changing Culture of Motherhood, 1851-1950* (Lawrence, KS: University Press of Kansas, 2000); Judith S. Modell, *Kinship with Strangers: Adoption and Interpretations of Kinship in American Culture* (Berkeley, CA: University of California Press, 1994), chap. 2.

[29] See Jane Russell, *Jane Russell: My Path and My Detours* (New York: Franklin Watts, Inc., 1985), esp. chap. 12.

[30] Christina Crawford, *Mommy Dearest* (New York: William Morrow, 1978).

[31] Michael D'Antonio, *Hershey: Milton S. Hershey's Extraordinary Life of Wealth, Empire, and Utopian Dreams* (New York: Simon and Schuster, 2006), 127-30, 150-52.

[32] Alicia Dujovne Ortiz, *Eva Perón* (New York: St. Martin's Press, 1995), 222-25.

[33] Susan Glaspell, *The Road to the Temple* (London: E. Benn, Ltd., 1926), 239.

[34] Jill Ker Conway, *True North* (New York: Alfred Knopf, 1994), 132.

[35] Anne Taylor Fleming, *Motherhood Deferred: A Woman's Journey* (New York: G.P. Putnam's Sons, 1994), 254-55.

[36] Robert A. Neimeyer, ed., *Meaning Reconstruction and the Experience of Loss* (Washington, DC: American Psychological Association, 2001).

[37] Mardi Ireland, *Reconceiving Women: Separating Motherhood from Female Identity* (New York: Guilford Press, 1993), 126.

[38] Richard G. Tedeschi, Crystal L. Park, and Lawrence G. Calhoun, eds., *Posttraumatic Growth: Positive Changes in the Aftermath of Crisis* (Mahwah, NJ: Lawrence Erlbaum Associates, Publishers, 1998).

[39] Judith Herman, *Trauma and Recovery* (New York: Basic Books, 1992), 207-8.

[40] Hermione Lee, *Virginia Woolf* (New York: Alfred Knopf, 1997), 328-29.

[41] Glaspell, *Road to the Temple*, 239.

[42] Elliott J. Gorn, *Mother Jones: The Most Dangerous Woman in America* (New York: Hill & Wang, 2001).

[43] Marginality can stem from gender, social isolation, socioeconomic status, physical differences, membership in a minority group, or from cultural and geographic dislocation, and an infertile woman may be marginalized in multiple ways. Marginality can be culturally assigned, as with gender, or it can be chosen, as in electing to move to another continent or live in a different culture.

[44] Letty Cottin Pogrebin, *Debra, Golda, and Me: Being Female and Jewish in America* (New York: Crown Publishers, Inc., 1991), xv.

[45] John Kotre, *Outliving the Self: Generativity and the Interpretation of Lives* (Baltimore: Johns Hopkins University Press, 1984).

[46] Erik H. Erikson, *Childhood and Society* (New York: W.W. Norton, 1950, 1963), 267.

[47] Dan P. McAdams and Ed de St. Aubin, *Generativity and Adult Development: How and Why We Care for the Next Generation* (Washington, DC: American Psychological Association, 1998). Abigail Stewart and

Elizabeth A. Vandewater, "The Course of Generativity," in McAdams and de St. Aubin, *Generativity and Adult Development.*

[48] Norma Taylor Mitchell, "Making the Most of Life's Opportunities: A Slave Woman and Her Family in Abingdon, Virginia," in Janet L. Coryell et al., eds., *Beyond Image and Convention: Explorations in Southern Women's History* (Columbia, MO: University of Missouri Press, 1998), 79.

[49] Mitchell, "Making the Most of Life's Opportunities," 98.

[50] McAdams and de St. Aubin, *Generativity and Adult Development,* 31.

[51] Herman, *Trauma and Recovery,* 207-8.

Juliette Low in 1912, Courtesy of the Library of Congress,

Carl Van Vechten Collection.

Chapter 2
The Girl Scouts:
"Something for All the World"
Juliette Low (1860-1927)

Juliette Low was a remarkable person. Although accomplishing little in a worldly sense in the first five decades of her life, Low in her later years helped bring new skills and new ways of socialization to growing numbers of young and adolescent girls by founding the Girl Scouts of America. A childless woman, who never raised any daughters of her own, she wound up heading a national organization that made her a virtual mother to thousands. On the surface it appears highly improbable that Juliette Low, born into a wealthy family in the nineteenth-century American South, and married into an even wealthier one in Victorian England, would eventually choose the course she did and touch the lives of so many. As her chief biographers state, it was certainly a great contradiction that "this social butterfly and world traveler, flitting restlessly from country to country and country house to country house, suddenly in middle age threw all her capabilities, driving power and a large part of her financial resources into an effort completely foreign to anything she had ever done before, showing a tenacity of purpose and an organizing and executive genius that those who knew her best had not dreamed she possessed."[1] Yet as one looks at the details of Juliette Low's existence before her mid-life change of direction, there are certain hints that following this alternative path was not so inexplicable. It is clear that early on she exhibited the quality of identifying with the needs of others and a disposition toward performing charitable works. Over the years she herself had experienced physical and emotional pain from various illnesses, from the failure of her marriage, and from her inability to bear children. In the aftermath of these losses, she began to look beyond her immediate and narrow social environment and toward the pursuit of meaningful goals in the larger society. Over the course of this transition, Low went from a circumscribed role as a woman of leisure to that of an influential figure on the national and even international stage, helping prepare young women to meet the challenges of the modern world. Though she died after fifteen years of service to the organization she founded, before accomplishing all she had hoped to, her legacy through the Girl Scouts continues to expand down to the present day.

The second eldest of six children, Juliette Gordon Low, always called Daisy by her family, was the daughter of a prosperous southern businessman and Confederate officer, William Gordon, and his northern-born wife, Eleanor (Nellie) Kinzie. Low was born in Savannah, Georgia, in October 1860, just on the eve of the Civil War. She came of age in the latter part of the nineteenth century known as the Victorian Era, when a woman's role was generally restricted to the home. At that time, women were looked upon as essentially different from men—the weaker sex, unsuited by nature for the harsh, male-dominated outside world. As prescribed by Sarah Hale, editor of the most popular women's magazine of the age, *Godey's Lady's Book*, the path to female respectability was achieved through being "pious, pure, submissive, and domestic."[2] Women of the middle and upper classes were expected to marry at an early age, take care of the household, and devote much of their time and energy to the bearing and rearing of children. Only the few women who entered the professions such as nursing, teaching, or social work were exempt from these expectations.

From the beginning it seemed certain that Juliette Low, coming from a large, respectable, well-to-do southern family, would take the conventional path. Even if a bit stubborn sometimes, she never acted in an overly rebellious manner. Early on Low had helped her mother to raise her two youngest siblings, Arthur and Mabel, and it was anticipated that she would someday be raising children of her own. Although the Gordon family accepted the idea of formal education for its daughters, it was not with careers in mind. Low attended a private primary school near her home in Savannah and then was sent to a boarding school in Virginia for a few years. While her brothers followed in their father's footsteps and went on to college at Yale, Low and her sisters enrolled in an elite finishing school, Mesdemoiselles Charbonnier's, in New York City. There they led a very sheltered and closely chaperoned existence; classroom activities included learning French, dance etiquette and other social graces, and studying the arts. Upon completion, Low returned home to Savannah and made her societal debut at age twenty. Until marrying six years later, she enjoyed entertaining guests, attending local social events, and traveling both near and far to visit friends and relatives. She clearly had no thought of forsaking this carefree life and venturing into the workplace, as some of her contemporaries such as Jane Addams were beginning to do. Nor was she attracted by the emergence of social and political causes like temperance or suffrage reform that engaged a growing number of educated women of her generation.

Yet a look at Low's family tree provides examples of women who did not always follow convention. Both the Gordons and Kinzies have a rich and varied history in North America, dating back to at least the eighteenth century.[3] Especially relevant to the life story of Juliette Low is the long tradition of adventure and innovation in the Kinzie family. Low's maternal great-grandfather, John Kinzie, established the first trading posts by white settlers in Ohio and Illinois, and is credited with building the first house in the city of Chicago. His wife, Eleanor Lytle McKillip, according to family lore, was taken captive in 1779 by the Senecas, a branch of the Iroquois, when she was nine and adopted by the chief of the tribe, known as Cornplanter, as his sister. She lived with them for four years and was given a Seneca name meaning "Little Ship Under Full Sail," a name the family later applied both to Juliette Low's mother and to Low herself to characterize their spirited temperaments. The son of Kinzie and McKillip, John Harris Kinzie, married Juliette Magill, Low's maternal grandmother, an adventuresome and artistically talented person who wrote and illustrated a book, titled *Wau-Bun* and still in print, about her adventures in the Wisconsin wilderness.[4] Juliette Low in some ways followed in this active mode as a youth. She loved the outdoors and all through her growing-up years was consistently seen as fearless and adventurous; as a girl she once saved a drowning child who had fallen into the nearby Savannah River.

The family's tradition of service is another important feature of Low's background. In addition to participating in many local projects in Savannah, Low's mother, in middle age, accompanied her husband to the military camps in Florida during the Spanish-American War. There she became alarmed about the harsh living conditions faced by the U.S. forces, including a major outbreak of typhoid fever. In response she helped facilitate the construction of a convalescent hospital and then nursed many of the patients who were brought there. Following in her mother's footsteps, Juliette Low also aided people in need throughout her life, often reaching out to individuals in her environment who were ill or suffering, both in the U.S. and Britain. At the time of the Spanish-American War, she came to assist her mother in the army convalescent hospital by cooking soup and making tea for the hospitalized soldiers, and each morning she scoured the countryside in hopes of obtaining eggs, butter, and milk.[5]

Earlier, as an adolescent, she had founded a club called "Helpful Hands," with the goal of improving the life of others. Her first project was to teach fellow club members to sew in order to make clothing for local Italian immigrant children. The club broke up a short time later, however, as a yellow fever epidemic took the lives of a club member and a number of the immigrant children.

Juliette Low was similar in personality to her mother; both had a zest for living and very high levels of energy, as well as being interpersonally charming. In fact, the two were often at odds because of their intensity and stubbornness, and Low, in times of crisis, tended to look more to her solid and steady father for support and consolation. Her mother was said to have very changeable moods, and as a youth Low herself was known to have "sulks" and was nicknamed "Crazy" by her older sister Eleanor for her sometimes strange and unconventional behavior. Her nephew, Rowland Leigh, later characterized her as follows: "Her methods were as curious and attractive as those of Alice in Wonderland, the results equally astounding but far more useful."[6] She was variously described by family members as being unpunctual, original, adventurous, and "killingly funny."[7] Whereas her mother was essentially a realist, Low seemed more of a romantic and had flights of fantasy that allowed her to dream on a large scale. Her brother Arthur noted that "Two and two by no means made four for her. They made anything she chose to imagine they made, and once she had an idea in her head facts could not change it."[8]

Unlike her mother, Juliette Low possessed substantial artistic talent, which she exhibited first as a painter and then as a sculptor. Her bronze sculptures, ceramics, wood carvings, and hand-painted china can be seen on display at the family home and her birthplace in Savannah, now called the Juliette Gordon Low Scout National Center. As an adolescent, she obtained her own set of wood-burning tools, called a "Pyrographic Outfit," which she used to carve designs on the family furniture, including feet on her poster bed. Later on, as an adult, at her home in Warwickshire, England,

Low employed her carving ability in creating a unique mantelpiece for the smoking room. Throughout her life she enjoyed learning new practical skills. One time during her marriage, while her husband was away on a hunting trip, she took lessons from a blacksmith, and constructed a pair of highly artistic iron gates that now stand at the entrance of the Gordonston Memorial Park in Savannah. In the process of engaging in this physical work the muscles of her upper arm developed to the point that she no longer could fit into the narrow sleeves of the fashionable dresses of the era.[9] After her husband died, Low devoted a great deal of her spare time to sculpting and continued to do so until a few months before her death. Had she grown up in a later age, this artistically gifted woman might have received serious training in the visual arts and made her mark in the world through that medium.

In contrast to her highly developed visual abilities, Juliette Low had lifelong difficulty with spelling, word usage, and arithmetic. As a youth, she frequently used a word in conversation other than the one she meant, which her family members found amusing and sometimes disconcerting. She called sneakers, for example, "creepers" or "rompers," and once told a salesman she did not like the "snout" on a teapot. Another time, on a visit to inquire about a school curriculum, she asked to see the "school funicular." Later in life, upon completing a tour of Egypt, she remarked that the most interesting groups she had observed were "the pneumatic tribes," meaning the nomadic tribes.[10] Today, Low would probably be identified as having a verbal learning disability. Her combination of talent in the visual arts and difficulty with linguistic expression suggests that she was a strong visual-spatial thinker. In fact, her brother Arthur commented upon her unusual thinking style and how she would at times stubbornly hold onto an idea once "she visualized it."[11] She has also been described by her biographers as being quite disorganized and having a mind "that did not work like that of the average person."[12] But it was this unorthodox manner of looking at the world that allowed her to accomplish what she did. In her later years, Low used these very qualities of broad vision and innovative thinking to successfully launch and develop the Girl Scouts.

Along with her learning difficulties and unusual ways of thinking, Low had a series of life experiences that set her apart from others. Her sense of being different may have laid some of the groundwork for her subsequent pioneering efforts in changing societal expectations regarding the education and training of young women. Low's initial connection with being an outsider began at birth, when her family, especially her mother, felt disappointed at her not being a boy, and also thought her a very unattractive baby. Her grandmother responded, saying: "I am sorry the new baby is not a beauty. You may remember that the first was not, until a week or more had elapsed. But I am sure that after a very little while she will cease to look like a 'freak' and do credit to the stock from which she is descended."[13] Indeed, her physical appearance did improve over time but not enough to fully satisfy her parents or herself. For years Low suffered from feelings of inadequacy about her looks because she was less conventionally attractive than her female siblings. Only after she reached adulthood and made her social debut did she begin to be considered somewhat pretty.

Low also felt marginalized by a number of health problems, beginning at age four, with a critical illness then called "brain fever." She was not expected to live, and when she recovered, she was catered to and pampered, a situation her family later felt contributed to that certain stubborn and determined quality of hers. As a young adult, Low developed serious abscesses in both ears and was partially deaf for the remainder of her life. Her auditory problems started at age twenty-four when a physician, apparently at her insistence, administered silver nitrate for an ear infection and inadvertently punctured her eardrum. Then, at age twenty-six, a day or two after her marriage, she began to experience pain in her other ear due to a grain of rice, thrown by one of the wedding celebrants, having become lodged there and causing severe inflammation. The family claimed that another physician then injured this second eardrum in removing the rice grain, leading to total deafness in that ear. Over time, Low's hearing difficulties continued to mount, adversely affecting her communication with others, as she had trouble taking part in normal conversation. During the next several years of marriage, additional health-related symptoms began to plague her as well. She injured her back while horseback riding and was instructed not to ride anymore, which cut her off from one of the main social activities engaged in by her husband and friends. In a letter to her sister in 1891, she wrote: "I can hardly face the loneliness of the coming winter, now that I can't ride anymore."[14] She also began suffering from various gynecological problems, which frequently forced her to bed. As a result, she was periodically in bad health for quite a length of time, further restricting her social life and taking away much of her natural enthusiasm.[15]

Another dimension of Low's being outside the mainstream comes from her not being rooted in a single geographic location. As an adult, she moved back and forth between her homes and those of relatives in England, Scotland, and Georgia, never residing for long periods in any one place. Her sense of belonging to multiple settings rather than being comfortably established in just one may reflect the division in her family during the Civil War, when Low was a young child. Her father was an active and devoted Confederate, while her northern-born mother, who had made a pledge when she married not to speak critically about the South, was not. Additionally, her mother's uncle, General David Hunter, was one of the Union officers most hated by southerners both for his alleged brutality and for his permitting runaway slaves to join military regiments. This family connection made Low's mother the object of some suspicion in Savannah at that time, as did her hosting of General William T. Sherman during his march through Georgia. Toward the end of the war, Low, age four, accompanied her mother and sister to stay for a time with relatives in Chicago, and in the months of separation her parents' marriage grew very strained. While Low's adult travels were influenced by her own temperament and sense of inner restlessness, this early model of being pulled by separate places and traditions is consistent with her subsequent pattern of moving back and forth between continents. In fact, this very lack of a single geographic and cultural identification may have facilitated the growth of her international vision for the Girl Scouts later on. Over the years, Low had gained an appreciation for cultural differences and for the possibility of strong relationships developing between people of disparate backgrounds.

In the course of her travels across the Atlantic in her early twenties, Juliette met William Mackay Low, the son of Andrew Low, one of the wealthiest men in Britain. The elder Low, of Scottish origins, had immigrated to Savannah as a young man. He became extremely prosperous in the cotton trade and a good friend of the Gordon family. Later, after marrying a Savannah woman, he returned to the British Isles and acquired large estates in both England and Scotland. Andrew Low had two children by his first wife and then four by his second before she died in childbirth. Willie, the only boy, was raised mainly by his sisters, who apparently doted on him. At school, he showed no real interest in his studies and little inclination to pursue a profession, perhaps partly because he always assumed he would inherit his father's fortune. Following a second visit by Juliette, the couple became secretly engaged and continued a long courtship until they married at her parents' home on December 21, 1886. They had a lavish wedding celebration and stayed in Savannah for the first few months of their married life, a time Juliette later recalled with much fondness. She had hoped they would remain there permanently, but as Andrew Low had recently died and Willie came into his inheritance, he felt it necessary to take his American wife to settle on his property abroad.[16]

Residing mainly in England during the next several years, the new Mrs. Low overcame doubts about fitting in and achieved a certain level of social success. Willie's friends were "devoted to Daisy," and there was always a stream of visitors to their home. Members of the English upper class seemed taken by her naturalness, her sense of humor, and her considerable warmth. Indicative of her acceptance into the aristocratic circles of Great Britain was her formal presentation to Queen Victoria in the year 1889. According to her sister, Mabel Gordon Leigh, who by then was also living in England, the marriage went well for a number of years. Juliette, she said, adored her husband, "and as she considered him perfect, gave way to him in every way."[17] Willie Low, or Billow, as he was sometimes referred to in letters, appears to have been a rather self-focused individual, though "generous and kind-hearted." He was very popular with both men and women, but before his marriage, "never had been interested in any one particular woman."[18] He was fair-haired, fair-skinned, and very good-looking; one contemporary described him as "handsome as a Greek god." He loved attending fancy parties as well as taking part in sporting activities like hunting and riding, pastimes much enjoyed by aristocratic Englishmen of that period. His charming manner and high social standing enabled him to be included at times in gatherings with the Prince of Wales, the future King Edward VII.

If the early years of the Lows' marriage brought a certain degree of contentment and social acceptance, one thing conspicuously missing from the couple's existence was the presence of children. Juliette's sister Mabel later commented, "They were both grieved that there were no children."[19] Unlike the other women to be discussed in the book who were much more revealing about their intimate lives, we have little knowledge of Juliette Low's personal response to her inability to produce offspring. Although she wrote frequent letters to her family, she never mentioned anything about the lack of children. The diary Low kept during her marriage and her letters to her husband, which may have shed some light on the subject, were later burned at her request by her brother Arthur, in order to protect her privacy. However, given the fact that she was living in Victorian times when discussion of such personal matters was not usually committed to paper, she may not have revealed anything about her childlessness in these sources either. The only information that is known comes from a long letter her sister Mabel wrote about the couple a decade after Low's death. She stated that sometime in the first few years of marriage Low became pregnant for a brief period and that her health declined after a miscarriage and what was referred to as a "series of internal abcesses [sic]."[20] Subsequently, she wrote, Low consulted many doctors in England and on the Continent for help with her infertility. Though they could not find any specific reason for the problem Low apparently never conceived again. According to her chief biographers, "What these [abscesses] were, in modern medical terms, is a mystery."[21] In those days, they note, people did not talk openly about "female disorders" any more than they did about pregnancy. Nevertheless, it is probable that they refer to reproductive tract infections, which may have caused or contributed to her infertility. However, it is not clear whether Juliette Low ever contracted syphilis or gonorrhea or some other venereal disease as her overall health eventually improved in the course of time.

As is the case with several of the other couples we discuss in the book, the inability to bear a child seemingly had a negative effect on the marriage over the long run. Each of the Lows, husband and wife, was extremely disappointed at this turn of events, both personally and as a matter of family standing. According to Juliette's biographers, "The hardest blow of all was to have the years go by, and the longed-for babies fail to appear. Both the Lows very much wanted children. To Willie Low, as an Englishman of position and substance, it was vastly important to have an heir to carry on his name and inherit his wealth. Juliette Low, from early childhood, had exhibited her Grandmother Juliette's capacity for nurturance. Her choice of the parents' wedding day for her own was more than a compliment to them. She had thought of it as presaging the start of a family life as happy as theirs had been."[22] But the outcome she hoped for was not to be, as

Juliette's health problems and failure to produce a child made her less and less desirable to her husband.

Although there were no children in the Low household, pets abounded and became the chief recipients of her nurturance. Extending this point a bit further, Juliette Low's biographers view her fondness for pets as being an outlet for "her great tenderness toward small, helpless things."[23] After settling down in England she had mockingbirds sent over from her native state of Georgia. She also acquired a blue macaw that followed her around and a parrot named Polly Poons that often slept on her chest; when she had a formal portrait photograph taken in her new surroundings the parrot was shown sitting on her wrist. Besides birds, Low possessed numerous dogs that accompanied her everywhere and generally slept on her bed. In fact, the picture album at her Wellesbourne home contained almost as many photos of dogs as there were of people. Her interest in the helpless was not limited to birds and animals. She also engaged in charitable work among the ill and elderly at places such as the workhouse at Stratford-on-Avon, doing it surreptitiously so as to avoid confronting Willie Low's opposition to her participating on charity boards or visiting slums.[24] Though her husband viewed her involvement in such activity as unsuitable for a lady of her position, Low's commitment to helping others would eventually expand as time went on.

It is not clear how her parents responded to the lack of children in Juliette and Willie's marriage. After all, the Gordons had begun to have grandchildren from their other offspring and may not have felt the absence so keenly. More difficult for them was eventually learning about their daughter's unhappy marital state. Her family had been concerned about her choice of a husband from the outset and had openly expressed their disapproval. Her father in particular had opposed the selection of Willie Low because he had no profession and did not seem to spend his time very productively. When newspaper accounts of his gambling activities had surfaced just prior to the marriage, Juliette wrote to her father in

September 1886, trying to reassure him that the reports were exaggerated. She said, "Perhaps you think me blinded by love, but in the long run I feel perfectly convinced that you will find I have not over estimated his character . . . his faults are not such as will make my future uncertain. They are minor failings that may exact self control & unselfishness from me, it depends on my self, therefore, & not on him whether I am happy."[25] Juliette Low was an optimistic individual, and apparently believed she had the ability to be happy in the impending marriage despite what she perceived as small deficiencies in her husband's character. This was not to be the case, however, as Willie Low's deficits in character, particularly his degree of self-focus, went well beyond the minor failings she felt prepared to handle. Over the years he became increasingly absorbed in his own pleasures, traveling and hunting with friends in far off places such as Asia and Africa. Since her health did not usually permit her to join them, she was frequently left behind.

But even when at home with her in England he was often distant or cruel. According to her biographers, as the marriage deteriorated, Willie began making fun of his wife and found it amusing to talk in a deliberately low voice so that the partially deaf Juliette had trouble hearing him. Increasingly he drank to excess and lost a great deal of money due to poor financial judgment. Although for a long time she defended her spouse in spite of his uncaring and erratic behavior, she eventually admitted that she was unhappy in the marriage. She confided to her brother in a letter of October 1900 that she had told her friend Margaret that "frankly he was a very bad husband."[26] By then Willie Low had entered into a long-term extramarital relationship with an attractive widow named Mrs. Bateman. Mrs. Bateman had been widowed as a young woman after being married briefly to a wealthy older man. She, like Juliette Low, never had any children, though it is not clear if she was infertile since it is possible that the marriage was never consummated. In any case, Mrs. Bateman, after meeting Willie Low, fell "desperately in love with him, and . . . eventually he became infatuated with her."[27] In the summer of 1901, when their affair became public, Willie sought to live openly with Mrs. Bateman and have her situated in the main part of the Low mansion and confine his wife to a smaller, separate wing. This was the last straw, finally prompting Juliette to leave the unpleasant scene and live apart from her husband. Soon she established her own household and began to take the first legal steps toward divorce. Her brother Arthur wrote to their mother that regardless of the outcome, this was a positive development: "I think, divorce or no divorce, money or no money, she will be a much happier woman. Believe me the worst is over. That, was when her eyes were opened to his real character."[28]

Many of the details of the Lows' unraveling relationship are unavailable, both because of the loss of her marital diary and because of her wish to avoid public discussion of her situation. As the marriage was dissolving, Low wrote frequently to Arthur, imploring him not to speak to others about her spouse's failings. Even though she obviously felt wronged and thought her husband's behavior despicable, she did not want to be part of an open scandal, which she believed would bring dishonor to her and to the Gordon family. She wrote to her relatives in November 1902, urging them not to reveal anything about the couple's marital problems or to publicly criticize Willie Low: ". . . please say as little against Willie as possible. He will blacken his own reputation without any assistance from us. . . . I get pity & Willie gets blame but I prefer dignified silence to either."[29] She did express her feelings about Willie's behavior, however, in a confidential communication to her legal representative, Sir George Lewis. "Considering he proposes to install another woman in the house that I have called my home and has enough money himself to gratify his every whim, one might have supposed that he would wish, as far as possible to make up to me in the future, for the injury he has done me in the past. It is the incredible meaness [sic] that disgusts me."[30] In addition to feeling angry about Willie's treatment of her, Low understandably feared the social ostracism she imagined would result from divorce. But she wrote to Arthur in 1902 informing him that her friends, Amy and Katri, were supportive, saying, "this shows me I was morbidly sensitive when I imagined I would be ostracised as a woman separated from her husband."[31]

At this point Willie Low was spending most of his time with Mrs. Bateman, who pressed him to seek a legal divorce from his wife as quickly as possible so that the two of them could marry. Naturally, Juliette was very disturbed by what had transpired, especially when she was far away from Savannah as the crisis developed. Yet from a distance family members did offer their practical, emotional, and monetary support throughout the proceedings. Her father and brother were especially helpful in advising her on the legal aspects of the divorce negotiations. On the other hand, she declined offers of a permanent stipend from her father and mother, saying that financial provisions were Willie's responsibility. Her standard of living declined during this troubled time, and she had to do without certain luxuries to which she had always been accustomed. Yet despite the rejection and dislocation Low was experiencing, she was able to find certain benefits such as relying more on herself to accomplish certain household tasks. As she wrote to her mother in August 1902: "P.S. I have made my self a very pretty dress bodice. They all say it is very nice. I begin to like sewing and being my own maid."[32] Learning practical skills and becoming more self-reliant in this period of transition may have been the nucleus for Low's strong emphasis on providing skill development for young women when she became involved with the Girl Guides and then the Girl Scouts. Low's long-held belief that she would always be fully cared for and that life would go well for her was obviously shattered by her husband's behavior and the dissolution of her marriage. It would take time for her to rebuild her world view and to develop a new and broader landscape upon which to focus her optimism.

Despite Mrs. Bateman's wish for a quick divorce, the Lows' legal proceedings dragged on for a number of years, as Juliette was reluctant to accept what she felt were humiliating conditions included in the proposed settlement.[33] During this time, Willie Low's neurological and psychological health deteriorated, and eventually he was placed in an asylum. While continuing to be institutionalized, he died suddenly from a seizure in June 1905, before the divorce was finalized. According to the stipulations of his most recent will, his wife and his sisters, nieces, and nephews were to receive little, with the bulk of the estate going to Mrs. Bateman. After long negotiations, based on the claim that Willie had been unduly influenced by Mrs. Bateman when he wrote his revised will, Juliette Low was finally able in November 1906 to obtain a more favorable outcome than had been originally proposed. Although Mrs. Bateman still got the largest share of the property, Juliette received a substantial sum of money that made her financially secure.

But obtaining an adequate settlement did not fully relieve her overall unhappiness. The transitional period turned out to be very difficult for her, both physically and emotionally, as she moved into middle age and found it hard to sustain her once cheerful disposition under all the pressures. She lost a lot of weight and may have been suffering from clinical depression during the prolonged divorce proceedings and aftermath. In one of her letters from this time she even joked about suicide. She wrote to her mother in October 1905, saying, "on the first of April I must commit suicide, for my money will only last until then, and if this will isn't settled I must just peg out as I'd rather die than go in debt again, so you see by sending me a present of money you unwittingly prolonged my life! Mabel thinks the 1st of April an appropriate date for me to die!"[34] Her brother Arthur confirms that she was frequently depressed in these years not only due to matters related to the divorce but also from being physically ill and alone—far away from her family of origin.[35] Juliette was probably affected as well by having observed her husband's sad decline and early death.

The nature of Willie Low's illness and premature death is somewhat ambiguous. It is clear that in addition to whatever personality issues related to self-absorption were already present, he underwent marked cognitive deterioration and personality change due to an underlying medical condition, then referred to as "general paralysis" or "softening of the brain." Even Juliette felt that her husband had not been fully responsible for his cruel behavior toward her in his last years because his personality alteration had been brought on by health problems. Whereas he had formerly been described as amiable, he now became highly irritable and morose. On one occasion while tarpon fishing off the coast of Florida, he attacked a member of his own fishing party with a knife. Toward the end of his life he was said to be "incoherent and agitated,"[36] and his own business agent tried to get Juliette to have him declared insane. Her attorney, Sir George Lewis, was of the opinion that Willie was not sane enough to write the new will he put forth in 1902. While there are numerous references in the family correspondence to excessive drinking and alcoholism, Juliette's sister Mabel claimed that "his softening of the brain had been going on for some years,"[37] and Juliette herself in describing her husband's condition in his last days referred to "his poor palsied body."[38] According to Low's biographers, early in the new century Willie was diagnosed with a progressive paralytic condition. Juliette wrote to her family in December of 1903, saying that Willie was taking a rest cure and the doctors could not determine how much his illness stemmed from alcoholism and how much was due to some other cause of brain damage.[39] A variety of neurological problems could have contributed to the deterioration in Willie Low's personality and health, including alcoholism, tertiary syphilis (syphilitic infection of the nervous system), or some other brain lesion.[40]

Given his symptom picture, neurological deterioration secondary to tertiary syphilis, or neurosyphilis, is a likely candidate for explaining his odd behavioral pattern and premature death. While the diagnosis obviously cannot be made retroactively in the absence of laboratory confirmation, neurosyphilis is consistent with the descriptions of his deterioration. The course of syphilis is widely variable, and in women it can lead to infertility, miscarriage, stillbirth, or the birth of a child with congenital syphilis. Syphilis was also frequently accompanied by other sexually transmitted diseases such as gonorrhea that can cause pelvic infection and infertility. Sexually transmitted disease may indeed explain the "internal abscesses" and infertility experienced by Juliette Low during her marriage. Willie Low may have already been infected at the time they wed or may have acquired a sexually transmitted infection subsequently through his extramarital activity. Interestingly, Willie's mistress, Mrs. Bateman, who like Juliette was childless, previously had a husband who was said to have "died out of his mind."[41]

For Juliette Low, now nearing fifty, life over the next few years provided few joys. While she may have eventually come to terms with her husband's death and the settling of his estate, she continued to be depressed, reaching a low point in the winter of 1909. Most weighing on her mind was the feeling that she had failed as a wife and had not brought any children into the world. She began to experience the success of her mother, sisters, and sisters-in-law in these realms as somewhat of a reproach to her. Like many infertile women and couples living in subsequent periods, she found it painful to be present at child-centered holiday gatherings. It proved especially difficult for her to be around her extended family during the Christmas season, and from 1907 onward she started to make other travel plans in order to absent herself from the annual end-of-year celebrations. She told her brother Arthur, who had by now married and become a parent, that she thought her sisters and sisters-in-law, when assembled together with all their children, "assumed a superior air toward this one childless adult of the family."[42] Whether or not her relatives deliberately behaved condescendingly toward her, she clearly felt excluded from the mainstream of family life.

Feeling further marginalized and grieving her many losses, Low started to analyze her past existence and ultimately find a solution to her predicament. Through these years of suffering, she began to look beyond personal concerns and to question the whole meaning of life. One can get a glimpse of her soul searching in the following poem that she wrote during this difficult period:[43]

> When we are young, and heart to heart
>
> Whispers of things untried, divine,
>
> Before the dregs are in the wine
>
> Or disillusion plays a part—
>
> When we are young, is it not true,
>
> That love's eternal, when it's new?
>
> When we are old and time has bred
>
> A callous tolerance in love's stead
>
> Blessed are the eyes whose clearer view
>
> Can read the wisdom of the whole,
>
> The deeper meaning of the soul,
>
> The Love Eternal—old or new!

Looking back, Low now felt that up to this point much of her life had been wasted. She realized that many of the social activities she had formerly engaged in had no real purpose. Her brother Arthur wrote that her strongest personality trait was her desire to be useful to others, a description reminiscent of psychologist Erik Erikson's concept of the generative individual's need to be needed.[44] Given this fact, Arthur noted, "As a childless widow, she was denied this outlet, and brooded over the fact that she was not essential to anyone."[45] Her concerns about the deeper meaning of her existence began to find active expression after she developed a close friendship with General Sir Robert Baden-Powell, a highly-esteemed former military figure in Great Britain, with whom she shared many interests, including sculpture. Baden-Powell had served as a high-ranking officer with the British Army in India and South Africa for many years, and then came back to England to found the Boy Scouts. He wanted to create an organization to provide young men with life skills that could be learned outside the classroom to enable them to become better citizens and, if necessary, future soldiers. Low saw Sir Baden-Powell as someone who had succeeded in shifting his focus from matters relating to his own needs to those serving the larger public good. As she reflected in her diary: "His activities are for mankind, and he has, perhaps, eliminated the effort to attain things for himself. . . . To him, his own life, as a unit, is apparently unimportant."[46] On one of these diary pages she labeled her life "a wasted life," and revealed that she had told Baden-Powell she felt a sense of shame about her lack of accomplishments.[47] But through their continued connection, Low soon found an opportunity to overcome her sense of inadequacy. In late 1909, in response to the barrage of requests from young women who wanted to be part of the scouting experience, Baden-Powell had persuaded his sister, Agnes Baden-Powell, to oversee the creation of a separate female scouting group to be known as the Girl Guides. Once the framework was established in the year or two that followed, Low decided to become personally involved with the Guides. She told her father, "I like the girls and I like the organization and the rules and pastimes, so if you find that I get very deeply interested you must not be surprised."[48] In the Girl Guides, Low must have immediately seen a role for herself that would provide a sense of meaning through engagement in mentoring-related activities.

Encouraged by Baden-Powell, Low set up a local Guides group in the vicinity of her summer home in Scotland in the valley of Glen-Lyon. Given the impoverished background of many of the girls in the area, Low focused on helping them learn work-related skills. This would enable them to find employment locally and not have to leave home at an early age to do industrial work in Glasgow, as was the usual custom. As a start, she had her troop raise poultry, and after acquiring the skills herself, taught the girls how to card and spin wool, which allowed them to generate enough income to stay home an average of two years longer than they would have otherwise. The young women went on to learn about a number of practical subjects—knitting, cooking, first aid, personal hygiene, mapmaking, signaling, and dealing with nature—as well as certain job skills. This was Low's first experience as an educator, learning the basics as she went along, perhaps hoping that the group she was helping would be better prepared to face life's challenges than the typical young women of her generation. For her efforts she received much praise in the local community. The following winter Low went on to establish two new troops of Girl Guides in the city of London, one of them in the very impoverished district of Lambeth. Further demonstrating her support for scouting, she held a number of charitable events in her home to help raise money for the rapidly growing organization.

Low may have been drawn to the Guides not only to do good works but partly because of her attraction to Baden-Powell. Although he was not the handsomest of men, he was a charismatic figure around the same age that she was, and there are hints in her correspondence that she would have liked to marry him. On the other hand, Low claimed that she did not press the issue because she felt he should have the opportunity to marry someone who could bear him children. Perhaps too, much as she liked and admired Baden-Powell, she may not have wanted in middle age to accept the restrictions that any marriage would have imposed upon her. In any case, even after Baden-Powell became engaged to a younger woman, Olave Soames, Low maintained and even increased her commitment to the scouting movement. She remained a friend of Sir Baden-Powell and his wife for the rest of her life. In fact, Olave, soon to be known as Lady Baden-Powell, would subsequently devote much of her time to the promotion of girl scouting both in England and internationally. She and her husband continued to encourage Low's efforts with the Girl Guides and later Girl Scouts, and they worked together with her on various scouting projects.

Girl Scouts Troop #1, with Juliette Low at right, 1917,

Courtesy of Library of Congress.

Early in 1912, when Sir Baden-Powell decided to come to the United States to promote scouting, Juliette Low chose to return to her country of origin as well, with a similar goal in mind. On March 9, back in her hometown in Georgia, Low called a friend, saying: "Come right over! I've got something for the girls of Savannah, and all America, and all the world—and we're going to start it tonight."[49] It was with these words that she started to arrange the first meeting of what became the first Girl Guides groups in the U.S., enrolling sixteen girls in two patrols. She offered the old carriage house and servants' quarters on her family's property as the Girl Guides' headquarters, and a nearby vacant lot she owned was adapted for outdoor activities. One of the girls who joined the initial group was her twelve-year-old niece, Eleanor, known then as Daisy Doots, who later as Daisy Gordon Lawrence co-authored her aunt's biography. Low had a close relationship with her niece, and even created a clay model of her, which is now preserved in the Juliette Gordon Low Scout National Center in Savannah. In the new organization, Low served not only as the chief administrator but engaged in many "hands-on" projects with the girls themselves. She took them camping and initiated other kinds of programs and special events. Within a short time, the number of patrols in Savannah had increased from two to six, and inquiries about the movement began to arrive from all over the country. As a result, Low started giving serious consideration to organizing the Girl Guides on a national basis. Unfortunately, for several months these plans had to be put on hold. Low had become inactive due to the death of her father, with whom she had been very close, and the need to care for her mother, who had even greater difficulty than she did in adjusting to the loss. As time passed, the two women who had sometimes been at odds became more reconciled and in sync with one another, especially as Low was now beginning to be something of a celebrity.

Low returned to public activity full time in 1913 and went to Washington, D.C., intent on establishing a national scouting organization for girls. Among other things, this meant creating a national headquarters (later moved to New York City) and forming a board of directors. As part of her campaign she enlisted the support of several nationally prominent women, such as Minna Edison, the wife of inventor Thomas Edison, and Corinne Roosevelt, sister of the former president, in addition to the wives of congressmen and other high government officials. Eventually, she even persuaded the wife of the U.S. president to serve as honorary president of the Girl Scouts, a tradition that began with the second Mrs. Woodrow Wilson and continues down to the present day. She also put together an elaborate handbook to describe the activities and regulations of girl scouting, which was given the patriotic title, *How Girls Can Help Their Country*. In the ensuing months, she visited numerous places around the country to promote scouting and helped to form additional troops, so that over 7,000 girls were registered within a couple of years. As she worked toward her goal of expansion, Low sought to have her Girl Guides merge with the Campfire Girls, a group similar in outlook, which had been formed a short time earlier. The merger, however, failed to materialize because neither side could agree on the terms of the union. But Low's organization continued to grow and ultimately far surpassed its rival; in 1915 it changed its name to the Girl Scouts of America. Naturally, Juliette Low, no longer called "Daisy" even by her family, became its first president. In her new post, Low labored tirelessly, giving virtually all of her time and energy to further the interests of the Girl Scouts. In her mid-fifties, with no other encumbrances, she was now functioning according to her childhood nickname of "Little Ship Under Full Sail."

The Girl Scouts started out with just a small staff with Low handling most of the administrative and financial matters. Actually, she financed much of the early operation herself, paying salaries, office rent, printing fees, eventually selling some of her jewels to cover expenses. But with costs mounting and the workload growing ever larger, Low realized that the movement had become too big for her to direct and support alone. The Girl Scouts clearly needed additional leadership, and fortunately she had the ability to recruit individuals who could help share the responsibilities and do a good job. Once selected, such people found it difficult to turn down someone as strong willed and determined as Low. As one later chronicler of the organization put it: "With Juliette Low thought and action were always simultaneous. The Girl Scouts needed more national leaders; therefore she went out and got them. She picked the person she wanted, and from that point on acceptance was a foregone conclusion. There was no denying her; if the desired man or woman hesitated or tried to refuse, it was useless. For Mrs. Low was deaf—the result of an early injury. . . . This handicap she readily converted into a tool. If anyone tried to say no when she wanted something for the Scouts, she would conveniently be completely deaf and remain so until the victim agreed to whatever she wanted."[50]

One area of scouting that always held great interest for the visually-oriented Low was the uniform. She in fact oversaw the creation of each and every aspect of the early uniform, realizing its importance in attracting attention to the group and in recruiting members. The original outfit consisted of middy blouses, dark blue skirts, and black stockings. While the skirt color had great appeal, it was soon determined that the dark blue was unsuitable for the camping experience and khaki was substituted. Low's own uniform was far more elaborate than the normal one. As one writer noted: "Like the girls it was khaki-colored, but hers had a Norfolk-type jacket and she wore a white shirt and black four-in-hand tie. Over her left shoulder was a fourragère of gold braid and attached to her leather belt were a scout knife, a whistle and a drinking cup."[51] Others may have thought the uniform extravagant but not Low, who wore it proudly on most public occasions. The uniform, in fact, had much meaning for her beyond being head of the Girl Scouts. It gave her a sense of identification with her beloved father, a military officer in two wars, and Sir Robert Baden-Powell, who had spent his career in the British army before starting the Boy Scouts. Like the Boy Scouts, Low's Girl Scouts engaged in a certain amount of paramilitary activity such as marching and parading, particularly after the country became involved in the First World War.

America's entrance into the world war in 1917 sparked the expansion of the Girl Scout movement, and in turn the Scouts' wartime activities greatly benefited the country. Thousands of young girls felt a strong need to join the organization in order to render national service. The Girl Scouts contributed to the war effort in many ways; they participated in food conservation drives and assisted the Red Cross in numerous emergency situations. They also helped out at canteens in railroad stations, served as messengers in both rural and urban settings, relieved overworked nurses in hospitals, and planted vegetable gardens. Perhaps most importantly, they raised a significant amount of money through the sale of Liberty Bonds. In fact, by the end of the war, when the figures for the final bond drive were tallied, the Girl Scouts stood sixth among the nation's women's organizations in terms of total funds raised. At the center of all these wartime projects was Juliette Low, who, in addition, was giving speeches, recruiting new members, and initiating the new girl scouting magazine, first called *The Rally* and later *The American Girl*. Even before any U.S. involvement in the war, Low was active during the time she spent back in England, working with her sister Mabel for Belgian relief and setting up a hostel in London for wives and other relatives visiting wounded soldiers.

One ideal that Juliette Low vigorously promoted after the war concluded was the establishment of scouting on an international basis. This had been a concept that fascinated her and many others in the movement and showed her as something of a visionary. From the outset Low and the Girl Scouts had cooperated with the Girl Guides of England, and she had always believed in stressing the similarities between peoples rather than their differences. As scouting became established in various other countries she hoped to use the scouting organizations to create lasting intercultural ties. Having lived through the horrors of the First World War, Low thought that the only hope for civilization's survival in the future was the removal of barriers among the inhabitants of different nations. Getting young people together from all over the globe was a key factor, she firmly believed, and felt scouting would provide a start. As one of her contemporaries in the movement described her view: "She believed with every ounce of her being, that if young people throughout the world could meet with and know one another; could learn about and understand the folk-lore, culture, and social habits of other lands, that the friendships so developed would create the best possible foundation for world peace."[52] Forming an international council and eventually holding international gatherings of campers became a priority. When, in 1919, the first International Council of Girl Guides and Girl Scouts met in London, Low, as might be expected, served as the official United States representative. To assure that the meeting would be well attended, she even helped finance the travel costs for some of the delegates who lacked sufficient funds.

Within America, Low and her associates also sought to break down barriers between people, making the Girl Scouts a more inclusive organization by reaching out to young women of different socioeconomic and racial backgrounds and to those with disabilities. Among the initial Girl Scout laws was the following: "A Girl Scout is a friend to all, and a sister to every other Girl Scout no matter to what social class she may belong."[53] Though the term "social class" was eventually dropped, the phrase, "be a sister to every Girl Scout," remains a strong concept in the present Girl Scout Law. The group was one of the few available from the beginning to disabled young women, and the first African-American troops were created in 1917, followed by Native American troops in the 1920s. The Girl Scouts did not become fully integrated, however, until the era of the Civil Rights movement.

In considering the many aspects of scouting, one can readily see Low had the capacity to grasp large concepts quickly. Somehow she was able to visualize changing conditions in the world and how they would affect young women. She saw that young women were moving in new directions and sought to prepare them for that eventuality. In conceptualizing the scouting experience, Juliette Low helped to broaden permissible roles and activities for growing girls. Her biographers commented that the scouting handbook she wrote "did a great deal to break down the restrictions then imposed on girls, especially in the South." Prior to this time, "Southern ladies were expected to do nothing more strenuous than 'sit on a cushion and sew a fine seam,' and their daughters were carefully shielded from a host of things considered unfeminine, including a more than rudimentary education. But the handbook pointed out that women had made a success in nursing, medicine, architecture—that they had even flown airplanes! Girls were inducted into the delights of outdoor life, vigorous sports, naturalizing."[54] In a general essay Low wrote on scouting and the programs available for its members, she listed thirty-four fields in which scouts could earn proficiency badges.[55] While a few of these, such as child care and needlecraft, were within the province of traditional women's work, many of the proficiency badge areas introduced Girl Scouts to non-traditional activities, among them aviation, seamanship, electricity, marksmanship, and telegraphy. Of course, some of the advances achieved by the young women such as engaging in team sports remained subject to certain restrictions. Although Low's Savannah troops could play basketball in the vacant lot she had provided for them, they had to wear wide bloomers and middy blouses and needed to play behind curtains strung on wires in order to prevent passersby from observing their black-stockinged legs.

Various speeches and writings she produced as Girl Scout leader on preparing young women to play expanding roles in the larger world demonstrate that Low was clearly ahead of her time. A statement from a draft of an address she delivered in Washington, D.C., in 1915, reflects her views on the inevitability of more and more women entering the work force: "No matter how much we wish to keep our girls at home modern life has so changed conditions that [a growing] percentage of girls have to become wage earners. So that besides every girl being capable of taking her place as a home maker she should be able to take her place Shoulder to Shoulder with men who are working for their living."[56] In a later essay that discusses the Girl Scouts as an educational force, Low declared, "Girl Scouts of today are the women of to-morrow. Even as young girls they are eager to do their share of the world's work."[57] The following poem, written during her early involvement with scouting, suggests the shift that had taken place in Low's view of the value of work for women and her belief that members of her generation and background, now in middle age, needed to support the new concept:[58]

A Call

Women of Ease before its too late

Shoulder your burdens & open your Eyes

Can mere amusement alone compensate

For the problems of life which you seem to despise

You whose sure instincts like sap in the trees

Rise, who knows how, to point out what is good

Shall you ignore—Oh women of ease

Truths as inherent as grain in the wood!

Women out number the men here below

To woman we look for whats good in a nation

Boy Scouts are trained in the way they should go

But tis girls who will count in the next generation

You who have children & you who have none

Don't shout for votes—let men vote as they please

Daily endeavor to train up the young

There tis your duty oh women of ease

Sacrifice self for the good of the whole

Fill idle moments in trying to please

Workers not shirkers should have the Control

The world is not governed by women of ease

As a former "woman of ease," Low could have been speaking to her previous self. She appears to be making a connection in the poem between doing meaningful work and having control over one's life. Viewing education for young women as facilitating their path to a better existence, her new concept of women's education contrasted sharply with the less than practical approach she was exposed to at finishing school four decades earlier. She was also appealing to women with children as well as those who were childless to devote their energy toward readying the next generation of girls for the challenges that lay ahead. Believing that education for women was more important for their futures than gaining the right to vote, she felt that only women who became adequately trained would be able to occupy a more influential place in society. She knew that "women of ease," like her earlier self without such preparation, would never have the authority or capability to "govern" the world.

Low had truly found her calling in helping young women, but contemporaries and later commentators often viewed her attachment to the Girl Scouts primarily in terms of creating substitutes for the children she could not have. Her chief biographers strongly stated that ". . . not only had Daisy found at last something into which she could throw her vast array of unsuspected abilities. More than this—far, far more than this—in 'her girls,' Daisy was to find the children she had never had."[59] The theme of the Girl Scouts as compensation for childlessness was also expressed in a tribute by a friend: "Mrs. Low having no children determined to give her life to the service of the Girls of America, and, with this in view, she started a troop of Girl Guides. . . ."[60] Viewing Low's activities somewhat more broadly, but still emphasizing the child-substitute theme, another writer said, "She found in the Girl Scouts a purpose which appealed to her eternal youthfulness, drew upon her particular organizational ability and intelligence, and to some extent compensated for the disappointments in her marriage and her failure to have children."[61] Olave Baden-Powell in a farewell testimonial stated: "She loved her growing family of the Girl Scouts of America just as she would have loved her own child."[62] Even Low herself sometimes referred to the young women in scouting as "my girls," telling her sister Mabel, who had helped supervise her original groups in Britain during the war: "Thank you for all your work over my Girl Guides—Yes, I am more than glad to have Mrs. Francis look after my girls as deputy Commissioner."[63] After her death, a cottage was set up in England as a memorial to Low and named "The Link" to symbolize the connection between the British Girl Guides and the American Girl Scouts. Inscribed in the guest book of The Link is the following tribute to Low: a woman who "had no children of her own, and so devoted her great love of young people, first to her nieces and nephews and afterwards to her worldwide family of Scouts and Guides."[64]

While the Girl Scouts clearly provided Low with strong emotional ties to young women, her involvement with the organization and what she derived from it is far more complex than her acquiring substitute children. Scouting gave her the opportunity to express her visual-spatial and interpersonal intelligence in an endeavor that provided deep meaning in her life as well as in the lives of the young women who joined the Scouts. Advocating skill development for girls for the purpose of increasing self-reliance flowed from several aspects of Low's past experience. She taught both the hands-on skills that she excelled in, and the survival skills she had previously lacked. Throughout her life, Low loved learning new practical skills, and these proficiencies brought comfort to her in times of loneliness and despair. Her focus on practical skills in scouting was consistent with her strong visual-spatial talent and orientation to the external world. Additionally, in confronting her new status after the dissolution of her marriage, she found she was forced to rely on herself more than she ever had before. Low's expectations in life—to have a devoted husband and several children—had been shattered over the course of time, and she essentially rebuilt a new world view based on an expanded role for women. One of the chief aims of scouting, as she mentioned in a 1913 speech, was "to teach girls how to be self-helpful."[65] While today we might use the words "resourceful" or "self-reliant," "self-helpful" is a vivid descriptor for the concept of young women developing skills for a more independent life. In the reconstruction of her own identity, Low's work with the Girl Scouts also reflected more than the maternal aspects of her self-image. As previously mentioned, she was fascinated by the scouts' uniforms and by paramilitary activity; images connoting strength and masculinity became vital new aspects of her identity. One can argue that Low in fact helped to promote a more androgynous role for women in the twentieth century.

By 1919, the year of the first meeting of the International Council, which she attended as U.S. representative, Low, now nearing sixty, realized that the time had come for her to turn the reins of leadership over to a younger and broader group of women. The Girl Scouts of America now had five times the number of members (35,000) as it did at the beginning of the war and the rate of expansion showed no signs of leveling off. The organization was becoming too big to be run on the somewhat casual and personal prewar basis. Firmer rules and regulations for safety and conduct had to be established which fit in with the larger institution and the increase in camping facilities. There were also calls for the creation of programs for younger girls, leading to the formation of the Brownies. Fund raising had to be improved and put on a strict accounting basis. In previous years, Low herself had provided much of the funding, but with the growth of membership and new projects to pursue her finances seemed insufficient to keep pace. During the war, she had economized by adopting such measures as turning off her lights in the daytime and serving recycled cakes at her famous teas. But these efforts were hardly enough to offset the group's rising costs.[66]

When Juliette Low retired from the office of president in 1920, the national convention of the Girl Scouts gave her the title of "Founder," and her birthday was made Scouts Founder's Day. In this position, she continued to work on the national and international level to promote scouting. Even though Low suffered from metastatic breast cancer in the last few years of her life, she told very few people and maintained an active schedule when she was well enough to do so. In the summer of 1926,

66

just months before her death, she was still undertaking preparations for another world-wide Girl Scout camp experience. By the time she died at the age of sixty-six in January 1927, the Girl Scouts of America had expanded to almost 170,000 members, with troops operating in every state, and a national training center for scout leaders established in upstate New York. During the next few decades, the scouting movement would continue to grow and engage in valuable local and national service. In the years of the Great Depression of the 1930s, Girl Scouts took part in the relief effort, collecting clothing, food and other items, and they also began selling Girl Scout cookies to raise money for the local organizations, a practice that continues to the present-day. In World War II, they again worked in various ways to support the war effort, volunteering in hospitals and growing "Victory gardens."

Today the Girl Scouts, now officially called the Girl Scouts of the U.S.A., is the largest organization for girls and young women in the world. It has approximately 3.5 million members, including almost one million adult volunteers in areas such as group leadership, child development, outdoor education, and administration. It is open to girls of all races and those with physical or mental disabilities, ages five through seventeen, or in kindergarten through twelfth grade. Its focus is to meet the needs of its members through offering a broad range of activities aimed at building skills and self-confidence. The Girl Scouts offers over 300 proficiency badges in areas such as the arts, camping, computers, health and fitness, mathematics, science, and sports. Girl Scouts of the U.S.A. is part of a worldwide organization of 8.5 million girls and young women living in 128 countries, known as the World Association of Girl Guides and Girl Scouts. With the re-emergence of the women's movement in the 1970s, Cecily Selby, then the national executive director of the Girl Scouts and concurrently a professor of science education at New York University, claimed that "Girl Scouting has been liberating American girls since 1912." Selby persuaded well-known feminist Betty Friedan to join the national board. Friedan, who had loved hiking with her Peoria, Illinois, troop in the mid-1930s, said, "The meetings were hatefully bureaucratized, but it was important for me to be there, and I saw the Scouts really evolve into a new consciousness of personhood, really prepare girls for leadership, in a way that isn't patronizing, doesn't infantilize real commitment to quality, real reaching out to black and white."[67]

Although the Girl Scouts continue to thrive and Juliette Low is repeatedly cited in all of the Scouts' literature, beyond the Scouting community her name is not as well known as many other historical women of major accomplishments. While she has had an important naval vessel named for her and her picture has appeared on a commemorative postage stamp, she remains a not very recognizable figure to the public at large. She is not mentioned in most history books and few people actually know her name. Perhaps part of the reason is that she is not considered a feminist in the sense of directly participating in the various movements for women's rights. This view underestimates Low's individual achievements and her vision for young women's increasing self-reliance, goals that were radical in her day but accepted as the norm over time. Clearly Juliette Low was an innovator and a feminist in transforming herself from a society matron into an international figure who helped to expand women's roles and opportunities, provide practical training in life skills, and promote intercultural cooperation.

NOTES

[1] Gladys Denny Shultz and Daisy Gordon Lawrence, *Lady from Savannah: The Life of Juliette Low* (New York: Girl Scouts of the U.S.A., 1958, 1988), 17. Hereafter cited LFS. Though somewhat dated and by no means thorough, this is the only book that attempts to cover Low's entire life. The essay by Martha Saxton, "The Best Girl Scout of Them

All," *American Heritage* 33 (June/July 1982): 38-47, provides a brief introduction.

[2] For a modern discussion of Sarah Hale and her influence on a "woman's place" in the mid- to-late nineteenth century, see Ann Douglas, *The Feminization of American Culture* (New York: Random House, 1977).

[3] LFS, 15-91.

[4] Juliette M. Kinzie, *Wau-Bun: The "Early Day" in the Northwest* (Urbana, IL: University of Illinois Press, 1992).

[5] LFS, chap. 14.

[6] Rowland Leigh, "Daisy Low," Gordon Family Papers, Box 15, Folder 172, Item 3275, 1, Georgia Historical Society, Savannah Georgia. Hereafter cited GHS.

[7] Arthur Gordon, Gordon Family Papers, Box 15, Folder 172, 7, GHS.

[8] LFS, 115.

[9] LFS, 200-1.

[10] Arthur Gordon, Gordon Family Papers, Box 15, Folder 172, Item 3271, 15-16, GHS.

[11] LFS, 115.

[12] LFS, 115.

[13] LFS, 67.

[14] LFS, 167-71, 177, 200.

[15] LFS, 201-2. An assessment of Willie Low's character and the Lows' marriage appears in a long letter from Mabel Gordon Leigh to Daisy

Gordon Lawrence, October 1937, Gordon Family Papers, Box 15, Folder 172, Item 3276, 2, GHS.

[16] On Juliette's courtship and marriage to Willie Low, based in part on the previously cited letter, see LFS, chap. 11.

[17] Letter from Mabel Gordon Leigh to Daisy Gordon Lawrence, October 1937, 2.

[18] *Ibid.*, 2.

[19] *Ibid.*, 3.

[20] *Ibid.*, 2.

[21] LFS, 201.

[22] LFS, 202.

[23] LFS, 202.

[24] LFS, 203.

[25] Letter from JGL to WG, September 6, 1886, Gordon Family Papers, Series 1.5, Folder 107, Southern Historical Collection, University of North Carolina, Chapel Hill. Hereafter cited SHC.

[26] Letter from JGL to AG, October 23, 1900, Gordon Family Papers, Series 1.6, Folder 158, SHC.

[27] LFS, 235.

[28] Letter from AG to NKG, September, 11, 1902, Gordon Family Papers, Series 1.6, Folder 174, SHC.

[29] Letter from JGL to AG, November 21, 1902, Gordon Family Papers, Series 1.6, Folder 176a, SHC.

[30] Letter from JGL to Sir George Lewis, undated response to letter of October 13, 1903, from SGL to JGL, Gordon Family Papers, Folder 153, GHS.

[31] Letter from JGL to AG, July 4, 1902, Gordon Family Papers, Series 1.6, Folder 176a, SHC.

[32] Letter from JGL to NKG, August 3, 1902, Gordon Family Papers, Series 1.6, Folder 176a, SHC.

[33] LFS, 246-49, 252-59.

[34] LFS, 255.

[35] Letter from AG to NKG, September 11, 1902, Gordon Family Papers, Series 1.6, Folder 174, SHC.

[36] Letter from JGL to MGL, December 23, 1903, Gordon Family Papers, Folder 153, GHS.

[37] Letter from Mabel Gordon Leigh, October 1937, 1.

[38] LFS, 247.

[39] Letter from JGL to MGL, December 23, 1903; Letter from JL to WG, December 23, 1903, Gordon Family Papers, Folder 153, GHS.

[40] *The New Sydenham Society's Lexicon of Medicine and the Allied Sciences*, vol. 5 (London: The New Sydenham Society, 1899).

[41] Letter from Mabel Gordon Leigh, October 1937, 4.

[42] LFS, 283.

[43] LFS, 257.

[44] See Erik Erikson, *Insight and Responsibility* (New York: W.W. Norton, 1964), 20, 132.

[45] Arthur Gordon, Gordon Family Papers, Folder 172, Item 3271, 22-23, GHS.

[46] LFS, 298.

[47] LFS, 298-99.

[48] LFS, 299.

[49] LFS, 305. See also Ethel Mockler, *Citizens in Action: The Girl Scouts Record* (New York: Girls Scouts of America, 1947), 11.

[50] Mockler, *Citizens in Action*, 24, 26.

[51] LFS, 307, 351.

[52] Mockler, *Citizens in Action*, 23.

[53] LFS, 323.

[54] LFS, 321.

[55] Juliette Low, "Girl Scouts as an Educational Force," *Bulletin No. 33, Department of the Interior, Bureau of Education* (Washington, DC: Government Printing Office, 1919).

[56] Speech by JGL, Gordon Family Papers, Box 14, Folder 211, Item 3935, GHS.

[57] Juliette Low, "Girl Scouts as an Educational Force," 6.

[58] Juliette Low, "A Call," Gordon Family Papers, MS 318, GHS.

[59] LFS, 316.

[60] Speech, unlabeled, Gordon Family Papers, Box 15, Folder 172, Item 3277, GHS.

[61] Anne F. Scott, "Juliette Magill Gordon Low," in Edward T. James et al., eds., *Notable American Women, 1607-1950*, 3 vols. (Cambridge, MA: Harvard University Press, 1971), 2:433.

[62] Anne H. Choate and Helen Ferris, eds., *Juliette Low and the Girl Scouts* (New York: Girl Scouts Incorporated, 1928), 245.

[63] JGL to MGL, February 25, [1919?], Gordon Family Papers, Box 15, Folder 163, GHS.

[64] LFS, 359.

[65] Unlabeled speech, [1913], Gordon Family Papers, Box 14, Folder 211, Item 3934, GHS.

[66] Mockler, *Citizens in Action*, 40.

[67] Jane Howard, "For Juliette Gordon Low's Girls, a Sparkling Diamond Jubilee," *Smithsonian* 18 (October 1987): 46-55.

Josephine Baker, 1949, Courtesy of Library of Congress.

Chapter 3
Boundaries and Brotherhood: "The Rainbow Tribe" Josephine Baker (1906-1975)

The acclaimed African-American entertainer, Josephine Baker, never one to do things on a small scale, responded to her infertility in a grand fashion, by integrating mothering with social change. In midlife, she began adopting children, eventually twelve in number, of diverse origins and adverse circumstances, whom she called the Rainbow Tribe, and devoted much of her later years to raising them and promoting international brotherhood. Born at the turn of the twentieth century, Baker had risen from poverty in segregated America and gone on to become a famous dancer and international celebrity in Paris starting in the mid-1920s. She remained a sizzling stage performer for several decades, but also served the Allies as an anti-Nazi spy during World War II, and on trips back to the United States in the 1950s and 60s played an important part in the emerging civil rights movement. While perhaps best known through her early sexualized image as an exotic dancer, it was her mothering of others that increasingly occupied her energies over the last half of her life. These others included her family of origin, the French nation, wartime refugees, and the neglected children who became her Rainbow Tribe. As a young woman, she had longed to bear her own children, and had consulted many gynecologists in trying to overcome long-term infertility. After several miscarriages and a stillbirth, though still wanting to be a mother and also accomplish something larger in scope—to reshape society by removing long-standing exclusionary barriers—Baker came up with an ambitious plan. Together with her French husband Jo Bouillon, she proceeded to adopt children of different races and religions in an attempt to show the world that people of disparate backgrounds can live together in peace and harmony. As she went on performance tours across several continents, Baker would hear about cases of abandoned or impoverished infants and seek to bring them home and care for them. In adopting and raising this unusual multi-cultural group of youngsters, she tried to ensure that each child would be fully accepted and not stigmatized by their background. As Baker herself stated, "My babies will never be ashamed of their origins. They will be loved."[1] Over the course of twelve years, she and Bouillon adopted a dozen children, ten boys and two girls, from various countries in Asia, Latin America, Africa, and Europe. The members of the Rainbow Tribe initially grew up on Baker's large estate in the south of France called *Les Milandes*, which she hoped to transform into a "World Village" and a "showplace for brotherhood."

From the time she was an adolescent, Baker had wanted to be the mother of several children. But only as she was approaching forty and unable to have any did thoughts of large-scale adoption begin to take shape in her mind. Late in life, when reminiscing with her friend and musical director, Stephen Papich, she explained how the concept of the Rainbow Tribe took shape. The idea, she said, came to her as she returned to France in late 1944, on a slow-moving transport ship from North Africa, where she had spent most of the Second World War:

. . . I had plenty of time to start thinking about what I was going to do in the future. . . . Then I was thinking about myself and what was going to happen to me. I wasn't getting any younger. I thought if only I could marry the right guy, one I really loved, then I would settle down. Maybe even retire from the theater. After all, I had had twenty good years, and was still a famous star. I thought it would have been wonderful to have some children. But now, I knew that would be impossible. After all those operations I had had in Morocco, I knew that was a dream.

I envied those men and women who had children. Of course many had been lost in the war, but how happy it would be for those that returned. I wouldn't be able to share in any of that. I didn't have a husband, and I didn't have any children to come home to. *I was really alone.* [italics added]

But then, I remember it was evening and the sun had set quickly, and I had been in the chair daydreaming about my life for a long time—about the past, and about what would be happening to me in the future. And that is when and where it all came to me about the children.

I was sitting in a deck chair on the back of that ship when I thought first about an adopted child, at first a little girl. Then I thought about a boy. But what kind, where? Then I began to think about a lot of little children, and slowly the plan came to me. And I began to think of children being brought up in a totally different environment.

I thought, Now that the war is over, maybe people will have some sense. Maybe we can all work together and prevent wars like the one we had just come through. But you cannot prevent this sort of thing unless you have harmony and peace within yourself.

I knew that then. That's what I thought, at least. Little did I realize that I was in for a rude awakening. If anything, people were worse.

Then I said that someone has to start somewhere and in some little way. After all, experiments are made in many fields—in medicine, on the kind of weather we have, on new inventions, and all that. Why not an experiment in brotherhood? And then all at once it hit me that I should be the one to do it. After all, I was still young enough—and I could afford it.

I thought about it a great deal the rest of that voyage, and by the time I got off the boat in France I knew what I was going to do. And I would do it at the *Milandes*. It would be my own experiment in brotherhood, and I would use a unique formula. I decided to adopt as many children as I could, and to segregate them from the environments that they were in; and not only would I teach them, but I would bring in people to teach them all sorts of things I did not know. As they grew up with each other in close harmony, not knowing anything about what life was really like in the outside world, as they grew up they could go out as emissaries of peace and brotherhood themselves, and pretty soon their children, and even their children, could spread the word of brotherhood. I figured that if someone didn't start all this no one ever would, and I decided then it would be me.

I would get children from every race, every creed, every religion. They would be every color of the rainbow. Then it hit me all at once. They would be the Rainbow Children of Josephine Baker.[2]

In telling this story, Baker began with the theme of being an outsider, with no family to come home to as the war drew to an end. Her solution involved creating a new kind of family explicitly based on the principle of inclusion, where her unique expression of generativity was aimed at ending the negative legacy of racism and religious persecution.[3] As Baker said in her statement above about creating the Rainbow tribe, "if someone didn't start all this no one ever would, and I decided then it would be me." Someone had to initiate the process if society was ever going to change and she determined that she would be the one. In making this decision, Baker illustrates the concept of an "intergenerational buffer," recently introduced by psychologists John Kotre and Kathy B. Kotre, to describe individuals who decide that they will not pass on the damage done to them as children.[4] To consider oneself a buffer means locating oneself in the middle of a sequence that extends beyond one's own life. For Baker, the damage she wanted to stop was racial and religious exclusion—the devastating effect of such practices had been laid bare in the long war that was now finally in its last stages. In multiple ways she would fight to eliminate this harmful pattern of mistreating minorities, particularly through political action and innovative parenting.

Being a famous entertainer in Europe, working for the Allies during the war, and then promoting international brotherhood were a long way from Josephine Baker's origins in turn-of-the-century black America, where few opportunities for advancement existed. The specific details of Baker's birth and early struggles are much less documented than her adult years, when she became a well-known celebrity. Indeed, some basic facts are almost impossible to verify, and the problem is further complicated because she herself often put forth contradictory statements about her childhood in later interviews and autobiographical writings. The ambiguity of her birth in a sense foreshadows what became a major theme in her life story, the defiance of boundaries and the fight for inclusion. There is even an uncertainty about her original name—whether she was born Josephine McDonald or Freda Josephine McDonald. In any case, there seems little doubt that she was born in St. Louis, Missouri, in June 1906, the first of four children of a young African-American domestic worker named Carrie McDonald, who had been adopted by Baker's grandparents. Baker's grandmother, Elvira, was born into slavery on a plantation in Arkansas. Later on after gaining freedom, Elvira married a man from Virginia, Richard McDonald; they were infertile but adopted a baby girl called Caroline or Carrie in 1886. The identity of Josephine's father is not at all clear, though Eddie Carson, a local musician, is the man most commonly listed in biographical accounts despite his absence after Carrie McDonald became pregnant. Both Carson and McDonald were musical; Carson played the drums while McDonald was said to be a "terrific dancer," according to Baker's sister Margaret. "No one could dance like she could, with a glass of water balanced on her head, never spilling a drop. She was still dancing two months before Josephine was born." Regarding her sister's origins, Margaret rejected the idea that Carson was the father. "What had happened was this: Mama was swept off her feet by a handsome, olive-skinned boy—a 'spinach,' as we called Spaniards—with disastrous results. His family wouldn't hear of marriage to a black girl."[5] Jean-Claude Baker, who was informally adopted as a teenager by the legendary performer and later took Baker's surname, disagrees with both these theories of her parentage. After doing research for his biography *Josephine*, he concluded that her father must have been white, something he claims she and many members of her family also believed. According to the records of the city of St. Louis, he says, Carrie McDonald spent six weeks in the almost exclusively white Female Hospital at a time when most African-American women gave birth at home with the help of a midwife. The baby's father was listed as "Edw.," and the baby's birth was registered by the head of the hospital, at a time when most African-American births were not formally registered at all.[6] (Of course, "Edw." could refer to Eddie Carson.) This unresolved issue of her racial origins remained alive for Baker, and she later said that she envied the birth of her brother Richard, born to McDonald in 1907, saying, "He had black skin . . . he was the welcome one."[7]

In any event, Baker grew up under difficult economic circumstances as her mother and new stepfather, Arthur Martin, whom Carrie McDonald married after the birth of her first two children, struggled to earn a living. With Martin, McDonald had two more daughters, Baker's half-sisters, Margaret and Willie Mae. Baker was known as "Tumpy" in her youth, derived from the character, Humpty Dumpty. As the oldest child, she felt responsible for watching over the others as much as she could and would organize her siblings to provide cleaning services and find pieces of coal to sell. By the age of seven Baker was sent away to do domestic work to help out the family and received little formal schooling after that time. Her first employer physically abused her, however, reacting to some minor offense by plunging Baker's arm into a pot of boiling water; the injuries and subsequent hospitalization ended her first out-of-home employment. Her childhood experience also included the trauma of living through the East Saint Louis race riots of 1917, in which dozens of African-Americans were killed and thousands of others left homeless.

While her formative years may have been filled with deprivation and uncertainty, Baker was already displaying several talents and exhibiting a high level of energy and persistence. From early childhood onward she loved to sing and dance, and enjoyed watching the many black vaudeville performers who came to town, giving her ideas about a future livelihood. She herself staged little shows for friends and family, in which she utilized her creative and improvisational ability. One example took place while she was employed as a live-in servant for a childless white couple, the Masons. After being taken once by Mrs. Mason to a local play, she constructed in the basement of their home a miniature theater from boards set on bricks and old curtain material, nails, and string. She then made a costume out of Mrs. Mason's dress and a big hat with a feather, and performed for the neighborhood children. She also liked the new school she briefly attended while in the Masons' employ. The teacher, she said, told stories of kings and queens, enabling her to use her imagination to visualize romantic historical figures and realize there was a world beyond that of her present existence. This placement ended, however, when Mr. Mason began visiting Josephine's bedroom at night and Mrs. Mason brought her back to her family, according to Baker, before any actual sexual abuse occurred. Afterwards, Baker made another theater in the cellar of her own home and put on similar shows for her siblings and friends.

As a youth Baker continued to work at various jobs, such as waiting on tables and baby-sitting, usually for long hours and very little money. She occasionally did baby-sitting for white families but, as she wrote later, did not always follow their warning, "Be sure not to kiss baby." She later described her close interaction with the young children in her charge, saying, "It was hard to resist that rosy, delicate, almost transparent flesh. How I longed to have a fair-skinned baby of my own, but I knew that this was one thing that would never happen."[8] At age thirteen, perhaps wishing to have a child of any kind and in general find a better life, she married a somewhat older African-American man named Willie Wells, whom she had known for a short period. Nevertheless, the marriage did not last very long, as Baker felt that her husband was too demanding. The couple had no children, though Baker later claimed that during the brief marriage she had become pregnant and suffered a miscarriage. Her sister Margaret denied this, telling Jean-Claude Baker that Josephine never became pregnant at this time or any other time.[9] Her brother Richard provides a different version, having told biographer Lynn Haney that shortly after the marriage Baker began knitting baby clothes and acquired a bassinet. After Wells left, she became very sad, according to Richard, who was twelve at the time: "All the life went out of her face. The baby clothes disappeared." Although she may have suffered a miscarriage, he drew a different conclusion. "She must have had an abortion, 'cause nothin' arrived."[10] The stories surrounding Baker's later pregnancies likewise contain questionable theories and speculation as to what actually transpired.

At some point after Wells's departure, Baker, though still in her early teens, started actively pursuing a career in show business. Being on stage represented one of the few opportunities for African-Americans at that time to escape from low-paying menial work. Baker began performing locally with a group known as the Jones Family Band, and then went out on the road with them. She soon switched to another, better-known group, the Dixie Steppers. Along with other music and dance ensembles, they played the black vaudeville circuit, touring mainly through the South. Baker eventually moved up the ladder to work on the same stage with bigger-named artists, and while still lacking in experience, gained some notice as a comic dancer while traveling with the legendary blues singer, Clara Smith. Even when she wed William (Billy) Baker, who had a steady job as a Pullman porter, in 1921, and took her husband's last name, Josephine did not want to stop performing. After several months, the marriage continued in name only, as she realized that her career, and the hope of future stardom, meant everything to her. Her major break came in 1922, when she was hired by the creative team of Noble Sissle and Eubey Blake to dance in the road company of their first all-black Broadway musical, *Shuffle Along.* Despite the fact that Baker was only sixteen, she became a standout in the chorus line, and was on her way to stardom. Some later commentators, in explaining Baker's rise, saw her as being a "natural," simply using her God-given abilities. But it was more than just natural talent that made Josephine Baker successful. Always driven, she worked hard at becoming a top-notch entertainer. Over the years, she had watched other performers very closely, noting what clicked with audiences and what did not. She experimented with many different movements and routines, adding comedy to ordinary dance numbers, crossing her eyes, falling down, and in the process drawing huge bursts of laughter.[11] Baker was determined to make it big—to be rich and famous—and in so doing help out her family. Even before she earned huge sums she began sending money home, designating a portion of it for her younger sister Willie Mae's education, a sign of her early commitment to improving life for the next generation.[12]

Of course, being a black performer in America in that period—the 1920s—was not easy. Besides the low pay and difficult traveling conditions, Baker had to contend with the effects of racism and segregation, which meant being treated as a second-class citizen. Not only did she experience discrimination from whites, she sometimes had trouble getting hired for all-Negro shows, either because she was considered too dark-skinned or too light. Baker's response then and after was to try to transcend issues of race, fraternizing with people of all colors and backgrounds. Decades later during the civil rights struggle, while supporting racial equality, she opposed the trend among some in the movement toward separatism and "Black Power."[13] She also favored interracial marriage as a means of breaking down racial barriers—indeed her last two husbands were white. Part of her intense drive for fame and fortune appears to have been her belief that achieving an elevated status would enable her to overcome racial prejudice. In fact, being a celebrated figure did help her attain acceptance in many places, though in the U.S. her skin color long prevented that from happening. Over the years Baker functioned both inside the white world and also among people of color. Where exactly she belonged would remain an unresolved issue the entire course of her life.

In 1924, Baker, just eighteen, made her Broadway debut in another Sissle and Blake musical, *The Chocolate Dandies*. The show was not a major hit but Baker's stint as a comic dancer made a memorable impression on those who saw it, even if not always completely flattering. The poet E. E. Cummings described her as a "tall, vital, incomparably fluid nightmare which crossed its eyes and warped its limbs in a purely unearthly manner."[14] She also won considerable praise for her dancing abilities at the Plantation Club on Broadway and the Lafayette Theater in Harlem. The following year (1925), as Baker continued to make her mark as a rising entertainer in America, a wealthy white female producer named Caroline Dudley offered her the chance to star in an all-black musical to debut in Paris, France, called *La Revue Nègre*. After some hesitation, the nineteen-year-old native of St. Louis accepted the opportunity to go abroad, unaware that this decision would change her life forever. Although it seemed unclear beforehand whether she or the show would be a success, Baker's initial performance in Paris quickly became legendary. Encouraged to appear on stage virtually nude, with pink feathers around her ankles, thighs, and neck, Baker's dancing scandalized some but mesmerized others. In the most daring and dramatic moment, she was carried upside down and doing a split on the shoulders of her black male partner, Joe Alex. Together, they performed a fiery *pas de deux* called, "The Dance of the Savages." As writer Janet Flanner recalled the debut years afterward: "Her magnificent dark body, a new model to the French, proved for the first time that black was beautiful."[15] A few months later Baker left *La Revue Nègre* and was hired as the featured performer at the best-known Parisian music hall, the *Folies-Bergère*, attired in her most famous costume, a girdle of rhinestone-studded bananas and nothing else.

Almost overnight Josephine Baker became the rage of Paris and was hailed in other European cultural capitals as well. Audiences saw in her not simply an "American negro performer" but an exotic figure embodying the essence of primitive Africa. In her essay, "Remembering the Jungle," feminist scholar Wendy Martin discusses the French fascination with Baker in terms of the "admiring gaze of the white audience on the primitive Other, who represents erotic energy repressed by European civilization."[16] Through her sensuous movements on stage Baker created the legend of her own sexuality, the uninhibited and sensuous black woman who brought renewed vitality to an exhausted postwar European culture. Some of the foremost writers and artists of the time cheered her on. The French writer Colette, who became a friend, called her "a most beautiful panther." Ernest Hemingway described her as "the most sensational woman anybody every saw. Or ever will!" Picasso, another admirer, reputedly said, "She is the

Nefertiti of now." Alexander Calder produced a wire sculpture of her, with a spiral for her pelvis. French artist Paul Colin sketched her for many posters, and after seeing the flattering portrayals, Baker remarked that for the first time in her life she felt beautiful.[17]

Josephine Baker, undated, Courtesy of Library of Congress.

In the next few years, the young African-American expatriate became one of the most photographed women in the world, the subject of many exquisite portraits, including those by the great German photographer, Madame d'Ora. Her likeness was also used to promote various beauty products—perfumes and hair preparations were advertised with her name—and new styles of clothing. All the great French designers sought to create original outfits for her. Couturiers like Paul Poiret saw a new ideal in her lithe body, and she eagerly adopted the latest fashions created in her honor. With her newfound wealth and success Baker began acquiring a large collection of gowns, jewels, and other luxurious items. In time, she started letting go of her *danse sauvage* persona in favor of a more regal image, the first of many transformations before the public. At this point too, she developed her lifelong interest in exotic pets and eventually brought into her hotel suite a parrot, a parakeet, two baby rabbits, and a baby pig. She also added a baby leopard named Chiquita, who wore a diamond choker given to her by a male admirer. The association with unusual animals further contributed to her celebrity and Baker always attracted crowds as she walked with the leashed leopard on major boulevards like the Champs Elysées.

Eventually in 1929, with her wealth already estimated at over one million dollars, Baker, only twenty-three, purchased a huge house in Le Vésinet, a village just outside Paris. The thirty-room mansion named *Le Beau-Chêne*, built at the turn of the last century, is still standing. There Baker continued to acquire more animals and more luxuries, and to serve as hostess to her many newfound artistic and show business friends. She also took an active part in village life, supporting local charities, for which she received praise for her generosity and kindness. Yet she had trouble getting along with her employees, who often became victims of her unpredictable mood swings. At times seemingly small matters would push her into a terrible rage. "She was always in a crisis," remembered one former servant. "I never knew what started them. Sometimes there would be one per day; other times two per day or only one per week. Sometimes a crisis would last a week. They were like seizures that took hold of her." According to biographer Lynn Haney, "Josephine was high-strung and was always ready to fight at a moment's notice."[18]

Although only in her early twenties, her immense fame and the public's great curiosity about her past led Baker, in collaboration with French journalist Marcel Sauvage, to write an autobiography. The first of several such accounts, it does not totally stick to the facts and in some places is highly inventive. (She tells, for example, about her mother and father having met at school, and running away to marry because their parents objected.) Yet, as one of her biographers has written, despite the volume's shortcomings, "it nonetheless captures her febrile essence, uncontrived and unadorned, before she began to think of herself as a legend. In a chatty style she shows an independence of spirit, an unsentimental directness and a breezy curiosity about life."[19] Moreover, in the book, she accurately foresaw how she would later wish to leave the stage, buy property in the south of France, and raise a large family. Two decades before it started to happen, she wrote, "I will marry an average man. I will have children, plenty of pets. This is what I love. I want to live in peace surrounded by children and pets."[20] What she did not foresee, however, was that the children would eventually number a dozen and be adopted from many different countries, and that coupled with her other goals it would be increasingly difficult for her to "live in peace."

Baker's early fame perhaps resulted as much from her exotic looks and behavior as it did from her accomplishments on stage. Yet as a dancer she proved to be highly innovative and her new styles and methods influenced some of the leading choreographers of the time. Clearly her fusion of popular American dances such as the Charleston and Black Bottom with elements of ballet, combined with her own comic and erotic style, were important advances, as was her later incorporation of Latin American dance patterns into the blend. The Russian-born André Levinson, who became

France's leading modern dance critic, described Baker the performer as "a sinuous idol that enslaves and incites mankind." Captivated time and again by her extraordinary bodily movements, he wrote, "Thanks to her carnal magnificence, her exhibition comes close to pathos. It was she who led the spellbound drummer and the fascinated saxophonist in the harsh rhythm of the 'blues.' It was as though the jazz, catching on the wing the vibrations of this body, was interpreting, word by word, its fantastic monologue. The music is born from the dance, and what a dance!"[21] With private instruction from the innovative Russian-émigré dance master George Balanchine, Baker began dancing on point, and she was one of the first to integrate traditional French and Russian ballet with the new American jazz forms.

Besides the recognition she achieved as a dancer, Baker began to gain praise as a singer and actress as well. She made her initial vocal recordings in 1927, singing with a high-pitched, bird-like voice, but by the 1930s she had improved her range and power, enabling her to star in two major song-filled revues at the Casino de Paris—*Paris Qui Remue* (1930) and *La Joie de Paris* (1932). In the first of these shows, Baker introduced the song that became her theme over the years, *J'ai Deux Amours*—(I have two loves, my country and Paris). She was particularly admired for her performance as a singer in the revival of Jacques Offenbach's opera bouffe, *La Créole* (1934). Many critics, in fact, have considered this performance her greatest achievement on stage. As she got older, singing became a larger part of her act, and she made more and more recordings. During the war, she started singing with a microphone and began using a deeper mezzo-soprano delivery, offering popular international ballads such as *Bésame Mucho* and *Brazil*.

In addition, Baker appeared in a number of feature films, starting with the silent *La Sirene des Tropiques* (1927), and reaching a wider audience in two later productions, in which she sings and dances, *Zouzou* (1934) and *Princesse Tam Tam* (1935). *Princesse Tam Tam* has been recently analyzed by writer Elizabeth Coffman, who explores Baker's role as the "other," the "savage," a counterpoint to the artificial quality of European civilization.[22] The story begins in North Africa with Baker playing a poor Bedouin female "savage," who steals, begs for food, climbs trees to catch monkeys, and runs through the streets playing with children. The chief male character is a visiting French writer who fantasizes an "interracial" romance with the North African woman, to help him restore both his marriage and his creative powers. Referring to the strange, dark-skinned woman as "that little animal," the writer and his male comrade seek to civilize her by bringing her back with them to Paris. They are convinced that she will be treated with respect and admiration if attired in beautiful western clothing and given an exotic name. The movie recapitulates themes from Baker's own life: the rise from poverty to princess and her ability to dazzle white audiences on the dance floor. The enthusiastic reaction to Princess Tam Tam's exploits in Europe parallels the initial response to Baker's early career in France, especially the symbolic arrival of libidinous freedom to challenge the constraints of civilization. Along with her sexualized image, Baker/Tam Tam is also depicted as a mother figure to the street children of Morocco, whom she entertains and helps to feed. The movie ends with her character back home in North Africa, now wedded to a Muslim butler she had previously known, happily holding their young baby. (This last scene obviously represented a real-life wish on the actress's part.) Although moderately praised for her film performances, Baker never found the right vehicle to bring her the kind of success on screen that she found on stage. Indeed, she would never star in another motion picture. Perhaps her talents were better suited to the stage, where she could operate with fewer restraints and interact with a live audience.

During Baker's early years in Paris, along with the impact of her erotic performances on stage, she also gained notoriety for her uninhibited sexuality off stage. As one of her biographers, Phyllis Rose, put it: "For Josephine Baker, sex was a pleasurable form of exercise, like dancing, and she wasn't notably fussy about her partners."[23] Virtually all her lovers were white and included such famous Frenchmen as the mystery writer Georges Simenon and the renowned architect Le Corbusier. (Baker later claimed to have had a whirlwind romance with Crown Prince Gustav of Sweden, though most of her friends believed this tale was a product of her imagination—wanting to achieve royalty—or at best a one-night rendezvous.)[24] In reality, the most influential man in her life for many years was a street-wise Sicilian émigré with a good head for business, who passed himself off as an Italian count, Pepito Abatino. As her manager and sometime lover, Abatino added order and structure to Baker's existence. He handled her finances and encouraged her investment in a nightclub, which she named *Chez Josephine.* He also persuaded her to take French lessons to improve her speech, and engage in further study of music and dance. In general, Abatino helped her to achieve a transformation toward a more accomplished, worldly, and stylish entertainer. Though the two had many quarrels—Baker always complained that he was too controlling—the partnership lasted for almost a decade and coincided with her greatest acclaim as an artist. Eventually, in the winter of 1935-1936, Abatino helped arrange for Baker's return to the American stage—something she had long hoped for—to appear in a new version of the famed *Ziegfeld Follies.* Unfortunately, despite introducing an original dance number choreographed for her by Balanchine, the Parisian star received generally negative reviews when back on Broadway. Brooks Atkinson of *The New York Times* declared that "Miss Baker has refined her art until there is nothing left in it." Even more hostile was a bluntly racist review in *Time* magazine that declared, "Josephine Baker is a St. Louis washerwoman's daughter who stepped out of a Negro burlesque show into a life of adulation and luxury in Paris during the booming 1920's. In sex appeal to jaded Europeans of the jazz-loving type a Negro wench always has a head start." The well-known black newspaper, *Chicago Defender,* responded in an open letter to *Time,* saying, "We are loath to believe that the editor and managing editors of TIME live in such a low and degraded mental channel. . . ."²⁵ Baker was stung hard by all the criticism in the press and her lack of acceptance as a performer in her native land. She also disliked having to put up with segregated facilities during her sojourn in New York. Subsequent to the show's closing, Baker severed her relationship with Abatino, whom she blamed for the unfavorable outcome. Abatino, suffering from cancer at the time, returned to Paris alone and died shortly thereafter.

Soon back in France herself, Baker continued to perform in the music halls, appearing in sparkling gowns and making several costume changes during her shows, which became bigger and bigger extravaganzas. What critics said about her in New York had no effect on her popularity in Paris. Offstage, she became more involved in the sporting activities of the wealthy, having learned to ride horses, drive a car, and fly an airplane. During this period, she fell in love with one of her sporting companions, a French Jewish businessman named Jean Lion. As she was now past age thirty, Baker began thinking seriously about settling down and starting a family. The affluent Lion, she thought, was someone who would be able to adequately provide for her and any children they might have. It was with Lion that she first visited the Dordogne region of southern France and stumbled upon an abandoned chateau called *Les Mirandes* (she changed the name to *Les Milandes* because she had difficulty pronouncing French "r's"). Baker loved the chateau and envisioned their children "running up and down the vast stairways."²⁶ She immediately rented the property and after the Second World War returned to purchase it. Baker and Lion married on November 30, 1937, and in so doing the American-born star became a French citizen. Shortly afterward Josephine announced her plans to retire from the stage and become a full-time wife and mother. In a later autobiography she claimed that she was soon pregnant, and started to knit baby clothes in preparation for the child's arrival. But, according to what she wrote, the pregnancy did not last. The following is her description of the ensuing miscarriage and its impact:

I lost my baby.

I lost the only thing that could have bound Jean and me together. Alice (Jean's mother) had been right. It's bad luck to furnish a nursery too soon. "Can I have another child, doctor?" "Of course, if you're careful." I knew what he was thinking. I had a dancer's body, long and narrow, with little place for a baby to grow. I burst into tears.

Mama Lion did her best to comfort me. Together we folded the little bibs and booties and locked them away in the closet. She did everything possible to set things right. But I knew that Jean and I were through. . . . I wanted to flee, like a forest animal that hides in the depths of the forest to nurse his grief. . . .[27]

For Baker, wedlock with Lion was closely linked with having children and since none seemed forthcoming, she felt that not enough existed otherwise to sustain the relationship. Unwilling to play the role of a fashionable housewife, Baker chose to resume performing. Once this happened, the marriage soon began to crumble—Lion disliked Baker spending her evenings at the music halls and Baker disliked Lion's long business trips where he was allegedly unfaithful. The couple separated after fourteen months together, early in 1939, but did not officially divorce until 1942.

Interestingly, when Baker married Lion, she began to embrace a Jewish identity to some degree, even though it was becoming increasingly dangerous for Europeans to be connected with Jews and Judaism. Prior to the marriage, she had joined the League Against Fascism and Anti-Semitism, and was strongly committed to its principles. In the period after she and Lion separated, when it became unsafe for him and his family to remain in France, she temporarily sheltered them at *Les Milandes*, and then helped them obtain exit visas. How committed she was to practicing her new faith is hard to know. Baker did carry a Hebrew-French prayer book with her throughout World War II and said that she had converted to Judaism when she married Lion. But, according to her later husband, Jo Bouillon, no written proof of her conversion was ever found.[28] Even if she did officially convert, Baker seemed to have an eclectic approach to religion, feeling equally at home when entering a synagogue, mosque, or church. Indeed, in her last years she started to embrace Catholicism and take part in its rituals.

Although childless before and after her marriage to Lion, Baker had already begun to nurture and care for children, seeking out and aiding the motherless youths she came across through her work. Japanese humanitarian Miki Sawada, who developed a deep friendship with Baker while studying painting in Paris in the early 1930s, later described the way Baker ministered to all the theater workers' families and toured the city's slums distributing gifts to the children.[29] In addition, Baker worked with the St. Charles orphanage not far from her home *Le Beau-Chêne*, and helped sponsor several charitable events, donating various items to be auctioned. Subsequently, she offered to become a godmother for all of the roughly fifty children in the facility, and arranged regular visits for them to her home. She had playground equipment—swings and slides—installed in her garden, and allowed the children to play with all the animals on the property. At Christmastime each year, she organized a big party and gave each child a present.[30] Later on, Baker sought to help children elsewhere in France and even outside the country as well. During the Spanish Civil War, she organized a fundraising effort to help the young victims of the bombings in northern Spain.[31] She also played numerous benefit performances to support the children's wings of French hospitals and on each occasion loved to visit the nursery and see the newborn babies. At one such stop, Baker walked with a nun through the baby ward, kissing and patting each child in its crib. Then, she turned to the nun and exclaimed, "I can't have a baby!"[32]

Whether her last remark was accurate at that point is unclear. As mentioned earlier, the details of Baker's fertility history are replete with contradictions. She claimed to have been pregnant during her marriage to Jean Lion but a one-time associate of hers, Albert Ribac, interviewed by Jean-Claude Baker, denies this.[33] She had said that her skeletal structure made it impossible to bear children, yet she wrote to a friend that she was unable to have a baby, not on account of physical deficiencies, but because "God doesn't want me to have a child."[34] Whatever the case, gynecological problems had long been part of her life. Lynn Haney notes that Baker suffered from menstrual cramps so severe that she sometimes "could not move."[35] According to Jean-Claude Baker's biography, Maurice Bataille, Josephine's one-time lover, claimed that "doctor after doctor had told her she could not [have a child]" and that his mother had sent her to a famous gynecologist, Professor Alexandre Couvelaire. Couvelaire was deceased by the time the author was doing his research, but he interviewed the son, urologist René Couvelaire, who said, "My father had told me she had a congenital malformation of the uterus, which was the size of that of a six-year old girl, and therefore could not conceive a child. He took care of her [gynecological problems] until the war started, then he destroyed his dossiers because he did not want them to fall into German hands."[36] However, Professor Couvelaire's diagnosis contradicts the later report of her delivering a stillborn child in North Africa, again adding to the inconsistencies surrounding her childbearing attempts.

Although the marriage to Jean Lion did not last, Baker took her new French citizenship seriously. As the Second World War began to spread through Europe, she used her status as an entertainer to take care of France and its rising numbers of displaced persons. She felt that since France had taken her in and given her so much she ought to extend a hand to those in her adopted homeland in their time of need. Then, as the fighting commenced on the Western front, Baker volunteered for the Red Cross, aiding refugees in their efforts to find food and shelter. She appeared at numerous charity functions in addition to her regular performances at the Casino de Paris. Around the time of the fall of the French armies in 1940, Baker was approached by the French Resistance to work for them as a spy. Her status as a popular performer who sometimes traveled to neighboring countries made her seem potentially valuable as an intelligence gatherer. Baker readily accepted this new role, and when in southern France, Spain, Portugal, and later North Africa, she served as a courier for the Resistance. Exactly what she did in this job is not well documented and even long after the war Baker appeared reluctant to talk about her clandestine activities. In addition to her involvement in intelligence gathering, she helped develop a network for obtaining Spanish Moroccan passports for Jews from Eastern Europe.

The war years seemingly brought an end to Baker's hope of bearing children. While situated in Morocco in 1941, she became ill and was brought to the Comte Clinic in Casablanca, where she apparently delivered a stillborn child, and then underwent an emergency hysterectomy. The operation also left her seriously ill with peritonitis and septicemia. Evidence for what transpired comes from Dr. Henri Comte, who claimed he performed the hysterectomy and treated the massive infection with sulfa drugs, and later told the story to biographer Lynn Haney. The paternity of the stillborn child remains unknown, but the Pasha of Marrakesh, El Glaoui, was very solicitous about her recovery, at times giving her a wing of his home for convalescing. Yet the most likely genetic parent was Jacques Abtey, the man who recruited Baker for the French Resistance and accompanied her on many of her secret missions. During much of her hospital stay, he slept on an adjoining cot, helped with the nursing care, and held her when she could not sleep. For additional assistance, the Red Cross in Casablanca sent a young woman named Marie Rochas to serve as Baker's private nurse. She recalled that her patient often had fits of crying, not so much from physical pain, but due to the hysterectomy and loss of reproductive ability. As Rochas told Haney: "Years later when

I read that she adopted all those children, I understood. To adopt one or two children is normal, but twelve! That's frustrated motherhood."[37] Baker remained hospitalized for over a year, and her medical problems were so severe that at one point a news report claimed she had died. Yet even while convalescing in the hospital she was useful to the Resistance, as her room became a convenient meeting place in Morocco for those persons needing to exchange confidential information.

By 1943, after the American army arrived in North Africa, Baker had more or less recovered from her illnesses. Although she still had to undergo several additional surgical procedures to remove intestinal blockages, she was beginning to feel better. Over the course of the following year, she entertained gatherings of Allied troops, regaining more of her vitality as she did so. At her performances she stipulated that black soldiers be allowed to sit together with white soldiers, something that went against the traditional pattern of segregation in the U.S. Armed Forces but was finally agreed to by the officers in charge. This marked the beginning of Baker's efforts to bring about integration among Americans. In addition to her performances on stage she also continued to work at times for the Free French in the anti-Nazi cause. When the Allied forces ultimately triumphed and the fighting came to an end, Baker, for her many endeavors on behalf of France during the war period, would receive an award known as the Rosette de la Resistance. Many years later, the French president Charles DeGaulle would present her with the Legion of Honor, the country's highest medal of distinction.

Baker returned to Paris following the city's liberation in late 1944 and resumed her performing career, initially at the *Theatre aux Armées*, and later on at the *Folies-Bergère*. Then, in 1947, after marrying her fourth husband, a bandleader named Jo Bouillon, she began implementing her postwar vision, which eventually included the Rainbow Tribe. She purchased *Les Milandes* and started the long process of transforming the three hundred-acre property into a tourist mecca and a "showplace for brotherhood."

Baker's plan called for the establishment of hotels, restaurants and various attractions, but most important to her was creating an atmosphere where visitors could observe a community of individuals of different backgrounds living and working in harmony. According to her last autobiography, which contains additional commentary by Bouillon and was published following her death, Baker first broached the subject of adopting several children early in the marriage after telling him that she was pregnant and ultimately wanted more than one child. The account of what transpired is perplexing—one wonders if the pains she said she felt were actually related to conception. If she had undergone a hysterectomy in North Africa six or seven years earlier, she obviously could not have conceived again. The alleged pregnancy did not last long, however, as Bouillon relates in the following statement:

> That night the pains began. I called a doctor at dawn, but by then Josephine knew that once again her hopes of motherhood had been destroyed, this time probably for good.
>
> I braced myself for her tears. But she remained dry-eyed, aloof in her grief, silent, grave-faced, her hands pressed to her empty womb. The doctor explained that due to Josephine's narrow pelvis, she could hope to carry a child to term only by spending her entire pregnancy in bed. 'If she ever conceives again, you've got to convince her to be very careful.' Forty-eight hours after her miscarriage, a stoic Josephine was back on the stage again.[38]

Whether there is any truth to this tale can never be known. It is possible that Baker invented the pregnancy story, and perhaps earlier ones, as a way of showing she was at least capable of conceiving, even if she couldn't bear a living child. Or she may have simply created this latest incident as a means of introducing the idea of children coming into the couple's life. She did, in fact, soon become very serious about developing

Les Milandes so as to set the stage for her subsequent adoptions. By the late 1940s, she and Bouillon were spending virtually all their spare time at the site, working with contractors and making improvements, such as bringing in electricity and modern plumbing. But the project turned out to be a very complex and expensive undertaking, far more than she originally thought. In order to raise money to cover the additional costs, Baker organized extensive performance tours over the next few years, visiting countries on several continents. In 1951, she came back to the United States, not only to help finance projects at *Les Milandes*, but also to promote civil rights for blacks in her nation of origin. "My greatest desire will always be to see my people happier in this country," she declared upon her arrival. While winning praise for her singing and dancing, Baker stirred up a great deal of contention with her criticism of racist policies and refusal to perform in segregated facilities. But her efforts did succeed in producing some changes. She became the first black entertainer to appear before an integrated audience at a Miami Beach hotel and at several other night clubs as well. She also used her influence with the management to try to improve employment opportunities for African-Americans at those establishments. For this work, she was acclaimed by the NAACP as the Most Outstanding Woman of the Year and was honored by black New Yorkers with Josephine Baker Day in Harlem in April 1952.

Nevertheless, Baker's uncompromising attitude on racial matters hindered her ability to continue performing in the United States, especially following a controversial incident in New York City later that year. When her request for dinner at the famous Stork Club was ignored, she complained bitterly to the press about the racial snub. Unfortunately, she included the influential newspaper columnist Walter Winchell in her attack for remaining a bystander that evening and not coming to her aid. Winchell responded in his next column by labeling her a Communist and an anti-Semite, after which Baker was branded as a trouble maker and found it hard to get bookings. The fact that she also spoke out about

American racial problems when appearing in other countries further hurt her chances of working in the U.S. Soon both the FBI and the State Department started using their influence against her, the history of which is detailed in a lengthy article by legal scholar Mary L. Dudziak.[39] Professor Dudziak asserts that "the restrictions on Josephine Baker's ability to travel and to perform did more than harm her career as an entertainer; they denied her the role she sought for herself as a personal ambassador for equality, furthering equal rights by winning the hearts of nations and their leaders."[40] Baker's difficulties were compounded by misguided statements she made in Argentina the following year. Her praise for that country's dictator Juan Perón led even a few American black leaders to denounce her, seeing her as someone being manipulated by foreign interests. In supporting the Perónist regime in Argentina, Baker identified, perhaps, with the work of the late Eva Perón, who had also been infertile and who had dedicated herself to mothering that nation's poor and neglected children. Both Baker and Mrs. Perón, in fact, independently acquired the label of "Universal Mother." Baker's efforts to improve race relations globally may have been slowed down by various obstacles but she persisted in going forward with her campaign. She continued over the next decade to contribute to the movement for racial equality on her visits to the U.S., culminating in an appearance at the famous March on Washington with Dr. Martin Luther King, Jr., in August 1963. One of the few women permitted to speak from the podium that day, Baker addressed the crowd in an impressive and moving manner.

It was after her return to France from Argentina in the early 1950s that Baker began devoting a great deal of her time and energy to *Les Milandes* and adopting the children who became the Rainbow Tribe. Dudziak offers the interesting hypothesis that Baker's focus on home and family was a direct response to the U. S. government making it difficult for her to perform internationally or to operate in the broader political arena. She also points out the parallels in the stage star's decision to be a stay-at-home mother with the shift of American and European women from the workplace back to housewifery and child rearing in the postwar years. Yet if some of Baker's activities coincided with the prevailing emphasis on female domesticity in western countries in the 1950s, others kept her connected to the larger world. Beyond being a mother, she was supervising the creation of a large-scale commercial enterprise, whose financial support often required her to work away from home. Moreover, Baker never let up in her efforts to promote racial understanding, and going forward with the development of *Les Milandes* was part of that process.

The attempt to transform *Les Milandes* into a "showplace for brotherhood" indeed started off on a positive note; the construction of many buildings was actually completed and plans for others were well under way. To staff the facility, Baker brought over several of her family members to work in the house and on the grounds, including her mother, her sister Margaret, and her brother Richard. She also hired a considerable number of townspeople from the local community to perform various jobs. For a time she retired from show business to personally direct the enterprise and take care of the children. But after years of struggle in which she devoted enormous amounts of time and money, the noble experiment did not work out as planned. Perhaps the biggest obstacle involved the size and complexity of the overall undertaking; the goal was too grandiose, too much for any individual or small group to achieve successfully without significantly greater resources. Even a highly experienced business person would have had trouble running such a multi-faceted operation at the same time she was trying to raise a large family. Baker herself did not possess good managerial skills and had trouble delegating responsibility. There was often near pandemonium on the estate due to the many projects going on at the same time and numerous workmen milling around. Baker proved unable to handle all the small details and her aspirations to succeed sometimes overwhelmed her. In larger-than-life manner, Baker once felt impelled, for example, to spell out the names of the cows on the barn in electric lights.[41]

When it came to managing the family, similar problems made it difficult to create a normal environment. The children often lacked discipline as Baker was usually too busy with other matters to exert much control over them. Inevitably, Josephine's sister Margaret and a few servants wound up providing most of the child care, but it was not sufficient. As time passed the bills kept mounting, and with no outside source of income Baker increasingly needed to spend several months each year away on tour. With her gone for considerable periods, she was unable to provide enough supervision for the business venture, much less for the members of the Rainbow Tribe. This led to strains on the relationship with her husband as well as with the many underpaid and overworked employees. Some of the staff chose to leave and Jo Bouillon threatened to go as well. Only his concern for the children's welfare made him stay on for as long as he did.

Although the dream of *Les Milandes* as a "World Village" and successful tourist attraction began to fade after a decade, Baker, in the mid-1960s, hoped to preserve her commitment to promoting interracial harmony through an alternative plan. She started thinking about using the property for the creation of an international learning center, a "college of brotherhood," a concept Baker claimed to have gotten from the children. She came to believe that it was probably impossible to change the world without first changing the educational system. "Our university," she said, "will be dedicated to nondiscrimination, be it racial, religious or social." Her proposal envisioned a diverse group of students, all on scholarship, coming from several nations, who would study ways of breaking down barriers between different peoples. "We can save Les Milandes and help the world at the same time," she told one of her sons. As her concept took shape, she even hired a well-known Italian architect, Bruno Fedrigolli, to draw up blueprints, and spoke to various world leaders including Fidel Castro about funding the project. But the *Collegio universitario della fraternità universale,* like many of the other plans associated with *Les Milandes*, remained an unfulfilled dream. When Baker revived the idea of such a school later in the 1970s, Marshal Tito, the president of Yugoslavia, offered her land on an island off the coast of his country, but by that point she had made a decision to stay close to home rather than embark on any projects abroad. In advancing a program of studies aimed at reducing discrimination and improving relationships between different racial and ethnic groups, Baker actually foresaw the trend of later educational developments.[42]

By the mid-1960s, the financial situation at *Les Milandes* kept worsening as Baker's expenses far surpassed her income. Jo Bouillon, after years of frustration, eventually left the household and moved to Argentina. The remaining employees became increasingly disgruntled at not being paid regularly and began stealing. Finally, in 1969, saddled with hundreds of thousands of dollars of debt, despite selling all her jewels and other valuables, Baker declared bankruptcy. *Les Milandes* and its contents were sold at auction for only a fraction of their worth. Baker herself, clutching a kitten and wrapped in an old blanket, had to be forcibly removed from the premises when it was boarded up by police. The once celebrated star had now reached her lowest point; the children had to be sent out and cared for by friends as Baker could not provide for them. But the famed entertainer was never one to remain mired and downcast for long. Princess Grace of Monaco helped come to her rescue, furnishing the down payment for a house in Roquebrune on the Riviera. Princess Grace also assisted Baker in obtaining work, so that she could resume her career. However, requests for her services were less frequent in the next few years, and Baker now in her sixties, was intermittently in poor health due to serious cardiovascular disease. But she never gave up and continued to perform when possible.

The last person to conduct a major interview with Baker was African-American writer and later Harvard professor Henry Louis Gates, Jr., who visited her in 1971 in Monte Carlo. Working as a correspondent for

Time magazine, which had approved his suggestion for a story on black expatriates, Gates described Baker as follows:[43]

> She had recently returned from a pilgrimage to Israel, and
> was looking forward to her return to the stage, her marvelous
> comeback. She was tall, as gracious and as warm as she was
> elegant, sensuous at sixty-five. . . . She was so very thoughtful, so
> intellectual, and so learned of the sort of experience that, perhaps,
> takes six decades or so to ferment.

During their evening's discussion, Baker talked about issues of identity and inclusion. When Gates asked her if the French people had offered her a respite from racial prejudice, she answered, "The French adopted me immediately. They all went to the beaches to get dark like Josephine Baker. They had a contest to see who could be the darkest, like Josephine Baker, they said. The French got sick, trying to get black—café au lait—you weren't anything unless you were café au lait." She expressed very mixed feelings about the United States, emphasizing both her sadness about leaving her country of origin and disappointment over America's failure to achieve brotherhood among its people, saying:

> But really, I belong to the world now. You know, America
> represented that: people coming from all over to make a nation.
> But America has forgotten that. I love all people at the same time.
> Our country is people of all countries. How else could there have
> been an America? And they made a beautiful nation. Each one
> depositing a little of his own beauty.
>
> It's a sad thing to leave your country. How very often I've felt
> like the Wandering Jew with my twelve children on my arms. . . .
> It's ironic: people ran from slavery in Europe to find freedom in
> America, and now. . . .

In selecting the metaphor of the Wandering Jew, the Jew of medieval legend condemned to wander over the earth until the Second Coming of Christ, Baker expressed her status as an exiled African-American and a mother to motherless children. She clearly saw the contradictions in America's ideals and still hoped that the country of her birth might change toward greater inclusiveness and racial brotherhood.

Never one to stay away from the stage very long and still needing to support her large family, Baker made another comeback as an entertainer in 1973, at age of sixty-seven. Despite her advancing years she could still move an audience, combining her earlier repertoire with new material designed to appeal to the younger generation. She toured several major cities in the United States, playing to enthusiastic crowds, including a sold-out performance at New York's Carnegie Hall. However, a heart attack that summer limited subsequent appearances and forced her to return to Europe to recover. The following year Baker started performing in what would be the last show of her career, a musical review called *Josephine*, in the Monte Carlo casino. Audience response was positive and in early April 1975, the show moved to Paris. Opening night drew an enthusiastic crowd and a party was held to celebrate Baker's fiftieth anniversary as a Parisian performer. A few days later, however, she suffered a massive cerebral hemorrhage and passed away on the morning of April fourteenth. Baker died in the manner that she always wanted. She had said in 1927, "I shall dance all my life, I was born to dance, just for that. To live is to dance, I would like to die, breathless, spent, at the end of a dance."[44] Her state funeral at *La Madeleine* church the following day drew twenty thousand people, with hundreds of thousands more watching on television. She would be the only American-born person ever to receive a military funeral and a twenty-one gun salute from the French government. At a memorial service in New York, she was eulogized as having "died in triumph, a woman nearing seventy seemingly transformed to her youth in voice, figure, and vitality, joining her damaged heart with the hearts of cheering audiences which welcomed her back to her beloved Paris."[45]

While Josephine Baker's career has always been viewed in a favorable light, the Rainbow Tribe experiment in diversity has often been regarded as a failure. Indeed, Baker herself sometimes referred to her child rearing efforts in less than positive terms. One can ask, however, by what standards can the adoption and raising of twelve children be deemed a failure? Although the financial collapse of *Les Milandes* certainly had a negative effect on the children's lives, the lack of economic security was only one aspect of the family's overall existence. Baker made a philosophical move to reclaim motherhood, from which she was biologically excluded, by her commitment to parenting and to broader inclusiveness. In some ways her parenting techniques were decades ahead of later trends in adoption, including open adoption and maintaining children's linguistic and cultural ties. She freely told her children about their origins, taught them about their birth parents' cultures, and hired tutors from their native countries to instruct them in language and customs. In addition, she introduced the children, where possible, to their genetic relatives, such as taking her Venezuelan-born son Mara to meet his grandparents. One of the boys, Jari, described the manner in which Baker (and Bouillon) explained things: "When we older ones were five, Daddy and Mother talked candidly to us. They said we were adopted, that our parents could not provide for us, and that Mother had taken us since she could not have children of her own. It helped us later on when we were growing up with a black brother, a yellow brother, a red brother. You were not shocked, you understood this other little child was from a family who could not feed him, and after a few months, he was your brother."[46]

Baker's original concept for the Rainbow Tribe was to adopt four or five two-year-old boys: one Japanese child, a black child from South Africa, a Peruvian child, a Nordic child, and an Israeli child, who, she said, "will live together like brothers."[47] She began implementing her plan by writing to her old friend, Miki Sawada, who was running an orphanage called the Elizabeth Sanders Home outside of Tokyo. Sawada had since lost one of her sons during World War II and had devoted herself, amidst great controversy and opposition, to aiding the abandoned offspring of American soldiers and Japanese women, referred to as *Konketsujii*, or postwar occupation babies. Between 1948 and 1954 Sawada took in over a thousand unwanted children, and Baker gave a series of twenty-three performances for the Home when she arrived in Japan in 1954, thus providing financial support for the orphanage at a critical time. She also gave lectures in Osaka and Tokyo as the French representative of the International League Against Racism and Anti-Semitism, and succeeded in founding a Japanese chapter of the organization. Baker left Japan with two children from the orphanage, Yamato Akio, later called Akio, born on July 7, 1952, and Kimura Teruya Seiji, later called Janot, born on July 15, 1953. Then, in September 1954, Baker went on a lecture tour to Scandinavia and found her third child. The adoption occurred in Helsinki, Finland, where families who were financially overburdened with children could place them in an orphanage, and she arranged to adopt Jari, who otherwise would have gone into foster care at the time of his upcoming second birthday. There are various versions of the circumstances of Baker's bringing home her next child, Luis, from Colombia in South America. Her version asserts that she originally selected a child whose "sickly mother [was] unable to tend him properly." However, it appears this child was taken back by the police because of community suspicions that he was being removed for the harmful purpose of drinking his blood. A different mother then appeared and volunteered to give Baker a baby boy, and Baker in turn offered her enough money to buy a house and garden. In December 1955, two French-born children were adopted from a foster home near Paris: Philippe, two years old, later called Jean-Claude, and Alain Jean-Claude, age fourteen months, who was renamed Moïse. Baker had been unable to adopt an Israeli child because of Israel's restrictive adoption policy, and there are, again, at least two versions of Moïse's origins. Most accounts state that he came from a French Jewish family, while Jean-Claude Baker claims that he was a Catholic-born child whom Baker simply decided would be Jewish. For her next children Baker traveled in December 1956 to North Africa. The entire population of a town called Palestro in Algeria had recently been massacred, but two six-month-old babies were allegedly found alive under a tree and brought to Algiers, where Baker received permission to adopt them. She named the boy Brahim and determined he would be raised Muslim, and named the girl Marianne and chose to have her brought up Catholic. By now there were eight children, and all of them were legally adopted in June 1957. The oldest one by this time was five.

The ever-increasing number of adoptees placed great stress on Baker's marriage, as Bouillon had previously agreed only to the initial four. The couple then established new limits but Baker would change them as soon as she was emotionally moved by the plight of the next child she saw. Bouillon tried to provide a voice of reality with regard to the practicalities and finances of running *Les Milandes* and raising so many children. But despite his pleas to stop, Baker continued adding to the family. In a village in Senegal, she was visiting a hospital when an infant's mother died, and she arranged to adopt the baby, named Koffi. The next child, (number ten) named Mara, was adopted, or possibly purchased, from an indigenous native community in Venezuela outside of Maracaibo. In one camp, she saw an eighteenth-month-old boy lying in a hole in the sand, who seemed like "skin and bones" and unable to walk due to severe malnutrition. Baker gave his parents some money, and they left, although she was arrested and temporarily detained before leaving Venezuela for Paris with him. Another addition to the group (number eleven) came about one night in Paris when a live baby boy was found in a trash can by a ragman, who saved him from being tossed into a garbage truck the next morning. When a journalist called Baker and asked what she thought about the situation, she went to the hospital and adopted the boy, naming him Noël. The final adoptee was a girl. For years Marianne had begged her mother for a little sister, and so

Stellina, the child of a Moroccan mother, born June 18, 1964, at a clinic in Paris, became the twelfth and youngest member of the Rainbow Tribe. All the children were given the last name of Bouillon, even though the last two were adopted after Baker and Bouillon had separated.

During their early years the Rainbow Tribe attended school near *Les Milandes* in Castelnaud-Feyrac. Monsieur and Madame Besse, who taught classes there, recalled Baker's children as very loyal to each other and very proud of their chateau and of their mother. The children also missed their mother terribly during her frequent absences while she was away performing. As they grew older, the oldest boys attended boarding schools in Switzerland. At one point some members of the "tribe" were sent to England during the summer and placed in the care of a childless couple, Harry Hurford Janes and his wife. Janes had worked with Baker in North Africa during the war, and now contributed to the Rainbow experiment through a form of substitute parenting.[48]

Given her vision of the Rainbow Tribe as a unified group and wishing to control her children's behavior even as they aged, Baker was unprepared emotionally for the normal developmental changes of adolescence, including separation from parents and shifts in identity. Particularly difficult for her was dealing with the cultural changes affecting teenagers everywhere in the late 1960s and early 1970s. She wanted conformity, and her older children challenged her with their individual forms of rebellion, perhaps reminding her of her own early adventures. Luis, for example, rebelled by wearing flowered shirts, which Baker had forbidden along with other changes in style such as long hair. She also became extremely distressed when Marianne, at age sixteen, fell in love with a nineteen-year-old boy and would stay out some nights until five a.m. When behavioral issues reached a point where they were more than Baker could cope with, she sent some of the children away. Moïse was put to work on a kibbutz in Israel, and Jari went off to live with his father in Argentina. A complicating factor was Baker's declining health during these years. She had sustained a right-hemisphere stroke in 1973 while performing in Copenhagen, which left her with cognitive deficits including spatial confusion, memory problems, and a tendency to "drift off." These cognitive difficulties sometimes made her more paranoid and erratic in her relationships with others, showing frequent flashes of temper. Never strong at managing finances and making practical decisions, she grew more and more disorganized as she aged, and the children often complained about the chaos in the house.

Yet in spite of the chaos, the children did mature and grow into adulthood. While none of them achieved their mother's fame, most went on to lead fairly productive lives. At age nineteen, Moïse was the first to marry; he wed Monique, who worked as a chambermaid at the hotel in Paris where he was employed as a waiter. Baker disapproved of the marriage and did not attend the wedding. At the time of her death, most members of the Rainbow Tribe were in their teens, though Stellina, who had been adopted when Baker was sixty, was only ten years old. After their mother died, Jari, Akio, Stellina, Noël, and Koffi went to live in Argentina with Bouillon. Luis, who had married, fathered a child shortly after Baker's death but it lived only briefly and was buried along side Baker in Monaco. Bouillon died in Argentina in 1984.

While Baker's parenting did not live up to her own aspirations, what she and her children experienced was in some ways not different from the ordinary struggles faced by many families then and now. The quality of her parenting was uneven, varying between overly strict and overly indulgent. She had great difficulty in setting limits and providing structure for her children, just as she had difficulty providing structure in her own life. She obviously loved the children very much and enjoyed mothering when she was around; nevertheless, she was often absent. Jo Bouillon is consistently described as having been a loving and caring parent, and his departure was a terrible loss to the children, compounding the original losses of their genetic parents and countries of origin. Baker did provide a home, family life (however unusual), and education to abandoned children who otherwise would have been considered "hard to place" or "special needs" because of their unwanted status as biracial (like Akio and Janot) or because of their age (like Jari). It appears that the two Latin American children, Luis and Mara, were removed from their parents, perhaps with the enticement of money, but at least one was acutely ill and might not have survived. Furthermore, the story is not over. Baker always hoped that her children and their children would be ambassadors for peace and brotherhood, and surely in some ways they have, especially in preserving the memory of their mother's efforts.

Unknowingly, Baker may have passed her own legacy of confusion on the issue of inclusion/exclusion to some of her children. Such confusion is evident in a fairy tale Baker wrote about the Rainbow Tribe called *La Tribu Arc-en-Ciel*, illustrated by Piet Worm. This book tells about a one-eyed hen named Kott-Kott, who travels around the world searching for her lost eye. She comes to rest in *Les Milandes*, a place where no one laughs at her anymore, and the cover portrays a black, one-eyed hen gazing up at eight children sitting in a tree. The hen most likely refers both to Baker herself and her half-sister, Willie Mae, who lost one eye in childhood. Baker, who was never sure where she fit in, with blacks or whites, Americans or Frenchmen, had only a partial understanding of the identity issues facing adopted children.[49] At times she appeared to follow carefully their cultural and religious origins and at other times to impose religious identification rather arbitrarily, based on her ideas about the mix of the group rather than the child's individual heritage. Her expectations about the direction of their life purposes made her especially unprepared for the process of identity development and differentiation during adolescence. She intuitively grasped that openness about adoption and ties to their cultural origins were important, but she minimized the degree to which her children, with their mixed cultural and racial origins, might have the same identity concerns that affected Baker. The two children who have altered their first names appear to have made changes that allow them to fit in more easily (Brahim to Brian, for example). Approximately half of the children have lived on more than one continent or moved back and forth between continents. Moïse appears to have had the most difficulty with Baker's preconceived ideas about his identity. He rebelled against her insistence that he wear a yarmulke to Catholic school, and he was actually excluded from the family because of his behavior twice during in his teenage years, the first time being sent to a kibbutz in Israel. During the 1950s, however, there was very little discussion of the identity concerns of adopted children, and one might argue that Baker was far more sophisticated than the average adoptive parent of her era. The dialogue on whether a child given up for adoption should be placed with parents whose ethnicity differs from that of the child is a more recent one, sparked by the 1980s position paper of the American Association of Black Social Workers opposing transracial adoptions and the ongoing debate over the outcome of such placements.[50]

Baker's life story reflects the transition of her generativity from the personal to the universal. She had always demonstrated a concern for the next generation and for the welfare of children, but her aloneness as an infertile woman moved her in the direction of her dual-purpose project of adopting children to create a family and to take political action against discrimination. By claiming motherhood for herself, she found a place of inclusion, as did Kott-Kott the mother hen, and recovered her lost eye/I.

NOTES

[1] Quoted in Lynn Haney, *Naked at the Feast: A Biography of Josephine Baker* (New York: Dodd, Mead & Company, 1981), 269.

[2] Stephen Papich, *Remembering Josephine: A Biography of Josephine Baker* (Indianapolis/New York: The Bobbs-Merrill Company, Inc., 1976), 134-35.

³ Dan P. McAdams, Holly M. Hart, and Shadd Maruna, "The Anatomy of Generativity," in Dan P. McAdams and Ed de St. Aubin, eds., *Generativity and Adult Development: How and Why We Care for the Next Generation* (Washington, DC: American Psychological Association, 1998), 36.

⁴ John Kotre and Kathy B. Kotre, "Intergenerational Buffers: 'The Damage Stops Here'," in McAdams and de St. Aubin, eds., *Generativity and Adult Development*, 367-90.

⁵ Josephine Baker and Jo Bouillon, *Josephine* (New York: Harper & Row, 1977), 5.

⁶ Jean-Claude Baker and Chris Chase, *Josephine: The Hungry Heart* (New York: Random House, 1993), 12, 16-17.

⁷ Baker and Chase, *Josephine*, 18.

⁸ Baker and Bouillon, *Josephine*, 9-10.

⁹ Baker and Chase, *Josephine*, 37. Regarding this statement, it must be remembered that her sister Margaret was a Continent away from Baker, who was living in France and then North Africa in the late 1930s and early 1940s when pregnancies quite probably did occur.

¹⁰ Haney, *Naked at the Feast*, 26.

¹¹ Baker and Chase, *Josephine*, 37-38.

¹² Haney, *Naked at the Feast*, 40; Baker and Chase, *Josephine*, 178.

¹³ Baker and Bouillon, *Josephine*, 230.

¹⁴ Quoted in Haney, *Naked at the Feast*, 40-41.

¹⁵ Quoted in Haney, *Naked at the Feast*, 61.

[16] Wendy Martin, "'Remembering the Jungle:' Josephine Baker and Modernist Parody," in Elazar Barkan and Ronald Bush, eds., *Prehistories of the Future: The Primitivist Project and the Culture of Modernism* (Stanford, CA: Stanford University Press, 1995), 310-25.

[17] The statements of awe and praise are found in Haney, *Naked at the Feast*, 67.

[18] Haney, *Naked at the Feast*, 177.

[19] Haney, *Naked at the Feast*, 126.

[20] Quoted in Haney, *Naked at the Feast*, 128.

[21] Quoted in Haney, *Naked at the Feast*, 64.

[22] Elizabeth Coffman, "Uncanny Performances in Colonial Narratives: Josephine Baker in Princesse Tam Tam," *Paradoxa* 3 (1997): 379-94.

[23] Phyllis Rose, *Jazz Cleopatra: Josephine Baker in Her Time* (New York: Doubleday, 1989), 107.

[24] Papich, *Remembering Josephine*, 81-90.

[25] The quotes can be found in Haney, *Naked at the Feast*, 202; Rose, *Jazz Cleopatra*, 169.

[26] Baker and Bouillon, *Josephine*, 111.

[27] Baker and Bouillon, *Josephine*, 113-14.

[28] On her religious practices, see Baker and Bouillon, *Josephine*, 136, 154.

[29] Elizabeth Anne Hemphill, *The Least of These* (New York: Weatherhill, 1980), 56-57.

[30] Haney, *Naked at the Feast*, 181.

[31] Bryan Hammond and Patrick O'Connor, *Josephine Baker* (Boston: Little, Brown, 1988), 145.

[32] Quoted in Haney, *Naked at the Feast*, 183.

[33] Baker and Chase, *Josephine*, 222.

[34] Quoted in Haney, *Naked at the Feast*, 183.

[35] Haney, *Naked at the Feast*, 183.

[36] Baker and Chase, *Josephine*, 211.

[37] Haney, *Naked at the Feast*, 226.

[38] Baker and Bouillon, *Josephine*, 157-58.

[39] Mary L. Dudziak, "Josephine Baker, Racial Protest, and the Cold War," *Journal of American History* 81 (September 1994): 543-70.

[40] Dudziak, "Josephine Baker," 569.

[41] Rose, *Jazz Cleopatra*, 240.

[42] On the university project, see Baker and Bouillon, *Josephine*, 242, 253; Haney, *Naked at the Feast*, 292.

[43] After the article was finished, *Time* magazine rejected it on the grounds that "Baldwin is passé, and Baker a memory of the thirties and forties." Gates wrote that this decision made him so angry that he decided to give up journalism to study English Language and Literature at Oxford, earning his doctorate five years later. See Henry Louis Gates, Jr., "An Interview with Josephine Baker and James Baldwin," *The Southern Review* 21 (Summer 1985): 594-602.

[44] Quoted in Haney, *Naked at the Feast*, 128.

[45] Quoted in Kariamu Welsh Asante, "Josephine Baker," in Darlene C. Hine, ed., *Black Women in America: An Historical Encyclopedia*, vol. 1 (Brooklyn, NY: Carlson Publishing Inc., 1993), 78.

[46] Baker and Chase, *Josephine*, 491.

[47] Baker and Chase, *Josephine*, 326.

[48] Rose, *Jazz Cleopatra*, 247.

[49] For a discussion of the identity concerns of adopted children, see David M. Brodzinsky, Marshall D. Schechter, and Robin Marantz Henig, *Being Adopted: The Lifelong Search for Self* (New York: Doubleday, 1992).

[50] For a discussion of policy aspects of transracial and transnational families, see Elizabeth Bartholet, *Family Bonds: Adoption and the Politics of Parenting* (Boston: Houghton Mifflin, 1993). Bartholet is both a civil rights and family law attorney and an adoptive mother of two children born in Peru.

Joy Adamson and Elsa, Courtesy of the Elsa Conservation Trust.

Chapter 4
Nurturing Animals:
"One Long Safari"
Joy Adamson (1910-1980)

Joy Adamson, author and naturalist, helped to change the world's perception of the relationship between animals and humans. It was only in middle age, after years of unsuccessful attempts to have children, that Adamson began adopting and nurturing orphaned wild animals. Her story of raising a lion cub named Elsa to adulthood and successfully releasing her to the wild became widely known with the publication of *Born Free* in 1960 and the subsequent movie of the same name. Adamson eventually wrote nine other books about her experiences with wild animals, along with three related children's books. With the proceeds, she supported conservation efforts and established parks, touring the world to deliver her message about Elsa and wildlife conservation. Her infertility and lifelong quest for children and family made her uniquely receptive to caring for wild animals and promoting their needs for autonomy and freedom.

Naturalist Jane Goodall once praised the contributions of Joy Adamson and her husband, George, in studying and recording animal behavior:

The careful documentation by the Adamsons of individual animals, their unique personalities, and the events of their rich and varied lives, represents a major accomplishment for science. They have a special place in history because they had the courage of their convictions and their success is a beacon for the long term goal of breeding endangered species for ultimate return to the wild.[1]

Today, the Adamsons' work is not as highly regarded by animal behavior scientists, and Joy Adamson's accomplishments in conservation and animal studies are not viewed in the same light as those of Aldo Leopold, Rachel Carson, Desmond Morris, or Jane Goodall. Her approach is seen as out of step with the animal behavior experiments of her day in that she placed herself in the lives of the animals she studied. Adamson admitted at the time that her efforts were "amateurish," and she viewed her animal observation methodology as "subjective and primarily based on mutual trust and affection."[2] But for the same reason that her achievements have been downplayed by the scientific community, her story deeply touched a public nerve and led people around the world to react favorably to her appeals for wildlife conservation. Adamson had no training as a scientist, and her work with animals was not rooted in any conceptually based research plan relevant to contemporary issues in animal behavior. Rather, this phase of Adamson's long career arose from the serendipitous appearance of orphaned lion cubs in need of care, juxtaposed with her intense need to parent, her identification with lions and respect for their freedom, and her own search for meaning. She used her strong observational abilities, which she had already developed in botanical painting, to document and describe lion behavior, and her readers responded to the depth of feeling she communicated in her telling of the story of Elsa. Although she was largely a popularist and not a great scientist, Adamson's personal accounts of interaction with animals brought worldwide publicity to the issues of animal rights and wildlife conservation. Adamson wrote at the end of *Born Free* that her relationship with Elsa "continues to be one of absolute equality quite different from that between a dog and his master."[3] She developed a special bond with Elsa and the big cats of Africa that she came to love and worked hard to protect. Her relationship with Elsa, as depicted in *Wild Lives of Africa*, by Juliette Huxley, suggests some of the flavor of her interaction with the young lion. Huxley was visiting the Adamsons, and they drove to the spot where they usually met Elsa and her cubs. The group walked towards the river "to the enchanting place of great trees spreading over rocks with sandy beach and murmur of water, where Joy used to do her writing and sketching, while Elsa played with her cubs." After two rifle shots into the air, they heard the chatter of baboons. "Elsa is coming," said Joy, "the baboons always give warning."

> At last, bounding out of the bush in great easy strides, there
> was Elsa, leaping towards Joy whose outstretched arms moved
> forward to defend herself from too powerful an embrace; even
> then she was nearly knocked over. The two of them, Elsa's paws
> on Joy's shoulders, stood there like old friends meeting again.
> The cubs were close behind, led by Jespath, the favourite son.
> He was a gallant little lion, with ears cocked and eyes alert, ready
> to protect his mother. Joy did not touch him, but kept stroking
> Elsa's sleek head, calling her name and fondling her gently,
> while Elsa returned all this affection in her own manner, her tail
> sweeping in wide curves as she nuzzled up to Joy.[4]

After her intensive work with Elsa the lion, Adamson went on to repeat the process with a cheetah and a leopard, in each case adopting and caring for an orphaned animal, releasing her to the wild, and observing the birth of her cubs. She had the capacity to see beyond the usual mode of relating to potentially dangerous wild animals, based on fear and domination. As was reflected in a broader ongoing cultural shift from exploitation to interdependence of organisms, on an individual level Adamson entered into an "I-thou" relationship with the animals she parented.[5] In addition to her infertility and longing for children, there are several other threads in Adamson's life leading to her ability to enter into an equal-to-equal relationship with a wild animal. She empathetically identified with lions from childhood, as can be seen in accounts of her growing up. Born Frederike Victoria Gessner in 1910 and called "Fifi," she was raised in Silesia, a region of the former Austro-Hungarian Empire. She and her two sisters often spent summers with their extended family on their wealthy grandfather's large estate. The children's favorite form of play involved a game of lion hunt, and Adamson was always assigned the role of the lioness and her cousin Peter the male lion. The other children had a prescribed time limit to capture the "lions," and if they were not successful, the hunt was over and the lions had won. Adamson wrote in her autobiography, "It was an exciting game; if we saw the pursuers closing in on one of our dens the other lion would roar to distract their attention and then run for dear life."[6] In this childhood play, Adamson acted not only as the hunted but also the rescuer of her fellow animal, foreshadowing a lifelong empathy for various creatures whose existence seemed threatened. She came to see beyond the aggressive potential of lions, cheetahs, and leopards, and to promote their needs for habitat in a landscape that was changing rapidly due to population growth and modernization.

From an early age, Adamson also had a feeling of being different from others. Despite coming from a background of relative security and affluence, she observed the disparity between her own middle-class standing (her father was a civil servant), and that of her mother's wealthier family, the Weisshuhns. While her summers with the relatives were generally positive formative experiences, Adamson felt emotional pain when her cousins laughed at her for having nails in the soles of her shoes to make them last longer. She also felt embarrassed on another occasion when her cousin Peter asked her if she would not "rather be a Weisshuhn like him."[7] More serious than these awkward incidents with her cousins were her feelings of rejection and alienation from each of her parents. Adamson later wrote in her autobiography how as a child she came to be frightened of her father, whom she described as a sadistic person who would often ignore, tease, or punish his daughters. Her father had always wanted a son, and throughout her childhood he called her Fritz and encouraged her to wear boys' clothing. In contrast, she felt closer to her mother, whom she idolized and who seemed like a goddess to her. Yet Adamson indicated that at times her mother could be indifferent or callous toward her feelings, as seen in the following story involving her beloved pet albino rabbit named Hasai. One day during the First World War, when meat grew scarce, she remarked at the dinner table that the stew was excellent, to which her mother replied "unconcernedly" that it included Hasai. In addition, her mother was often absent from the home, something that became permanent when she left Adamson's father for another man. Over time mother and daughter became increasingly detached.

Her parents' divorce constituted the first of many losses Adamson suffered during her life. Others would involve giving up her home, language, and culture. After World War I, her native land, Austrian Silesia, became part of Czechoslovakia, and residents were expected to speak Czechoslovakian in public instead of German. After World War II, she learned that the valley of her childhood had become permanently flooded, preventing her from ever seeing it again. She did visit Vienna following the latter war, but returned home to Africa feeling "extremely depressed," having witnessed much destruction, the loss of Jewish friends, and observing her mother and sisters living in poverty. Living in a British colony in Kenya in the years that followed, she felt the need to stop speaking German entirely and switch to English, although she sometimes had trouble being understood.

Despite feeling alienated from both her parents, Adamson did have two nurturing individuals available in her early life, the family's cook,

Milli, and her maternal grandmother, Oma. Adamson wrote that it was to Oma that she owed anything good about herself, an insight consistent with psychologists' thinking about the crucial role of an alternative parental figure in building a child's resilience in neglectful or abusive families. After her parents divorced she and her older sister lived with her grandmother, while her younger sister Dorle resided with their father, as all three sisters seemed unable to tolerate their stepfather. Her mother's infidelity was apparently not unusual within the extended family. Adamson wrote in her autobiography, "In our large family there were several unsatisfactory marriages and so from childhood I had learned to accept what might be called long-leash relationships, provided they were conducted with tact and did not hurt anyone."[8] Her statement surely underplays the obvious pain and turbulence caused by her mother's affairs and the subsequent psychological loss she felt after the divorce. Adamson remained exquisitely sensitive to loss her whole life, experiencing major depressive episodes in response to other severed relationships. She also followed her family's pattern of infidelity in each of her three marriages.

Adamson's childhood and adolescent experiences of marginality were amplified when she moved to Kenya, where as an Austrian citizen living in British colonial society in an African country, she was perceived as an outsider. During World War II she was briefly detained as a native German-speaker before being released. Later on, even though she acquired British citizenship through her marriage to George Adamson, she was not fully accepted by the local British community. This sense of feeling different and not getting along well with people, however, may have made a fundamental contribution to her love of the African landscape and her work with wild animals. On her very first visit to Africa, she stated that she "felt curiously at home."[9] Her love of open space and tolerance for being alone helped her to feel comfortable spending many hours a day in the wild observing plants and animals.

Adamson was "off-time," referring to a different life-course pattern from the one she expected, in failing to create her own genetic family as a younger woman, and then parenting animals during the last third of her life.[10] The nurturing of orphaned animals became a pervasive theme as she entered middle age, and her writing frequently made a connection between her frustrated desire for children and the numerous animals, large and small, she cared for in Africa. For a time she even carried her pet mongoose in her pocket like a fetus while sitting on a mule as she traveled. To some degree Adamson conceptualized the adoption of animals as an emotional replacement for lost children. She was extremely attached to her pet Cairn terrier, Pippin, given to her by her second husband following a miscarriage. During her third marriage, to game warden George Adamson, she specifically linked her pregnancy losses with compensatory animal adoptions. As she stated in her autobiography: "However varied and interesting our life often was, it was also restless and insecure, and I had another miscarriage, the third now by three husbands. I badly wanted a child, but evidently had not the mentality of a brooding hen, and I was distressed. As if to help me over my dilemma we were given a newly born rock hyrax, an animal that looks like a marmot though zoologists insist that by its feet and its teeth it must be related to rhinos and elephants."[11] She also referred to a baby buffalo that had lost his mother as "an affectionate, if boisterous, baby who sucked my thumb and followed us about wherever we went."[12] When offered a young mongoose, she insisted that she and George had no choice but to take him because he had adopted them on sight, "making it plain that from now on we were his foster parents." Interestingly, Adamson even facilitated the adoption of orphaned animals by other animals. On one occasion she rescued two female Colobus monkeys who had been illegally purchased and held in captivity for five months. She added that it took another five months for the mother Colobus who lived on her property to put her arms around the shoulders of the two orphaned monkeys. Adamson's use of animal analogy, in saying that she did not possess "the mentality of a brooding hen," suggests that she may have blamed her reproductive problems on her own mental state, an attitude not uncommon among infertile women even today.

Adamson's relationship with Elsa began in February 1956, when her husband, George, who found it necessary to shoot a female lion that had killed a Boran tribesman, brought home her orphaned cubs. Joy described the prelude to this new adoption as follows: "I had of course looked after other baby animals: among them two elephants, a bushbuck, an impala doe, a serval cat, three ostriches, many mongooses, and Pati, the hyrax, but I had no experience of tiny lion cubs and these we judged could not be more than three weeks old."[13] Among the three lion cubs was the one she named Elsa, whose adoption marked the beginning of the couple's intensive animal parenting that made them famous. In a subsequent interview, Adamson said that Elsa had become "almost like my child," as she devoted much of her time and emotional energy to her care, treating her in some ways like a human infant. In *Born Free*, Joy described how she adapted a flexible rubber tube from the "wireless set" to serve as teat for feeding the lion cubs before they were able to obtain baby bottles and other supplies. She claimed that all her emotion was directed to Elsa and their other animals because she had no children. A parent-child relationship was perceived by visitors as well, as in Juliette Huxley's recounting: "Joy continued with the Elsa saga, as one talks of a wonder child."[14] Even her husband George started acting like a father. As he later wrote in his autobiography: "There is no doubt that our shared devotion to Elsa had brought Joy and me as close to each other as we had ever been, just as a child might have done—and Elsa took the place of a child in our family album."[15]

The theme of large cats as the virtual offspring of Joy and George Adamson continued into their later years when they were considering divorce, and, more than once, decided to remain married for the sake of the animals. At a time when they were separated, Joy once wrote to

George at his camp to console him over the return of lion cubs to the wild with the following words: "Do not despair; have faith they are happy. We love our animals as our children but we have to try not to be possessive, and regard their lives as more important than our own need for them."[16] Adamson's writings indicate that she experienced maternal satisfaction not only in raising orphaned cats, but especially in providing a bridge to their successful reproduction in the wild. In her last book, *Queen of Shaba*, she described how the leopard she named Penny had been found abandoned at age one month and had no one to teach her how to mother her cubs. So she performed the task herself. The following passage affirms her maternal role: "The fact that Penny had kept closer to me this morning than she had done recently might suggest that to her I represented 'mother'—the supplier of food and security. . . ."[17]

Adamson's nurturing of animals was actually the third phase of her work involving African habitats and cultures. She had two previous careers, the first as a botanical painter and the second as a portrait painter of Kenyan tribal groups documenting ethnic costumes. All together, she completed about five hundred paintings of African flora and seven hundred tribal portraits. With her second husband's encouragement and tutoring, Adamson had started painting the flowers he collected on their honeymoon, as she put it, "To make myself useful."[18] Adamson was then asked by Dr. Arthur Jex-Blake, the editor of *Gardening in East Africa*, and his wife, Lady Muriel, to illustrate the second edition of the book. She wrote that she originally felt terrified to take on the project and believed that Lady Muriel had arranged for an exhibition of her paintings primarily in order to boost her self-confidence. Adamson eventually illustrated seven books on the flora of East Africa, including *Some Wild Flowers of Kenya*, *The Indigenous Trees of Uganda Protectorate*, and *Kenya Trees and Shrubs*. In February 1947, Adamson was awarded the Grenfell Gold Medal, the highest honor given to a painter by the Royal Horticultural Society in London. Her success led to her being offered a post as floral painter at the prestigious Kew Gardens, which she turned down in order to return to Kenya. At the time of her exhibit by the Royal Horticultural Society, a major art critic stated that "she combined artistic layout with scientific accuracy not seen since the day of the great Dutch herbalists." One of her biographers, Adrian House, has written that Adamson's botanical paintings have yet to receive the attention they deserve, either in terms of quality of reproduction, preservation and cataloging, or museum display.[19]

After marrying George Adamson, Joy spent the next five years (1948 to 1953) concentrating on the creation of tribal portraits, a project which required her to be apart from him much of the time. She began this series of paintings on her own, in response to her observations in northern Kenya that the traditional culture was slowly disappearing. Renowned anthropologist Louis Leakey was enthusiastic about this work and supported her efforts to find financial backing. Eventually Adamson obtained a government contract in 1949 to do portraits of between fifteen and twenty-two tribes; others were financed privately. In preparing to sketch each individual or group, she took detailed notes about her subjects, and required that each ritual or costume be authenticated by at least two elders. Despite suffering from malaria, she would paint from dawn to sundown, living on a diet of eggs, fruit, and local vegetables. To whatever area she traveled, she set up camp with a tent and established her makeshift studio. Besides using brush and canvas, she also took photographs of her portrait sitters, some of which are in the British Museum. Of the approximately seventy tribal groups in Kenya at that time, Adamson wound up painting nearly sixty. Through Leakey's intervention, the Kenyan government ultimately purchased all the works. Some are on display in the State House and most of the rest at the National Museums of Kenya in Nairobi. Adamson insisted that these portraits remain in Kenya rather than allowing them to be sold for more money to private individuals, an early example of her generativity and generosity. When some of Adamson's paintings were transferred from the Coryndon Museum to the future State House, Jomo Kenyatta, first president of independent Kenya, and his colleagues "rejoiced to see these fragments of the past given a place of honor in their new official building."[20] Later, when Adamson attended a reception with Kenyatta after the filming of *Born Free*, she found more than seventy of her portraits on the State House walls.[21]

That Adamson stands out as an unusually gifted individual is evident from the descriptions of her childhood interests and achievements as well as from her diverse adult accomplishments. In addition, a family history of giftedness and creativity is apparent from the information known about her relatives. Her maternal great-grandfather, for example, was an energetic and inventive person who introduced the first water turbine into the country of Austria. (He later received an offer from Thomas Edison to form a business partnership, but turned it down.) Her mother was an accomplished pianist, a talent that Adamson seems to have inherited and displayed at an early age. She loved music, her mother said, and could sight-read before she knew the alphabet. Music so moved her that if she felt any physical discomfort, she asked her mother to play Chopin to ease the pain. Playing the piano always comforted her, and Joy played regularly until she lost the use of her right hand in an accident she suffered in her last years. Adamson's manner was always intense and stoic from childhood through adulthood. Her mother wrote that in her youth she never complained when injured and seemed to be totally fearless. High-spirited and energetic, she longed to explore new places and discover strange animals. She lived her life with unusual courage, responding to the intensity of her interests and taking risks most people would never consider.

Adamson's rapid succession of career interests and paths of study indicates her ability to master a variety of fields, a phenomenon not uncommon among highly gifted people. She, like many of those talented in more than one area, often had difficulty in choosing which field to pursue. She later described her multiple interests by saying, "As I grew up, I found myself torn, like so many others, between an insatiable curiosity about the bewildering world around me and an urge to discover the medium through which I could express myself and in doing so be constructive."[22] Through her field work in Kenya she ultimately proved able to integrate her visual-spatial, naturalist, and kinesthetic abilities. She observed and recorded nature, paying great attention to detail and using her artistic talents to make lasting records of disappearing flora, fauna, and tribal customs. She had enormous strength and endurance and was said to be able to out-walk and out-climb any of her male contemporaries, excelling in fields that were traditionally considered masculine. Her stamina allowed her to carry out long-term projects such as the tribal paintings and to tolerate living without amenities. She enjoyed and needed challenging activity regardless of the time and energy involved. Her friend Elspeth Huxley once described how "Joy sat for hours sketching her loved one [Elsa]. . . ."[23] Adamson never retired, and though nearing age seventy, she had just completed her work on raising a young leopard when she died.

Despite her many starts and stops, one can find a thread of continuity in Adamson's intellectual and artistic interests, and over time she increasingly achieved an integration of her personal strengths. In her early teens, she was fortunate to spend four years at an experimental boarding school established by the Austrian government after World War I. At this institution, innovative teaching methods were practiced and learning opportunities in the creative arts readily available. Adamson studied painting and sculpture, as well as theater and music, and she painted murals on the walls of the school's living quarters. She then left boarding school at age fifteen to study music full-time in order to qualify for the state piano certificate. But by age seventeen, having satisfied all the requirements, she realized that her hands were too small for her to succeed as a concert pianist. As she had no wish to teach music, she soon gave up the idea of further musical training. Shifting to the visual arts, Adamson enrolled in a two-year course in fashion and dressmaking and acquired the Gremium diploma. She learned to do metalwork, poster and book-jacket design, and also studied art history, drawing, painting restoration, sculpture, woodcarving, and photography. Her work in photography, she wrote later, helped her to appreciate small detail, a skill she subsequently used to advantage in her botanical painting.

Adamson became the first woman in her family to undertake such a broad range of studies. However, it is unclear from her later writings whether her early training in so many fields was career-driven. In her introduction to *Joy Adamson's Africa*, published in 1972, she wrote, "All these occupations were no more than explorations through which I hoped to find my true fulfilment [sic]."[24] Her most serious life endeavors all began rather casually. She once stated, "In general, I seldom plan anything but, instead, find myself driven by my curiosity to find out about things which I see happening around me. Anything I have carefully planned has never worked out while, on the other hand, I have often found myself deeply enslaved to something which started as a hobby."[25] Her description of painting flora on Mount Kenya provides an example of her unplanned, spur-of-the-moment style. At some point between her second and third marriages, Adamson suddenly felt the need to be alone, and, as she put it, simply "decided to camp on the moorlands of Mount Kenya and paint the flowers there."[26] She appeared unconcerned that the moorlands begin at 14,000 feet of elevation, which presented formidable logistical problems in terms of supplies and safety. Nor did it seem to matter that she had chosen the rainy season so as to observe the richest flora. She had figured on a month's camping expedition but then remained for four months because she "found so many flowers to paint that I decided to stay on."[27]

In choosing and developing her work within the social context of relationships, Adamson's pattern of career development was consistent with that of other gifted women of her era. Feminist psychologist Carol Tomlinson-Keasey, in her study of a cohort of forty gifted women from the Terman Study of Genius in the United States,[28] found that individuals who, like Adamson, studied art and music "seldom pursued a career in that direction, but rather married and developed their interest in the arts into an avocation that gradually took on more and more of the characteristics of paid work." The recurring themes among this group of women included a lack of confidence in their abilities, a random aspect to career choice, and the importance of relationship context to work life. When Adamson began her work as botanical painter, for example, it was within the context of her marriage to botanist Peter Bally. She felt uncertain about her talent and did not have a lifetime career in mind. Later, when married to George Adamson, a game warden, she found the opportunities for a safari life and interaction with wild animals, and began moving in this new direction.

Joy Adamson's infertility problems originated in her early twenties at a time she was still undecided about future goals. Before any of her marriages, she had become pregnant during her first serious relationship with a young man. When he refused to marry her, Adamson obtained an illegal abortion, after which she fell "dangerously ill." She wrote obliquely in her autobiography about this first relationship, saying, "When, after two years, it ended, I was left with a little dachshund called Plinkus and a deep wound in my heart, which took a long time to heal."[29] According to biographer Caroline Cass, Adamson was never able to have children as a result of the abortion procedure, and it proved to be "one of the great sadnesses of her life."[30] Following the abortion and subsequent breakup with her boyfriend, Adamson grew increasingly depressed and attempted suicide by taking an overdose of drugs. Fortunately, her grandmother found her and took her to the hospital for emergency treatment. Cass quoted her sister Dorle as saying she was "sure that Fifi just wanted to die after the loss of her lover and her baby."[31] Becoming "dangerously ill" after an abortion suggests the possibility of infection and subsequent tubal scarring, which would be consistent with the "tubal insufflation" procedure Joy underwent much later in September 1951 at a hospital in Mombasa, upon the recommendation of her gynecologist. (A very painful procedure which has since been replaced by techniques that visualize the fallopian tubes, it involved insufflating carbon dioxide gas into the cervix, uterus, and tubes until the woman experienced shoulder pain, meaning that the gas had successfully traveled through the fallopian tube or tubes.) Although Adamson eventually recovered psychologically from the breakup with her first lover and her aborted pregnancy, she hoped that she could still become a mother, and the problem of bringing a child to term would continue to plague her.

In her mid-twenties, Joy had temporarily given up the arts and started studying medicine. But she found the pre-med curriculum difficult and the courses somewhat boring, and she focused instead on the attentions of an affluent young businessman named Victor von Klarwill. He was deeply interested in sporting activities such as skiing and canoeing, and he was very impressed with Adamson's athleticism. He proposed after a brief courtship, and they were married in the spring of 1935 when Adamson was twenty-five. With his encouragement and assurance that she would never need to earn her own living, she quit her pre-medical studies and set up housekeeping in Vienna. But she soon felt bored with her leisurely life style. She hoped that having a child would provide fulfillment despite her husband's lack of interest in starting a family.[32] However, when she did finally become pregnant, she had a miscarriage and subsequently became depressed. Meanwhile, with the rise of anti-Semitism, von Klarwill, who was Jewish, grew increasingly concerned about his safety in Austria. Together they secretly decided to leave the country, and they selected Kenya in east Africa, based on their correspondence with an acquaintance who had emigrated there. In May 1936 Adamson sailed to Kenya with the plan that her husband would join her if she felt that life there would be satisfactory. Before boarding the ship in Genoa, Italy, according to her autobiography, she had written out two questions for a Carinthian fortune-teller highly recommended by friends. The questions were whether she would continue to live in the place where she currently resided and whether she would have children. Upon her return to Austria she received his answers—that she would ultimately live in the tropics and would not have children. She apparently refused to accept the second part of the old seer's response and tried hard to prove him wrong. Adamson later wrote, "I had had a miscarriage during my marriage to Ziebel[33] which affected me so badly that after I recovered I decided to attend a course designed to teach women who were living in isolated areas, with no doctor or nurse nearby, how to look after their baby. I determined not to be influenced by the fortune-teller's predictions and had all my dresses made so that they could be let out if I became pregnant."[34] From these remarks, we can see that Adamson continued to prepare for another pregnancy, educating herself for the possibility of childbirth in a remote country, as she attempted to ward off the negative prophecy of the fortune-teller.

On her voyage to ascertain whether life in Kenya would be suitable for von Klarwill and herself, she fell in love with Peter Bally, a Swiss botanist traveling to South Africa. Bally had been born into an upper-class Viennese family, and was described as a quiet, introverted individual with a lifetime love of nature. He had rejected his father's request to join him in his pharmaceutical business, and had moved to Africa, where he had just published a book called *Native Medicinal and Poisonous Plants of Tanganyika*. During the course of the journey, they decided that she would return to Vienna to discuss ending the relationship with von Klarwill and that Bally would wait for her in Africa. He also requested that she visit his older brother, Gustav Bally, a prominent psychiatrist, partly to help her resolve her marital situation but also for his brother's professional opinion of Adamson as a suitable mate. Gustav wrote to Peter giving his approval to the marriage, "stating that, although he perceived her to be a highly strung and emotional woman, Joy was also a person of great courage, determination and vitality."[35] She then proceeded to divorce von Klarwill in December of 1937, and return to Kenya to marry Bally, who had since obtained a job as a botanist at the Coryndon Museum in Nairobi. Despite the divorce, Adamson remained on good terms with von Klarwill, who later fled to Kenya with his mother during the war; she even helped to support them with proceeds from the sale of her botanical paintings.

Adamson and Bally married in April 1938, and their honeymoon consisted of a three-month expedition to explore the Chyulu Hills, a twenty-eight-mile-long volcanic range on the border of Kenya and Tanzania. During the course of the honeymoon Adamson became pregnant and then experienced her second miscarriage. She described how during a hike with her new husband she became aware of some abdominal discomfort that changed gradually to severe pain, signaling the loss of the fetus. The incident is recounted only briefly in her autobiography, probably understating the impact it had upon her. She wrote, "For as long as I could I put up with the pain, but finally I could no longer walk and soon afterward had another miscarriage. Was the Austrian fortune-teller going to be proved right in the end? I was deeply distressed."[36]

With money from Bally's mother, Adamson and her husband built a Moorish-style house in Nairobi and planted a garden full of rare plants that was described as "spectacular." They also became friends with Mary and Louis Leakey and joined them in their archeological excavations in the Rift Valley. During World War II Adamson spent much of her time with Bally in the Coryndon Museum painting flowers. As a foreigner married to another foreigner, British officials saw her as an outsider and, as previously mentioned, she was also looked upon with suspicion for being a German-speaking Austrian. In addition, she and her husband began experiencing marital problems, and Adamson, now approaching thirty, may have begun to have increasingly serious mood swings. Apparently Adamson felt her husband could not satisfy her sexually and claimed that he was impotent. Bally grew depressed and was sometimes physically ill. In response, Adamson sought out other men and acquired a reputation for possessing a "voracious" sexual appetite, according to biographer Caroline Cass, who wrote, "Joy's carnal needs were to become legendary."[37] Moreover, she gained a reputation for being demanding and irritating to others, for example, repeatedly insisting on gasoline for flower-painting expeditions during the war when fuel was in very short supply and unavailable to other civilians. Bally then went to South Africa for rest, and Adamson visited a government family in the Northern Frontier District, where she remained for four months. The family recalled Adamson as moody, crying a lot, and tiring to be around.[38] During this time, she fell in love with the landscape of northern Kenya. When Bally and Adamson reunited, she was unhappy with his lack of attention, and he pulled further away. Cass wrote, "While Peter took refuge in working long hours at the museum, Joy threw herself into yet another painting commission. Her extraordinary knack for finding just the right antidote for her immediate emotional ailment would serve her more than once in times of trouble."[39]

From this time onward, it appears that Adamson alternated between episodes of severe depression and heightened creativity. Her extraordinary achievements took place within the context of her mood swings, which contributed to her high energy level and productivity and at the same time disrupted her interpersonal relationships. The description of her vacillating moods, suicide attempts, pressured speech, sleep disturbance, and risk-taking suggests that she was on the continuum of bipolar disorder, or manic-depressive disorder, for which there was no effective treatment at that time. Bipolar disorder would be consistent with many of her behaviors that were viewed as peculiar or immoral, such as her hyper-sexuality and impulsive decision-making. Gerald Nevill, her surgeon in later years, considered her "almost a manic depressive,"[40] probably meaning that she had mood swings but was not psychotic. A good friend as well being as her physician, Nevill recalled that over the years of their acquaintance, "Joy didn't just cry, she would sit there and weep. Often one had no idea why she was weeping."[41]

Adamson made considerable efforts to get assistance for her mood disorder, but the type of treatment available in that era was not especially helpful to her. Adamson entered psychoanalysis twice, the first time in

Vienna, where she saw a total of four psychoanalysts. She described her first analysis as follows: ". . . I duly spent an hour every day relaxing on the couch of a famous psychoanalyst. There, at his request, I talked about everything that came into my mind. It was believed that in doing this one would unknowingly reveal reactions that had been suppressed and had thereby damaged what should have been one's normal responses. I tried to let my thoughts pour out at random but the psychoanalyst kept interrupting, asking me to concentrate on my childhood."[42] She wrote further, "I found this quite unsatisfactory and went to another analyst, but after more than a year, having derived no benefit—except that of obtaining a patient listener of my problems—I stopped the treatment. As far as I could judge the only advice I had been given was to get married."[43] Later, after the breakup of her second marriage, when she grew extremely depressed, Adamson agreed to undergo psychoanalysis once again, this time in London and Vienna, but the experience did not provide a cure.[44] Today, bipolar disorder is understood as a largely genetically-based biological condition that can be treated with medication and supportive psychotherapy, but the approach followed in Joy's era, daily psychoanalysis, may have aggravated her condition rather than improved it. Relying on a free flow of thoughts and images, psychoanalysis can exacerbate the already flowing stream of unconnected ideas present in the thinking style of a creative individual with bipolar disorder such as Joy Adamson.

Without effective help for her mood disorder, Adamson's interpersonal relationships became increasingly unsatisfying and unstable. She showed little insight into her own shortcomings and generally blamed other people or circumstances when anything went wrong. On many occasions her impulsive behavior led to situations that exacerbated her mood disorder. The most notable example involved her response to meeting George Adamson, leading to the breakup of her marriage with Bally and her marrying George. The Ballys were invited to a Christmas party in 1942, where Joy first met George Adamson, a northern Kenyan game warden with a reputation for great courage in the face of danger. He invited the Ballys to accompany him on a camel safari, during which he and Joy initiated a sexual relationship that was soon discovered by Bally. She then decided she wanted to stay married to Bally, but he refused, offering to pay for all divorce expenses so that she could marry George Adamson if she wished. But Joy had serious doubts about marrying George, a man who spent most of his time living in the wild and seemed to lack any kind of domestic side. Stuck in this quandary and feeling totally depressed, she made another suicide attempt in 1944 by consuming a bottle of sulphanilamide tablets. Dr. Jex-Blake explained to George Adamson that the medication was an antibiotic that would not cause any lasting harm, and suggested that he leave Joy alone for a month to give her time to decide whether to marry him or not. According to biographer Adrian House, apparently George then threatened to shoot himself if she did not marry him immediately. Joy conceded and they were quickly married, and moved into George's small, Spartan-like dwelling near Isiolo in the game reserve. Their best times were spent on safari together while Joy painted and collected fossils, insects, and small reptiles for the Coryndon Museum. It was also during this time that she began adopting orphaned animals. She remained very ambivalent about George, and through much of the marriage avoided sexual contact with him, preferring affairs with other men except when actively trying to conceive.

Despite the problems that existed in the relationship, Joy Adamson continued to wish for children. Although she wrote in her autobiography about her longings for a child and her intense distress after each of her reproductive losses, the actual details surrounding her failed pregnancies are ambiguous. She claimed that she had three miscarriages, one during each of her marriages, and her husband George referred to the third miscarriage in his autobiography. Adrian House, who knew both Joy and George Adamson and had access to Joy's private diaries and calendars in writing the story of their lives, speculated that one or more of these experiences may have been fantasized or invented. In an unpublished draft of her autobiography, Adamson claimed that she and George went on a second honeymoon right after the 1951 procedure to open her fallopian tubes, and that she soon became pregnant and later miscarried. According to House, however, her calendar records noted a menstrual period occurring two weeks before the procedure and two weeks afterward, suggesting that no pregnancy occurred during that cycle.[45] Adding to the complexity were Joy's reservations about having a child with George because she felt a child might inherit his mother's mental condition (his mother had been institutionalized following mental deterioration due to pre-senile dementia and/or alcoholism). Joy had undergone an infertility workup, after which she approached several other men, apparently unsuccessfully, with the request that they serve as a sperm donor.[46] When Peter Bally remarried a much younger woman in 1951 and his new wife became pregnant, Adamson at age forty-one resolved once more to try to start a family. After being told by a psychiatrist that there was no danger of a hereditary mental condition being transmitted to a child, and following through with the recommended tubal procedure, Joy hoped to finally achieve motherhood. Nevertheless, all her efforts to conceive over the next few years were unsuccessful and she remained childless.

It was in these circumstances that Adamson, forty-six years old and past the normal childbearing age, received three orphaned lion cubs from her husband and started on a different kind of parenting. The runt of the litter was her favorite, and Adamson named her Elsa after her former mother-in-law, Elsa von Klarwill. She and George raised the three young lions, with Adamson's pet hyrax as their companion, and allowed them to roam the house and grounds freely. As the three animals became too large to manage, the chief game warden, William Hale, insisted that they all be sent away. The Adamsons reluctantly allowed two of the lions to be given to the Rotterdam Zoo, but they refused to comply fully with the directive from George's superior and kept Elsa. Whenever they could they took Elsa on safari with them, spending long periods of time in the bush. When Elsa reached age two and grew increasingly aggressive, the Adamsons believed the moment had come to release her into the wild, despite opposition from some government officials. After a first abortive attempt in which Elsa became ill, she was ultimately released in the Meru County Council Reserve. The Adamsons taught her to kill and gradually left her on her own for longer periods, until finally letting her go completely.

With her memories still fresh and possessing many sketches, paintings, and photographs of Elsa, Joy Adamson decided that she wanted to write about the experience of first raising and then releasing her beloved young lion. When a publisher told her that she did not know English well enough to write a book, she approached Elspeth Huxley to write the book for her, and Huxley replied that for the best effect it should be written in the first person. She then approached her husband George to tell Elsa's story, but he said he was uninterested in taking on such a major project. In light of these rejections, Joy consented to write the account herself. Some of the content came from her husband's diaries and reports, which she duly noted in the acknowledgments. Moreover, in developing the material for each chapter, she received advice from Lord William Percy, a renowned naturalist, who also suggested the volume's title. But *Born Free* was primarily Joy Adamson's work and she labored over it for many months. Then, having completed the first draft, she went to London to try to find a publisher but was rejected thirteen times. Finally, Marjorie Villiers of the Harvill Press, impressed by Adamson's telling of the story in her own words, recommended the idea to Billy Collins, chairman of the publishing firm that owned Harvill, and Collins offered Adamson a contract. Villiers then helped Adamson to rewrite her book, improving both the style and language. Meanwhile, in late December 1959, Elsa gave birth to three cubs, and, remarkably, after six weeks she came back with them to the Adamsons' camp. When Billy Collins received news of Elsa's litter, he decided to go to Africa and observe the scene personally. During his visit, Collins and Adamson began an intimate relationship, which continued well beyond the publication of the book. They remained married to their respective spouses but maintained a long correspondence, and Collins tried to interest her in religion in the hope of helping her resolve her emotional problems. Adamson considered Collins along with Peter Bally to be the real loves of her life. Despite some ups and downs in their relationship, she remained deeply connected to Collins until his death a decade and a half later.

Born Free was published in 1960, accompanied by an enormous publicity campaign that Collins arranged. The book became an immediate best-seller. Posters of Elsa could be found in virtually every bookshop in London, and the *Sunday Times* serialized the pictures. Within months the book had been translated into twenty-five languages. A children's book, *Elsa*, illustrated with the Adamsons' photographs, was released the following year. The success of *Born Free* helped bring the issues of animal treatment and wildlife conservation to the public's attention, and Adamson promoted these concerns with all her energy and resources for the rest of her life. *Born Free* netted 500,000 pounds for Adamson within its first ten years, all of which supported conservation efforts. With the help of Julian Huxley, she went on to write the first of her two books on Elsa's cubs, called *Living Free*, which appeared in October 1961. Ted Hughes, then Poet Laureate of Great Britain, reviewed *Living Free* and evidently felt touched by it:[47]

> That a lioness, one of the great moody aggressors, should
> be brought to display such qualities as Elsa's, is a step not so
> much in the education of lions as in the civilisation of men. And
> insofar as it is more important to throw one's energy into forming
> traditions of kindness and summoning a spirit of sympathetic
> understanding, even in the smallest things, rather than exercising
> any further the overdeveloped weapons of the hand and the head,
> this book is a small gospel.

Back in Africa, with George Adamson's impending retirement from the game department, a new home needed to be found for Elsa and her cubs. But before this could be accomplished Elsa became ill and died of unknown causes in early 1961. Joy was greatly saddened by the event, as seen in her comment: "With Elsa's death a vital part of myself died too."[48] Another crisis occurred when the game warden ordered Elsa's cubs to be shot after they had attacked some livestock. Yet after enduring lengthy battles with the authorities, the Adamsons were finally able to save the cubs and take them to the Serengeti Game Reserve in Tanzania.

Upon the publication of her third book, *Forever Free*, in 1962, Adamson went on a publicity tour in England. However, her first lecture, before three thousand people, titled, "Man: The Inferior Species," did not fare well. She seemed difficult to understand because of her Austrian accent, rapid speech, and idiosyncratic vocabulary. But her speaking gradually improved as she took elocution lessons and arranged for her tutor to sit in the front row and hold up a small red flag to indicate when to slow down. In 1963, at the suggestion of Billy Collins, the now celebrated author went on a world tour and undertook a lecture schedule with the same intensity she had always demonstrated in other endeavors. She gave three talks a day, in addition to breakfast, lunch and dinner interviews, autograph sessions, and television and radio programs. But after a while the pace became too strenuous. Following a trip around Australia she left for New Zealand on a stretcher, and a physician canceled her public appearances and insisted that she rest. Later on, she was invited to visit the USSR, Japan, Thailand, and Hungary, where she spoke to people on behalf of endangered wildlife and was taken on tours of parks and wildlife sanctuaries. She wrote that she sometimes felt like a detached observer during her lectures and thought that she might be "a medium for conveying Elsa's message," although she made the decision to keep quiet about this perspective when she spoke.[49] Fame brought a variety of reactions. Although she was admired for pursuing her cause she was sometimes criticized in the press for her manner and style, especially for wearing inappropriate clothing such as a leopard-skin coat that she ultimately agreed to discard. In December 1963 she was satirized on the London stage with a song called "Pride and Joy," containing the lyrics, "Oh, I'm in love with a lion/And a lion's in love with me. . . . I'm relyin' on a lion/And a lion is lyin' on me!"[50]

More positively, a charitable foundation called the Elsa Wild Animal Appeal was established that year and had a major impact on conservation in many countries, including her adopted homeland of Kenya. The Kenya Wildlife Service, formerly the Kenya Game Department and Parks Department, began receiving financial backing from the Elsa Wild Animal Appeal. Now having substantial income from her books, Adamson made sound decisions about the financial management of both the trust and her private finances. The trust's funds were controlled by a board of trustees in London, with recommendations for project support coming from an advisory committee in Kenya. Adamson's personal financial affairs were handled by an accountant, Peter Johnson, who said, "My role was to enable her to do her job. I dislike rows, so we never had one, but so few people tried to understand her. Joy was an idealist and was striving for the perfect conservation world. Such an ideal being unattainable naturally led to her unhappiness, and of course, Joy was also continually looking for love."[51]

One of the biggest boosts to Joy Adamson's promotional efforts on behalf of animal and wildlife conservation was the creation of a movie version of *Born Free*. In 1964 Columbia Pictures agreed to make a feature film of the popular book, to be shot on location at a farm at Naro Moru, on the plains of Mount Kenya. British actors Virginia McKenna and Bill Travers, who had strong sympathies for the wildlife conservation cause, were chosen to portray Joy and George Adamson. Twenty-one circus and native lions were hired to play Elsa and the other lions in the movie. In 1966 Adamson flew to London for the royal premiere, which was also attended by the Queen. While the film did not receive many accolades from motion picture critics in London and elsewhere, it became a worldwide success at the box-office and won an Academy award for its music. Later, in 1984, McKenna and Travers founded the Born Free Foundation, a British-based group with goals of stopping cruelty to captive wild animals, conserving wild animals in their natural habitat, and ensuring the long-term survival of species.

Ironically, Adamson's message to the world about respect for the freedom and autonomy of wild animals was juxtaposed with the loss of freedom and autonomy she experienced in her third marriage. There appears to be substantial evidence that at times George severely abused her, probably in conjunction with his heavy alcohol consumption, which had become a major issue of contention between the two of them. She did file a complaint at the local police station, which at first was not taken seriously. But when she started to pursue the matter she became convinced that taking her case to court would cause George to lose his job and be sent to prison, so she decided to keep quiet about her suffering. Bruises over her entire upper torso were noticed on one occasion by John MacDonald, a Scottish veterinarian, who mentioned his observation to his predecessor George Low, who told him, "Oh, George would have taken his rifle butt to her." According to MacDonald, "George was a gentle man most of the time but when he did explode it was bad."[52] Some episodes of violence took place in front of others, for example, a guest of the Adamsons reported later, "He flew at Joy and started to throttle her, beside himself with anger. He would have killed her if I hadn't yelled for the servants, who pulled George off her."[53] Joy made several efforts to obtain legal help or to divorce, but was persuaded not to follow through. Whenever she tried to leave, George constrained her, either through physical violence or by locking up her possessions. At the same time, she also felt very lonely when she was away from George, and she perceived herself as dependent on him. In their early years she may have feared being unable to support herself or having to leave Kenya if divorced, and later she may have wondered about her general ability to manage living on her own. Looking back over her life, she once said, "I had to marry George because of Elsa." While on the surface her statement seems inaccurate, as the Adamsons were together for over a decade before Elsa came into their lives, it reflects the emotional reality that her marriage to George gave her the opportunity to pursue the safari life, to parent Elsa, and to engage in conservation work. Her sensitivity to issues of freedom for wild animals may also have provided some balance for her in response to the experience of feeling trapped within her personal life.

From 1965 onwards, Joy and George resided in separate camps, which she explained as stemming from the needs of caring for their differing animals: "We could not camp nearer to each other because of the enmity between lions and cheetahs."[54] They lived twelve miles apart in what is now the Meru National Reserve, a 700-square-mile park. With the gift of an orphaned cheetah, which she named Pippa, Adamson continued to make observations of animal behavior, and a book about Pippa and her cubs, *The Spotted Sphinx*, was published in 1969. A sequel, *Pippa's Challenge*, appeared in 1972. Adamson's goals were to see if she could rehabilitate a tame cheetah to live in the wild again and to help save the cheetah from extinction. Cheetahs are a genetically vulnerable species and do not consistently breed well in zoos, and Adamson felt that by releasing Pippa to the wild and seeing her have several litters of cubs, she was making a contribution to the management of cheetah breeding. She further recommended more protected game sanctuaries as a priority in conservation planning. Today the cheetah continues to be an endangered species, with a remaining population of about 20,000 to 25,000, about half as many as when Adamson was working with Pippa. While cheetahs are now considerably protected, an illegal traffic in their skins still exists and habitat encroachment remains a problem.[55]

As the Adamsons lived in their separate camps, there were also theoretical disagreements between the two. For example, she disliked George's habit of keeping his lions domesticated and felt that this practice was both dangerous and contrary to their joint work of returning animals to the wild. As it turned out, in 1971, his favorite lion, Boy, did kill one of his assistants, a twenty-eight-year old man from the Meru tribe referred to only as Stanley in George Adamson's autobiography.[56] When the Adamsons' agreements with park authorities for animal research terminated, they moved to the small stone house on the shores of Lake Naivasha in the Rift Valley, a purchase Adamson had made on the advice of her financial advisor, Peter Johnson. For twenty-six years they had either lived in government housing or in camps. She named the house Elsamere, and she invited George to live with her again. During this time, she continued working on a sequel to her first book about Pippa. However, after more incidents of domestic violence, Adamson again considered divorce. Rumors of the impending breakup were reported in London newspapers, as "Straight from the Lion's mouth—Adamsons split."[57] But through the intervention of a mutual friend, Joy dropped the case, having been convinced that a divorce would alienate her from the conservation movement and that she needed her husband's connection with the game and parks departments of Kenya to continue her work. They remained legally married, though George went to live in a camp in the remote, northeast corner of Kenya, where his brother Terence built a house for him. Joy continued to live at Elsamere and began studying the geology and botany of Hell's Gate, a nine-mile gorge nearby. In 1971 a second motion picture about the Adamsons and their animals, *Living Free*, was produced, this time with Susan Hampshire and Nigel Davenport in the leading roles, though the film did not attract as much interest as its predecessor. In September 1973 Joy went on a world tour again to promote the Elsa Appeal and the Elsa Clubs in schools in Great Britain, the United States, Canada, and Japan. She worked to have Hell's Gate made into a national park, which finally took place in 1984.

As Adamson aged, her physical and emotional problems worsened, and she became increasingly isolated. Most difficult to handle was the serious injury she sustained when the Land Rover she had been driving plunged into a ravine, crushing her right hand between the car and a rock. After this, despite repeated surgeries and physical therapy, she could not hold a pencil or a paintbrush and could no longer play the piano. As her right hand continued to be painful, she needed large amounts of analgesic medication for relief. By now, she had multiple health problems, including repeated broken knees, arthritis, a hip replacement, osteoporosis, malaria, and low blood pressure. Not long after Adamson's return from medical treatment in England, Pippa broke a leg and died of complications. Although there were always new animals for her to nurture, she never forgot that she had no human offspring.

That she was still thinking of her infertility at this stage of her life emerged through a friendship with a woman whom she came to regard as a daughter, Ros Hillyar. According to Cass, when Hillyar's son was born, Adamson said, "You know, Ros, with all the things I have achieved I have never produced a beautiful child like Charles."[58] While walking together one day as they frequently did, the two women became lost and Adamson fell and broke her ankle, and that same day her publisher and lover Billy Collins died of a heart attack, after which she became severely depressed. In October 1976 she had a visit from her friend, Elspeth Huxley (the Huxleys had first visited Elsa's camp in 1969), and Adamson confided that "she had been suffering from depression, feeling that her life was dwindling away, and was unable to break new ground with the leopard research."[59] She explained that she felt divorce was impossible because she, George, and Elsa were so connected in the mind of the public. Apparently Huxley recommended a medication for Adamson's depression, which she was unable to obtain, but she did start taking some kind of medicine prescribed by her physician.[60] Around that time Adamson was given a one-month-old female leopard cub by a game warden, and the leopard, which she named Penny, gave her a new reason to continue living and working. She was eventually given permission to move Penny to Shaba, part of the Samburu and Isiolo game reserves, and she rented out her home in Elsamere for two years. With a possible premonition of the end of her life, she once woke up in the middle of the night and wrote down an epitaph, which came to her in German, to be placed on a small bronze plaque on Elsa's grave in the event of her death.

The wind, the wind, the heavenly child

Is fanning the solitary stone,

It strokes and caresses

In the moonlit night,

And watches over the mysterious deep.

Wind, wind, thou heavenly child,

Secret are thy ways.[61]

She sent the inscription, along with her wish for her ashes to be scattered on Elsa's grave, to her cousin, Felix Weisshuhn.[62]

At Shaba, Adamson lived in a camp in a grove of acacia trees, where she observed, photographed, and made notes on Penny, and also worked on her autobiography, *The Searching Spirit*, published in 1978. She reportedly suffered wide fluctuations of mood, sometimes acting pleasantly, at other times being irritable and abrupt to those in her employ. She had difficulty retaining assistants, the last one being a young South African named Pieter Mawson, whom she had hired despite the fact that he was considered untrustworthy. Even with the animals and household helpers around her, Joy was often lonely, especially at holiday time. Among her few friends were an American and his wife, Esmond and Chryssee Bradley-Martin, who, like her, fought against poaching and ivory trading. When the leopard Penny conceived and had a miscarriage, Adamson wrote of her distress to Elspeth Huxley, saying that George had tried to console her with the fact that one of his lionesses had experienced a miscarriage but later always had healthy cubs. Adamson commented that in her case she had three miscarriages and no children afterwards.[63] The subject of her childlessness was evidently on her mind, never far from the surface even in her last years, and she clearly identified with the leopard in her experience of reproductive loss.

On January 3, 1980, Adamson, then sixty-nine years old, went walking alone in the evening and did not come back. Her assistant, Pieter Mawson, found her dead and declared she had been killed by a lion. It was later determined by autopsy that her death was caused by a small dagger, and human rather than lion prints were discovered near the body. An employee whom she had recently fired because of suspicion of theft, Paul Ekai, was arrested and confessed to the murder after being tortured by police. Later he led the police to objects stolen the night of the killing, and he was convicted of murder on October 28, 1981, though he escaped the death penalty due to his young age. Her assistant, Mawson, was suspected of conspiracy to murder, but he left for Botswana and died in an automobile accident on December 8, 1982; his possible involvement in the crime was never clearly established. Following her wishes, Adamson was cremated and her ashes scattered over the graves of Elsa and Pippa. Nine years after Joy's death, George Adamson was shot and killed on August 20, 1989, presumably by Somali poachers, although no one was punished. He was buried in Kenya next to his brother.

Adamson's book about Penny, *Queen of Shaba*, was published posthumously in 1980. She had written to her editor at Collins four days before she died, saying, "I have just found out that female cats are called queens, and this gives us the title for the book on Penny—Queen of Shaba."[64] The following poem by African sculptor Francis Nnaggenda, which Adamson used to keep beside her, was included in the postscript:

The Dead

The dead are not under the earth

They are in the tree that rustles

They are in the woods that groan

They are in the water that runs

They are in the water that sleeps

They are in the hut, they are in the crowd

The dead are not dead.[65]

In her foreword to *The Searching Spirit*, Elspeth Huxley declared that Adamson stood out as a pioneer "in the sense of one who leads toward new ways of looking at our surroundings," especially with regard to the relationship between humans and wild animals.[66] Huxley emphasized the point that Adamson was not a scientist but acted from "the dictates of her heart," and that she had fully committed herself to the conservation of natural resources in Africa. Among Adamson's other contributions was the idea for a national "orphanage" for damaged or orphaned animals, which functioned under the supervision of anthropologist Richard Leakey, Louis Leakey's son and then Director of the Wildlife Services of Kenya. Adamson also set up The Elsa Wild Animal Appeal, later called the Elsa Conservation Trust, which promoted wildlife conservation. She herself spoke frequently of the need for action and in 1977 the government of Kenya banned the hunting of wild animals. Kenya became a leader in the fight against ivory trading, and in 1989 Richard Leakey was appointed to combat the ivory poaching that was threatening to destroy Kenya's elephant population. Four parks in Kenya were created with the help of Adamson's generosity: the Samburu Reserve, the Meru National Reserve, the Shaba Reserve, and Hell's Gate. Elsamere, her house on Lake Naivasha, was eventually converted into a conservation center and remains open to the public.

While Adamson's work is mostly forgotten from the viewpoint of animal behavior science, she did bring world attention to the plight of wild animals. To demonstrate this, Desmond Morris, Curator of Mammals at the London Zoo, compared the differences in responses to a questionnaire broadcast on television before *Born Free* was published and repeated two years after it had appeared. Looking at the 80,000 responses from children listing their ten best loved and ten most hated animals, Morris stated:

> There was only one significant shift: the lion was now more loved and less hated. Joy Adamson's promotion campaign on behalf of the lion had worked. She had achieved the difficult goal of not merely providing a passing entertainment, but of actually shifting public feelings toward an animal species. Elsa the lioness had become an ambassador for her kind. She had also done something else. She had made people start to query the morality of keeping animals in captivity—in zoos and, even more so, in circuses. The essence of Elsa's story was her freedom. . . .[67]

In raising an orphaned lion, a cheetah, and a leopard, and successfully releasing them into the wild, Adamson entered into an equal-to-equal relationship with these animals and their cubs. Her human-to-animal relationships constituted a departure from the usual linkage between human beings and the large cats based on exploitation and fear. She empathically identified with animals and their needs for autonomy and space, concerns that remained alive in her personal life as well. She also identified with them as mother cats that successfully raised litters, the life experience that she had always wished for. Her nurturing energy went into her work with Elsa, Pippa, and Penny, and she perhaps achieved a kind of unfettered attachment to her cats that she could never achieve in the world of human relationships. As she once said, "I love Elsa more than I have any man."[68] While all three of her careers depended on the integration of her intellectual strengths, it was her work with animals that best combined her longing for family and children with the use of her talents and her generative impulses.

Joy Adamson with Elsa, Courtesy of the Elsa Conservation Trust.

Joy Adamson must be seen as a person of enormous complexity and contradictions. Adamson, perhaps as much as any of our main subjects, led a life of many voices, though the major publications about her life do not properly reflect this. Her own autobiography is written in the tradition of suppressing the private aspects of her existence and presenting only her entertaining adventures and exemplary achievements. Caroline Cass subtitled her biographical portrait, "Behind the Mask," and made an attempt to bring to light the previously unknown and darker aspects of Adamson's personal life. Adrian House's joint biography of George and Joy clearly portrays George as the more sympathetic of the two, seeing his violent outbursts as rare and her mood-disordered behavior as frequent and deplorable.

Yet, whatever one might say about her shortcomings, Joy Adamson led a creative life, driven by her intellectual curiosity and her unusual energy level, and she left a legacy in the phrase, "Born Free," which has come to symbolize the rights of wild animals to exist in freedom. She possessed a focus and determination that drove her to meet her goals despite any obstacles. At the same time she was unusually unselfish in her disregard for her own comfort and in her generative concern for future Kenyans and for wildlife conservation. Her style of generativity was frequently abstract, as she was more loving toward her animals than toward her spouses and her servants. She was action-oriented and always took steps to determine her own future and pursue her dreams. Her activity, however, was bounded by the constraints she perceived, and she was both fiercely independent and dependent at the same time. She felt powerless to leave her abusive marriage, initially perhaps because she felt she needed her marriage to George Adamson to remain in Kenya and have access to the safari life she loved, and later because she felt a divorce would hurt her ongoing conservation work. She had a different sense of reality than that which is shared by most people, but her talent, energy and unusual risk-taking allowed her to do the work that led her to world fame. As a gifted woman coming of age in the 1930s she developed her intellectual abilities within the context of interpersonal relationships, gradually integrating her strengths and working more independently over the course of her life. Through her work with animals she achieved an integration of her talents and her lifetime longings for family, created by her parenting of the "big cats" and their parenting of their wild-born cubs.

NOTES

[1] Jane Goodall, Letter to Adrian House, August 28, 1992, in Adrian House, *The Great Safari: The Lives of George and Joy Adamson* (New York: William Morrow, 1993), 369.

[2] Joy Adamson, *Pippa's Challenge* (New York: Harcourt Brace Jovanovich, Inc., 1972), 9.

[3] Joy Adamson, *Born Free* (New York: Pantheon Books, 1960), 198.

[4] Juliette Huxley, *Wild Lives of Africa* (New York: Harper & Row, 1963), 196-97.

[5] It is possible that Adamson was familiar with *I and Thou*, by Martin Buber, as it was published in her native language of German in 1923, under the title *Ich und Du*. See Martin Buber, *I and Thou* (New York: Charles Scribner's Sons, 1958). Interestingly, Buber has a section on the language of an animal's eyes (pages 96-97).

[6] Joy Adamson, *The Searching Spirit: Joy Adamson's Autobiography* (New York: Harcourt Brace Jovanovich, Inc., 1978), 3.

[7] Adamson, *Searching Spirit*, 15.

[8] Adamson, *Searching Spirit*, 22.

[9] Adamson, *Searching Spirit*, 33.

[10] G. Hagestad and B. Neugarten, "Age and the Life Course," in R. Binstock and E. Shanas, eds., *Handbook of Society and Aging*, 2nd ed. (New York: Van Nostrand Reinhold, 1985), 35-61.

[11] Adamson, *Searching Spirit*, 136.

[12] Adamson, *Searching Spirit*, 100.

[13] Adamson, *Searching Spirit*, 170.

[14] Huxley, *Wild Lives of Africa*, 197.

[15] George Adamson, *My Pride and Joy* (London: Collins Harvill, 1986), 94.

[16] House, *Great Safari*, 364.

[17] Joy Adamson, *Queen of Shaba* (New York: Harcourt Brace Jovanovich, Inc., 1980), 150.

[18] Adamson, *Searching Spirit*, 38.

[19] House, *Great Safari*, 107-8.

[20] Julian Huxley, *Memories*, vol. 2 (New York: Harper and Row, 1973), 211.

[21] The portraits are published in *The Peoples of Kenya* (London: Collins Harvill, 1967) and *Joy Adamson's Africa* (New York: Harcourt Brace Jovanovich, Inc., 1972).

[22] Adamson, *Joy Adamson's Africa*, 11.

[23] Elspeth Huxley, *Out in the Midday Sun: My Kenya* (New York: Viking Press, 1987), 244.

[24] Adamson, *Joy Adamson's Africa*, 11.

[25] Quoted in Joy Adamson's obituary in *The New York Times*, January 5, 1980.

[26] Adamson, *Searching Spirit*, 76.

[27] Adamson, *Searching Spirit*, 78.

[28] Carol Tomlinson-Keasey, "The Working Lives of Gifted Women," in Hildreth Y. Grossman and Nia Lane Chester, eds., *The Experience and Meaning of Work in Women's Lives* (Hillsdale, NJ: Lawrence Erlbaum Associates, 1990), 213-39.

[29] Adamson, *Searching Spirit*, 25.

[30] Caroline Cass, *Joy Adamson: Behind the Mask* (London: George Weidenfeld & Nicolson Limited, 1992), 14.

[31] Cass, *Joy Adamson*, 15.

[32] Cass, *Joy Adamson*, 19.

[33] Ziebel was the nickname Adamson used for her first husband.

[34] Adamson, *Searching Spirit*, 36.

[35] Cass, *Joy Adamson*, 39.

[36] Adamson, *Searching Spirit*, 42.

[37] Cass, *Joy Adamson*, 54.

[38] Cass, *Joy Adamson*, 54.

[39] Cass, *Joy Adamson*, 56.

[40] Cass, *Joy Adamson*, 166.

[41] Cass, *Joy Adamson*, 167.

[42] Adamson, *Searching Spirit*, 25-26.

[43] Adamson, *Searching Spirit*, 116.

[44] House, *Great Safari*, 105, 110.

[45] House, *Great Safari*, 157.

[46] Cass, *Joy Adamson*, 86-87.

[47] Ted Hughes, *New Statesman*, November 10, 1961, quoted in House, *Great Safari*, 392-93.

[48] Adamson, *Searching Spirit*, 175.

[49] Adamson, *Searching Spirit*, 186.

[50] Cass, *Joy Adamson*, 144.

[51] Cass, *Joy Adamson*, 145-46.

[52] Cass, *Joy Adamson*, 85.

[53] Cass, *Joy Adamson*, 86.

[54] Adamson, *Searching Spirit*, 192.

[55] The Smithsonian National Zoological Park houses a cheetah research facility that studies cheetah behavior and offers a visitor education program focused on saving the cheetah from extinction.

[56] George Adamson, *My Pride and Joy*, 213-15. This was the second time that the lion, "Boy," had attacked Stanley. There were about six serious injuries inflicted by the lions, including the near-death of Adamson's brother Terence. The Director of Wildlife of Kenya eventually told Adamson to stop rehabilitating lions. In discussing his remorse over Stanley's death, Adamson wrote, "I remembered now the letter Bill [Travers] had written to me at Naivasha, eighteen months before, asking whether the pins in Boy's leg might not inhibit his movement or give pain, and so turn him into a man-killer. I was also reminded of Joy's frequent advice to let Boy loose at Kora and to leave him to fend for himself." (page 215)

[57] Quoted in Cass, *Joy Adamson*, 179.

[58] Cass, *Joy Adamson*, 194.

[59] Cass, *Joy Adamson*, 195.

[60] House, *Great Safari*, 374.

[61] House, *Great Safari*, 394.

[62] Cass, *Joy Adamson*, 198.

[63] Cass, *Joy Adamson*, 208.

[64] George Adamson, *My Pride and Joy*, 272.

[65] Quoted in Adamson, *Queen of Shaba*, 173.

[66] Elspeth Huxley, in Adamson, *Searching Spirit*, Foreword, ix.

[67] Desmond Morris, *Animal Days* (New York: William Morrow, 1980), 246-47.

[68] House, *Great Safari*, 243, and photo caption after 338.

Frida Kahlo, Courtesy of Corbis.

Chapter 5
The Visual Poetry of
Reproductive Trauma:
Henry Ford Hospital
Frida Kahlo (1907-1954)

Frida Kahlo, the Mexican artist whose popularity has grown dramatically over the last few decades, is noted in particular for painting the trauma of infertility and pregnancy loss. Her depiction of failed pregnancy not only constituted revolutionary subject matter but also reflected a fundamental change in her creative style. More broadly, in making herself and her internal experience the focal point of many of her paintings, Kahlo communicated her psychological reality as a woman. As a leading art historian, Sarah M. Lowe, has written, "Before Kahlo, Western art was unused to images of birthing or miscarriage, double self-portraits with visible internal organs or cross-dressing, as subjects for 'high' art."[1] The miscarriage that Kahlo endured and then painted at age twenty-five was not the first time she encountered physical trauma and serious loss. She grew up facing a constellation of health problems, starting with a congenital spinal defect, spina bifida occulta, followed by the atrophy and shortening of her right leg around age six, probably due to polio. Then, in late adolescence, Kahlo suffered massive injuries when the bus in which she was riding collided with a streetcar. An iron handrail had entered her body at her left hip; her lumbar vertebrae, pelvis, and right leg and foot were severely fractured. The accident victims had been taken to a Red Cross hospital and divided into two groups, the one containing Kahlo initially considered beyond help. She was hospitalized for over a month and underwent several difficult operations. It was during her long subsequent convalescence at home that she began to paint. Kahlo never could fully depict the horror of the bus accident, though she did produce one incomplete sketch of it the following year. She did, however, in the next decade express her experience of pregnancy loss, in the process changing her artistic approach as she dissected her grief in discrete and powerful images. Her husband, the famous Mexican muralist Diego Rivera, who had brought her with him on his sojourn to the U.S., said after seeing Kahlo's portrayal of her miscarriage, "Never before had a woman put such agonized poetry on canvas as Frida did at this time in Detroit."[2]

Rivera is not alone in affirming the major importance of this work, both in Kahlo's own creative development and in the future of women's art. Many art historians and critics point to *Henry Ford Hospital*, Kahlo's small but remarkably detailed painting of her pregnancy loss in the "Motor City," as initiating a transformative shift, moving beyond the modes of expression and types of subject matter that had characterized her earlier efforts. Her chief biographer, Hayden Herrera, called it "the first of the series of bloody and terrifying self-portraits that were to make Frida Kahlo one of the most original painters of her time. . . ." Sarah Lowe wrote that *Henry Ford Hospital* marked the beginning of the style and content that Kahlo developed to great acclaim over the next twenty years, and Salomon Grimberg commented, "Kahlo's art as we know it today did not exist until July of 1932, when she miscarried."[3] A recent expert summed up the artist's significance by saying that with this and several subsequent works, Kahlo painted the "previously unexplored subjects of menstruation, abortion, [and] miscarriage with forthright candor, long in advance of feminist art."[4]

With *Henry Ford Hospital*, Kahlo portrayed the elements of her miscarriage without perspective or realistic relationship to one another. In this work she also incorporated the Mexican votive style of painting, and began using her own personal experience as the essence of her art. Actually, this change in approach is foreshadowed to some degree in the earlier sketch Kahlo did of the bus accident, which presents the horrific scene more as she felt it rather than the way it would have been witnessed by an observer. Kahlo depicted the emotional and visual representations of trauma in a manner that discloses her inner world to the viewer. During her miscarriage, she may have relived crucial aspects of the bus accident, e.g., being hospitalized and operated upon, suffering pelvic injury and blood loss, and fearing an end to her fertility. The feelings associated with the initial event took on a larger-than-life significance, acquiring their own reality and losing their prior reality-based relationship to one another for a new one born out of the more recent trauma.

Unlike the scant attention given the subject in the life stories of many other infertile women, the issue of Kahlo's reproductive problems has not been neglected. Hayden Herrera, whose 1983 biography, *Frida*, has often been seen as most responsible for creating Kahlo's cult following in subsequent years, viewed her pregnancy losses and despair over childlessness as central to her life and art. She claimed that Kahlo wanted to die after the miscarriage in Detroit and the subsequent realization that she might never bear any children. "Painting was the best antidote to Frida's pervasive sense of barrenness—that barrenness that is seen in the desert backgrounds of so many of her self-portraits," she asserted.[5] Some feminists have criticized Herrera's conceptualization, however, for distilling a complex artist into a single essential "Frida," and for engaging in psychological reductionism by interpreting Kahlo's art primarily through her emotional suffering.[6]

Martha Zamora, in her 1990 study, *Frida Kahlo: The Brush of Anguish*, further argued that making the impact of infertility such a crucial issue in Kahlo's life is inaccurate. She declared that, "Contrary to widespread belief, Frida was not obsessed by frustrated maternity, although it was an idea she encouraged."[7] Even if Zamora's assertion goes too far in the opposite direction, it does raise the question of scholars perhaps exaggerating the effects of Kahlo's childlessness and using it as a means of reducing her art to an expression of grieving. Indeed, viewing her simply as a conduit for transmuted suffering undermines the breadth of Kahlo's creativity.

Frida Kahlo was born in the year 1907, though in adulthood she changed the date to 1910 to express her identification with the beginning of the Mexican Revolution. She grew up in Coyoacán, outside Mexico City, the third of four daughters of Guillermo Kahlo, a Hungarian-German Jewish immigrant, and Matilde Calderón, a native-born Mexican. Her only brother died as an infant, and Frida was conceived not long after his death. The youngest daughter, Cristina, was born when Frida was less than a year old. Of the four daughters, Frida was to become by far the most talented and successful, and also the most rebellious. She was baptized Magdalena Carmen Frida Kahlo y Calderón, though the name she chose to employ varied during her young adulthood according to subtle shifts in her identity. She often used the German spelling of her name, Frieda, while attending high school and on certain other occasions until the mid-1930s, when she wanted to separate herself from any association with Nazi Germany. Her husband suggested that she abandon the German-sounding name "Frida" altogether and use "Carmen," so for a time she was known as Carmen Rivera. Before she achieved international recognition in the late 1930s, some art critics referred to her simply as Frida Rivera or "Mrs. Rivera."

Frida's father, originally named Wilhelm Kahl, was born in Baden-Baden, Germany in 1872, just after his parents had emigrated there from the Austro-Hungarian Empire. Little is known about his childhood other than the fact that he must have been a good student since he was admitted to the University of Nuremberg around 1890. Yet shortly thereafter Kahl seems to have suffered a fall from a ladder resulting in a serious head injury and ongoing seizure disorder that made studying difficult. As his daughter Frida would later do during her adolescence, he gave up his formal education following a severe physical trauma. In 1891 at age nineteen, having also lost his mother, Kahl left Germany, moved to Mexico City, and changed his name to Guillermo Kahlo. He became a salesman in a variety of retail shops for the next several years, married a Mexican woman and fathered two daughters. Following the birth of the second child his wife died. He soon rewed, choosing as his new spouse a woman named Matilde, who had been a fellow employee at the jewelry store where he worked. The daughters from the first marriage were eventually sent off to a convent school and had only occasional visits with their father and his new family thereafter.

Frida's mother, Matilde Calderón y Gonzalez, was the daughter of Antonio Calderón, a native of Michoacan, and Isabel Gonzalez y Gonzalez, an immigrant from Spain who was the daughter of a general. Antonio Calderón worked as a professional photographer and persuaded Kahlo's father to join him in his business. At one point the two men traveled through the country photographing indigenous and colonial architecture, and Guillermo Kahlo eventually became known as Mexico's first official photographer. Although he never achieved great financial success in this endeavor, his camera-work was clearly admired both by contemporaries and people of later generations. His photographs came to be used to illustrate several books commemorating the centennial of Mexican independence, and many of them can now be found in the National Institute of Anthropology and History. He also painted in oils, and it was from her father that Frida learned to make close observations and to paint with very precise detail. Her attention to detail may also have been developed by their collecting various items, such as leaves, rocks, and insects, and then examining them under a microscope. Through this and other activities, Kahlo developed a special closeness with her father, who said of her, she is the "most intelligent of my daughters, the most like me." They were connected as well by assisting one another with their respective physical problems; she aided him when he fell during a seizure, raising him to his feet and rescuing his photographic equipment, while he helped her to recover from polio and later from the bus accident. Toward the end of her life, she wrote in her diary, "He was the best example for me of tenderness and workmanship (also photographer and a painter) but above all of understanding for all my problems which since I was four years old were of a social nature."[8]

During her childhood, Frida Kahlo struggled to find her place in life, and sometimes had trouble fitting in. She grew up in a household where her father created a German cultural world around him and encouraged her to learn to speak and read German, placing her outside the mainstream in her native country. At the same time she was often at odds with the traditional culture of her devout Mexican Catholic mother. Kahlo bonded with her mother in certain ways but felt alienated by her deep religiosity and overly strict manner. The two often clashed over questions of what was deemed proper behavior for a young woman. On the other hand, Kahlo recalled her mother providing nursing care and food to the *zapatistas* (followers of the legendary Emiliano Zapata during the Mexican Revolution), and realized that her own subsequent leftist political leanings had their roots in the sympathy toward the revolutionaries that she had experienced through her mother's actions. Kahlo also felt different and alone as a result of her atrophied right leg, especially when other children called her "Frida peg-leg." To cope with her impaired mobility, she tried to become more athletic, through skating and bicycling. Sometimes when feeling lonely she created an imaginary playmate, who she described in the following way: "She was gay—she laughed a lot. Without sounds. She was agile and she danced as if she weighed nothing at all. I followed her in all her movements and while she danced I told her my secret problems. . . ."[9]

Regardless of any differences or shortcomings in her early life, Kahlo developed into a smart, creative, and precocious young woman, one who showed great promise. At age fourteen she qualified by examination to enroll at the National Preparatory School in Mexico City, a government-sponsored high school that offered an advanced curriculum for those seeking a future professional career. At the time of her entry into the *"Prepa,"* as it was familiarly known, she planned on becoming a physician. Women had only recently been integrated into the public school system, under the direction of innovative education minister, José Vasconcelos, and at this institution she was one of only thirty-five females in a student body of two thousand. Not constrained by being in the minority or by the strict rules, she refused to conform to the behavioral expectations for women students, sometimes dressing in men's clothing and also participating in mixed-gender student organizations. One of these groups was a notorious band of seven young men and two young women known as the *Cachuchas* (the "Caps"), for the "proletarian, urchin-like cloth caps" they wore,[10] who showed disdain for formalities, agitated for reform, and played pranks on their teachers. The *Cachuchas* were followers of Vasconcelos, who sought to make the new educational system truly Mexican and to promote cultural nationalism. The outspoken Kahlo, who was good with words, soon became a leader of the group and was described by one member as "a master of pun."[11] When bored with a teacher's old-fashioned lecturing style, she sometimes amused herself by drawing satirical pictures of him and passing them around the classroom. Impulsive and high-spirited, she seemed to learn as much from her fellow Cachuchas as she did in her classes. The club's meeting place was the Ibero American Library, where its members read voraciously, dramatized their readings, and argued about the latest intellectual currents. By this time, Kahlo was able to read in three languages, Spanish, English, and German, which further broadened her intellectual reach.

Much later in life, in an interview with Olga Campos, recently translated by Salomon Grimberg, Kahlo stated that the first time she wanted to have a son was at the age of thirteen. The teenager allegedly told a close friend: "I would see Diego walk by, and I would dream of having a son of his. I would comment on it to my little girl friends, eating ice cream in the plaza of Coyoacán."[12] During her school years at the *Prepa*, she had an intimate relationship with fellow student and *Cachucha*, Alejandro Gómez Arias, who later became a highly respected Mexican journalist and intellectual. Handsome, intelligent, athletic, he was Kahlo's first real *novio* (boy friend). Fearful of her mother finding out, Frida sought to keep their relationship a secret, and when they exchanged passionate letters, she asked Alejandro to sign his with a woman's name in order to avoid suspicion. In an era when young women were supposed to keep the young men courting them at a distance, Kahlo behaved otherwise. Gómez Arias later recalled, "Frida was sexually precocious. To her, sex was a form of enjoying life, a kind of vital impulse."[13]

Kahlo's life at this point (prior to the bus accident) reveals a young person who was maximally engaged in the world both socially and politically. An independent thinker, she was defiant of authority and conventional morality, not afraid to act or speak out. Clearly gifted, Kahlo used her intelligence to learn and to participate in a wide variety of activities with her fellow *Cachuchas*. She had already developed the dark sense of humor that is evident later on in her letters and her paintings. She liked to swear in both Spanish and English, and she sometimes expressed herself in invented phrases that combined elements of Spanish, English, and German. The word, "*buten*," meant "lots of, or very much" as in, "I'm *buten, buten* bored!!!!!!"[14] "*Drepa*," a complimentary term meaning "great," was created by reversing the syllables of "*padre*," as in the sentence, "See *Vogue*: there are three reproductions in it, one in color I think is quite *drepa. . . ."[15]* Kahlo was a voracious reader, according to Gómez Arias, who said in 1977, *"Leia incansablemente. No solamente la biblioteca del padre sino cuanto tenian en sus manos sus compañeros.* [She read tirelessly. Not only from her father's library but from whatever was in the hands of her companions.]*"*

During her late adolescence, as her father's financial situation declined, Kahlo had to work after school and during vacations to help contribute to the family income. While the burdens of employment were sometimes onerous, they allowed her a certain amount of freedom to explore different fields and come into contact with different types of people than would have normally been possible. She was briefly employed as a cashier in a pharmacy and in keeping accounts at a lumberyard, but then more importantly as an apprentice in engraving with a friend of her father's, Fernando Fernández. According to Herrera, "Fernández taught Frida to draw by having her copy prints by the Swedish Impressionist Anders Zorn, and he discovered that she had, as he put it, 'enormous talent.'"[16] At this juncture she also studied shorthand and typing, and applied for a part-time job at the Ministry of Education library. It is alleged that after she attended an interview for the position, Kahlo was seduced by a female employee of the library. The liaison was eventually discovered by her parents and caused a small scandal.[17] Later in life, she had sexual relationships with women but her primary romantic attachment was to Rivera.

The adventurous and active existence that Kahlo led as an adolescent ended abruptly with the bus accident. While returning from school with her friend Gómez Arias one afternoon she experienced the horrific collision that forever altered her existence. The many operations plus the lengthy recovery period at home were extremely difficult for her both physically and emotionally. She kept reliving the event, attempting to make some sense of it, and also trying to cope with pain that never fully went away. While she always sought to present a joyful exterior in public, those close to her could sense the despair that existed below the surface, feelings that would later be expressed in her art. The accident not only changed her physical being but altered her personality, making her more serious and subdued. Alone a great deal, she became more self-focused, and learned to be still and to concentrate.

It was in this situation, no longer involved with school or friends, and forced to live a more sedentary life, that Kahlo began devoting herself to painting. Since she was largely confined to bed, her mother had a special easel constructed to allow her to work from a prone position, with a mirror placed under her bed canopy so that she could paint her own image. Her previous training had included only two required art courses at the Prepa and some personal instruction from her father and from engraver Fernando Fernández. She now learned mostly on her own, studying her father's art books and copying the works of other artists to further develop her technique. Her first paintings were relatively small and focused on subject matter she knew best—her friends, her family, herself. Almost half of the roughly two hundred paintings she produced during her lifetime would be self-portraits, though the early attempts were rather traditional in concept. Her first such creation, done with the aid of the mirror, was composed in the style of the Italian Renaissance, and showed her formally dressed in a burgundy velvet gown. On the back of the canvas she wrote in German, *"Heute ist Immer Noch*—Today still goes on."[18] The portrait was produced as a gift for Alejandro, done mainly to impress him with her recovery from the accident, and hopefully to rekindle their intimate relationship. They did remain friends of sorts, but over time Gómez Arias became less and less personally involved in Kahlo's life.

Sometime in the months following the accident, one of her physicians apparently informed Kahlo that she might never be able to bear a child. Whether or not this information was correct, it apparently affected her very deeply. Her response also foreshadowed a significant element of her later artistic style—the use of fantasy. When during her convalescence she received a lovely doll as a gift, she composed a unique birth announcement.

It was written in calligraphy and decorated with a winged turtle, describing the birth of a son born to Frieda Kahlo in the Red Cross Hospital in September 1925, the precise time she was being treated there for her injuries.

LEONARDO

Was born at the Red Cross

In the year of Grace, 1925, in the

Month of September

And was baptized in the

Town of Coyoacán

The following year

His Mother Was

FRIEDA KAHLO

His godparents

ISABEL CAMPOS

And ALEJANDRO GÓMEZ ARIAS[19]

In addition to being a forerunner of using visual expression and dark humor to respond to her perceived infertility and other losses, Kahlo's fantasy birth announcement in connection with the gift of a doll has other implications. It may be the earliest example of her employing dolls as symbolic replacements for the children she could not have, a practice she continued for the rest of her life. When friends traveled, she always asked them to bring back a doll for her, resulting in a large collection of dolls and doll accessories laying about her room. Her longing for offspring is also evident in some of the other objects she accumulated over the years in the Blue House at Coyoacán, now a museum. These include numerous books on childbirth, and, in another instance of her sometimes bizarre and unconventional manner, a human fetus in a jar of formaldehyde. The preserved fetus had been sent at her request in 1941, sometime after she had given up trying to conceive, by her close friend and physician in San Francisco, Dr. Leo Eloesser. She subsequently wrote him a letter of thanks for the "*child* that made me so happy. . . ."[20] In acquiring these numerous reminders of children and childbearing, Kahlo was apparently seeking to surround herself with objects associated with her pregnancy losses and her strong desire to give birth.

When at around age twenty Kahlo could finally move about and return to the outside world, she did not go back to school but did resume her political activities and contacts with some of her old friends and acquaintances. She grew particularly close to a leftist student leader, German de Campo, who introduced her to a group of individuals associated with the exiled Cuban Communist revolutionary, Julio Antonio Mella. Through Mella she got to know Italian-born American photographer, Tina Modotti, who had come to Mexico with fellow photographer Edward Weston in 1923 and had stayed on, sometimes participating in radical politics. As a result of her friendship with Modotti and other activists, Kahlo subsequently became a member of the Communist party. Joining the Communist party was not unusual at the time for Mexican artists and writers, who saw it potentially as a means of uplifting the poor and enhancing cultural nationalism. Soon afterward at a party meeting she formally met the celebrated muralist Diego Rivera, who was one of the painters involved in transforming Mexican art to make it more "authentic." Those engaged in this artistic effort sought to focus on indigenous traditions rather than European influences, and were particularly attracted by pre-Columbian artifacts, once thought too "primitive," and by modern folk culture.

Kahlo wanted very much to be associated with this movement, but was not yet sure of her ability or whether she could succeed as an artist. Looking for guidance, she soon visited Rivera at his worksite and brought along a few of her paintings for him to evaluate. As he later recalled the encounter, she said, "I didn't come here for fun. I have to work to earn my livelihood. I have done some paintings which I want you to look over professionally. I want an absolutely straightforward opinion, because I cannot afford to go on just to appease my vanity."[21] After a quick appraisal he stated that she was obviously an "authentic artist," and insisted that she continue to paint. According to his recollection, Kahlo invited him to her home the following Sunday to look at the rest of her paintings, although she recalled that it was he who initiated the offer. Clearly he was fascinated not just with her art but with her, and she, despite a twenty-one year age difference and his reputation as a lover of many women, was fascinated with him. They initiated a courtship and were married a year later in the summer of 1929; she was twenty-two and he was forty-three. Although it was not Kahlo's motive in marrying him, Rivera rescued her family financially by paying off the mortgage on the Blue House so that her parents and sisters could continue living there. Rivera would always remain a good provider and assist Kahlo in her quest to establish herself as an artist. But over time he would cause her considerable anguish as she came to realize that he was not the most faithful of husbands and saw she was not going to be able to change him in that regard. As Kahlo was once quoted as saying: "I suffered two grave accidents in my life. One in which a streetcar knocked me down . . . the other accident is Diego."[22]

In the first few years of their marriage, from 1930 to 1933, Kahlo accompanied Rivera to the United States, where he had been commissioned to work on murals in San Francisco, Detroit, and New York. Initially she lived in the shadow of his fame and as an artist clearly felt she was not his equal. In her large painting *Frida and Diego Rivera* (1931), which shows the two of them standing side by side, Diego is depicted as the central figure, bigger than life and holding an easel, whereas a diminutive Frida, situated to his left, looks meek and dependent. Although she was devoting more and more time to her own creative work as he labored on his massive murals, her smaller efforts, when mentioned in the press, were taken less

Frida Kahlo and Diego Rivera, 1932,

Courtesy of Library of Congress, Carl Van Vechten Collection.

seriously. The following headline in *The Detroit News*, for example, conveyed the prevailing attitude: "Wife of the Master Mural Painter Gleefully Dabbles in Works of Art."[23]

During this period Kahlo was more often noticed in public for how she looked. She had begun wearing *Tehuana* clothing, based on the native dress of the *Tehuanas*, women from the Isthmus of Tehuantepec in Oaxaca, who are mythologized as matriarchs. Drawing upon the new cultural nationalism in her homeland, she raised the *Tehuana* dress style to haute couture, wore Aztec jewelry, and arranged her hair in an indigenous manner supplemented by ribbons, combs, and flowers. Photographer Edward Weston described the impression Kahlo made during her stay in northern California: "Dressed in native costume even to huaraches, she causes much excitement on the streets of San Francisco. People stop in their tracks to look in wonder."[24] While her clothing style enabled her to hide her smaller right leg, she also made a political statement by associating herself with indigenous culture and communicating Mexican revolutionary ideals. In their analysis of Kahlo's attire, "Fashioning National Identity," Rebecca Block and Lynda Hoffman-Jeep pointed out that the vintage of her costume was actually based on a Victorian adaptation of the traditional *Tehuana* dress. "What Kahlo adopted was a culturally mixed costume from a racially mixed people."[25] Thus, in the artist's new dramatic appearance there were layers of mixed identities, complementing her own mixed identity.

The pleasure she derived from being observed in her indigenous dress could not mask a situation that increasingly troubled Kahlo as time passed: her continuing childlessness. Recounting the first year of her marriage, she said, "We could not have a child, and I cried inconsolably but I distracted myself by cooking, dusting the house, sometimes by painting, and every day going to accompany Diego on the scaffold. It gave him great pleasure when I arrived with the midday meal in a basket covered with flowers."[26] Though she did conceive once, Kahlo had to undergo a pregnancy termination around 1929 at about three months' gestation, because "the fetus was in the wrong position," (according to Herrera), or because she had a "malformed pelvis," (according to a retrospective medical record). Whatever the cause, the unhappy outcome led to Kahlo's first attempt at expressing her feelings about the failed pregnancy through art. This was a drawing done shortly thereafter of herself and Rivera. Inside her abdomen "she drew, and then erased, a baby Diego seen as if by X-ray vision."[27] Kahlo then produced an unfinished painting, called *Frida and the Caesarean*. Like the drawing, this canvas contains a Frida-like figure, here lying naked on a bed, with a fetus inside her. The woman on the bed is surrounded by a few other people, including Diego, with a small boy superimposed, and an unidentified woman standing to her right. In the upper left hand corner is a hospital scene depicting five medical practitioners performing the operation.

Kahlo's most famous attempt to portray her response to reproductive difficulties followed her second pregnancy loss, at fourteen weeks' gestation, on July 4, 1932, while she and Rivera were living and working in Detroit. This was not a pregnancy terminated for medical reasons; it was an actual miscarriage. The experience she underwent during her stay at Henry Ford Hospital devastated her both physically and emotionally. She spent thirteen days there in recovery, and was still distraught at the end of that time. But early on she felt the need to express her loss artistically and on the fifth day, using just a pencil, she created a self-portrait showing her face swollen with tears. Beyond this, according to Herrera, the grieving Kahlo wanted to "draw her lost child, wanted to see him exactly as he should have looked at the moment when he was miscarried."[28] Her doctors refused her request to examine medical books that contained illustrations of fetal development, but Rivera provided her with the desired texts. Kahlo then produced a pencil study of a male fetus, as well as two other pencil drawings of the miscarriage event considered by Herrera to be "more surrealistic and fanciful than anything she had done before."[29]

Henry Ford Hospital, Courtesy Art Resource and Artists Rights Society, ©2010

Banco de México Diego Rivera Frida Kahlo Museums Trust, Mexico,

D.F./Artists Rights Society (ARS), New York

Kahlo kept on working in this realm, and while still in the throes of her physical recovery, completed a highly original painting of her recent miscarriage, calling it *Henry Ford Hospital.* In it a dark-haired woman resembling Kahlo is seen lying naked and hemorrhaging in a hospital bed that is floating; she is isolated and detached. The industrial buildings far in the background reinforce a sense of isolation and lack of emotional connectedness. The various symbols of the miscarriage experience are shown as larger-than-life and vivid; their physical size in relation to the size of the woman illustrates their emotional magnitude. Her abdomen is still enlarged from the pregnancy, and a large tear runs down her face. From her hand come six vein-like tubes, each attached to an image related to the pregnancy and miscarriage. A male fetus is central (she had written to Dr. Eloesser afterwards saying that she had hoped for a little Dieguito), and around the bed are an anatomical side view of a woman's lower torso, a snail, a pelvis, an orchid, and an autoclave. The torso has two spinal columns, an intact spinal column interior to a fragmented exterior spinal column, perhaps her perception of her spine before and after the bus accident. On the surface of the torso are spermatozoa. Kahlo later told the art historian Parker Lesley that the snail referred to the slowness of the miscarriage: "soft, covered and at the same time, open."[30] Kahlo may have felt the tentative movement of the soft snail from its shell to be like the slow loss of the fetus from the uterus. The snail and shell motif continued to appear in other paintings of hers, including *Diego & Frida* (1929-1944) and *Moses (The Birth of the Hero)* (1945). Art historian Dina Comisarenco, in her analysis of Aztec imagery as it relates to both Kahlo's and Rivera's experience of reproductive trauma, has pointed out other associations to the snail, such as its place in Mexican folk Nativity scenes, its Aztec symbolism of parturition, and its Christian symbolism of sin.[31] The pelvic bones may be Kahlo's perception of the principal cause of her miscarriage. The uterine-like lavender orchid was given to her by her husband while she was in the hospital, and she said, "When I painted it, I had the idea of a sexual thing mixed with the sentimental." The machinery has been variously interpreted as her hips, a symbol for pain, or "anything mechanical," meaning "bad luck and pain," according to Kahlo.[32] Psychiatrist and art expert Salomon Grimberg has identified the machine as an autoclave, a device for sterilizing medical instruments. The autoclave contrasts with the tenderness of the snail; usually made of steel, it remains closed until its job is accomplished. As Kahlo felt she was sterilized in the machinery of the bus accident, the autoclave is also meant to be an instrument of sterilization. Finally, one other aspect of the canvas can be noted. Though Kahlo has failed at maternal reproduction, industrial production, as represented by the factory buildings situated in the background of the painting, continues.

Some might view Kahlo's juxtaposition of seemingly odd visual images in *Henry Ford Hospital*, such as the large snail floating over the bed, as an example of pathology, or "disordered thinking."[33] Disordered thinking is that which departs from reality and rules of logic; departure from realistic thinking around themes of content specific to trauma, however, is a frequent consequence of the aftermath of severe trauma. The unique and disturbing set of images that Kahlo created reflected her own emotional reality: in *Henry Ford Hospital* each element of the miscarriage is tied to the woman on the bed through vein-like ribbons, suggesting that these images flowed from her experience. Kahlo purposely used posttraumatic imagery in order to produce what appears in her paintings. As Andrea Kettenmann has described it, "Objects are extracted from their normal environment and integrated into a new composition. It is more important to the artist to reproduce her emotional state in a distillation of the reality she had experienced than to record an actual situation with photographic precision."[34]

A concomitant aspect of Kahlo's shift in artistic expression with *Henry Ford Hospital* was her emulation of traditional Mexican *retablo*, or ex-voto painting, a style dating back to the country's colonial period.[35] She eventually collected hundreds of ex-voto paintings, which commemorate divine intervention in the lives of individuals who have experienced a miraculous recovery from an accident or illness. Small-scale artwork done on tin or copper, sometimes cloth or canvas, ex-voto paintings offer thanks to the Holy Virgin or to a saint for the recovery, and they include the name of the person who was saved and the date and place of the miraculous intercession. As with *Henry Ford Hospital*, the essential elements of the traumatic experience are selected and re-integrated into the composition of the *retablo*. Generally disregarding linear perspective, a *retablo* records the facts of the distressing situation; it serves as a kind of a healing ritual in that it places the illness or accident in the past and expresses gratitude for survival. *Henry Ford Hospital* was Kahlo's first work on metal, following a suggestion by Rivera, and it was her first fully developed representation of her own trauma. What the painting is missing, however, is the traditional *retablo* element of faith and redemption. Later in life, Kahlo purchased an actual *retablo* that reminded her of the earlier bus accident, and then personalized it by adding her eyebrows to the injured woman and labeling the streetcar.

Kahlo also produced another artistic rendering of her pregnancy failure, when Rivera, hoping to alleviate his wife's depressed feelings after the miscarriage, arranged that she and her friend, Lucienne Bloch, be given access to a lithography workshop in a local arts-and-crafts guild. The resulting piece, called *El Aborto*, or *The Miscarriage* (1932) and signed Frieda Rivera, offers a powerful image of her grieving process and the meaning of her pregnancy loss. A naked woman is shown standing up, with her right leg tethered to a fetus, above which float drawings of embryonic cell division. A less developed fetus is located on her abdomen and large tears run down her face. Blood is dripping down her left leg to fertile ground, giving life to plants. A weeping moon, noted by Grimberg to represent Ixchel, the Mayan goddess of the moon and childbirth, looks down upon the woman. A second left arm is holding up an artist's palette in the shape of a womb, suggesting Kahlo's way of working through her enormous grief. According to Herrera, the palette perhaps implies "that painting is an antidote to maternal failure, that for Frida, making art must take the place of making children."[36] This is also the first work in which Kahlo reveals her withered leg, a choice consistent with the possibility of the miscarriage leading to a re-experiencing of prior trauma.

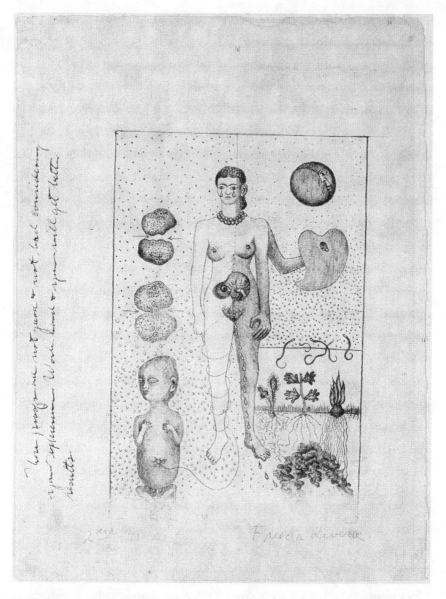

El Aborto, or *Frida and the Abortion*, Lithograph, 1932, Courtesy Art Resource and Artists Rights Society, ©2010 Banco de México Diego Rivera Frida Kahlo Museums Trust, Mexico, D.F./Artists Rights Society (ARS), New York.

The frequently expressed view of Kahlo as an icon of strength in reaction to physical and emotional suffering implies passivity; it emphasizes her quietly enduring life's harsh events as opposed to participating in the creation of her own environment. But early on Kahlo was clearly active in her orientation to the world, both in thought and sensual experience. In emphasizing the emotional aspects of her art, critics have tended to overlook the breadth of her intellectual interests and how they enriched her work. Kahlo scholar Ankori Gannit, writing about the covert Jewish elements in Kahlo's art, analyzed her library at *La Casa Azul*. While her collection includes many volumes on various aspects of Mexican culture, as one would expect, it also contains books on world history and art, communism, modern and classical literature, and Jewish subjects. Gannit stated: "Yet neither Kahlo's interest in her Jewish roots nor the literary and historical dimension of her art have ever been fully investigated. One reason for this oversight may be that while Rivera is always viewed as a painter of history, Kahlo, by contrast, has thus far been considered a 'personal painter,' whose profound physical and emotional suffering clouded her interest in the outside world. Rivera is portrayed as a man of the world; Kahlo, as his 'self-absorbed,' invalid wife."[37] While Kahlo's visual-spatial abilities and naturalist talents are obvious in her work, the contribution of her strong logical-analytical intelligence has often been overlooked.

During the same year as the miscarriage, Kahlo's mother died in Mexico, bringing her additional loss and anguish, and leading her to the creation of another artwork related to childbearing entitled, *My Birth* (1932). The painting shows a woman lying at the center of a large bed, legs spread apart, with a sheet covering her head and chest but otherwise naked. The head of the child (Frida's head) emerges from the womb on its side and appears dead, the sheet below heavily stained with blood. Hanging on the wall above the bed is the portrait of a grieving mother, the Virgin of Sorrows, pierced by swords and weeping. The painting thus appears to represent a condensation of images of both her mother's recent demise and the death of Kahlo's unborn child. As discussed by scholar Margaret A. Lindauer, this painting "depicts what would 'rationally' be considered mutually exclusive relationships between mother and child, birth and death."[38]

In the next several years, Kahlo attempted to become pregnant three more times, according to Rivera, despite the fact that he as her husband was not enthusiastic at the prospect. Perhaps because of her ongoing desire for a child, images of children and themes of reproduction continued to appear in her artwork, most notably in a 1937 painting, *Me and My Doll*. On this canvas, a woman who looks like Frida is sitting on a bed next to a small baby doll. The woman's demeanor is detached; she is looking away, and smoking a cigarette. The doll is clearly an inadequate replacement for a child.

As Kahlo's childlessness persisted over several years, says Herrera, she developed attachments to other people's children. Both Rivera's daughters from his prior marriage, Lupe and Ruth, and her sister Cristina's children, Isolda and Antonio, were by then frequent visitors at their Aunt Frida's house. Clearly, she doted on them and kept them close at hand. In addition, Kahlo acquired numerous pets, including dogs, monkeys, cats, parrots, doves, an eagle, and a deer. Henceforth, many of her most famous paintings, such as her self-portrait with a monkey, display her together with one or more of these animals. Her interest in nurturance and her attachment to other living things soon extended even further, according to Herrera. Consistent with her view of the centrality of reproduction to Kahlo's work, she wrote that Kahlo "tended the plants in her garden as if they were as needy as infants. Flowers and fruit she painted so that they look alive, projecting upon them the full force of her obsession with fertility."[39]

While Kahlo may have wanted children, she had mixed feelings about the idea of bringing a child into the world of an uninterested father and a less than healthy mother. One can appreciate her ambivalence in the letters she wrote to Dr. Eloesser before and after her 1932 miscarriage. The questions Kahlo faced were not very different from those that confront a present-day woman who is concerned about spousal indifference, health issues surrounding pregnancy, and the possibility of passing on genetic illnesses or transmitting communicable diseases. She had written a long letter to Eloesser on May 26, 1932, requesting his opinion on whether or not to abort her pregnancy, followed by a briefer letter on July 26th describing what had transpired in the weeks gone by. In her first letter she let Eloesser know that she felt her overall health was not good, and that Dr. Pratt, her physician in Detroit, had diagnosed her as having a trophic ulcer on her right foot. She also let him know that she was two months pregnant and had told Dr. Pratt that it might be better to terminate the pregnancy because of her poor health. In response, Pratt had given her quinine and castor oil, but the pregnancy continued, at which point he advised her to just persevere and then try to deliver by Cesarean section. Her concerns about whether or not to go on with it also included "the inheritance I carry in my blood," her general weakness, and the feasibility of returning home to Mexico at the end of the second trimester. Her statement about heredity has been interpreted by some as referring to her father's epilepsy, which would not have been hereditary if it resulted from an injury. But, in fact, she may have been referring to the congenital defect of her spine diagnosed by Dr. Eloesser, which would have implications for future offspring.[40] She contemplated staying in Detroit by herself to have the child but worried about having no one in her family to take care of her during or after the process.

Kahlo also pointed out that Rivera was preoccupied with his work and uninterested in having a child. Rivera, in fact, had a long history of abandoning his offspring. At age thirty, while living in France, he and his common-law wife, Angelina Beloff, had a son, Diego Jr. Rivera then left Beloff to move in with Marevna Vorobiev for five months. Shortly after he went back to Beloff, young Diego Jr. died (at approximately the age that Rivera's own twin brother had died). In November 1919, Vorobiev had a daughter, Marika, whom Rivera did not recognize as his child. Following his return to Mexico in 1921, he married Lupe Marín, with whom he had two daughters, but he left her in 1929 to wed Kahlo when the second daughter was only two.

Dr. Eloesser's reply to Kahlo's first letter has been lost but when she wrote to him the second time, she thanked him for his note and telegram, explaining that she had finally decided to allow the pregnancy to go forward, not knowing it would come to such an unpleasant and premature ending. She stated, "At that time I was enthusiastic about having the child after having thought of all the difficulties that it would cause me, but surely it was rather a biological thing since I felt the need to give myself over to the child." She then described the timing of the miscarriage, and wondered why the fetus had disintegrated, saying: "Until now I do not know why I miscarried and for what reason the fetus did not take form, so that who knows what the devil is going on inside me, for it is very strange, don't you think?"[41]

Kahlo's seemingly less than overwhelming desire for a child, inferred from this correspondence and from certain other behavior during this time, has been seen by writers such as Martha Zamora as evidence that she did not really have a strong wish for motherhood. Indeed, the fact that the original title she chose for her *Henry Ford Hospital* painting was "The Lost Desire" has been taken literally by some writers to imply that the artist lacked true maternal longing. A few contemporaries even seem to hold her partly responsible for the baby's death. A friend, Ella Wolfe, claimed at the time that Kahlo might have been able to bring the pregnancy to term had she been willing to stay in bed for five or six months rather than engage in normal day-to-day activities.[42]

But Kahlo's ambivalence as expressed in this correspondence does not imply that she did not want children or that she did not grieve intensely over her pregnancy losses. She appears to have taken great care in considering the potential problems, arriving at a decision she was comfortable with in spite of the challenges. The fact that she did not terminate pregnancies unless medically necessary and kept trying to conceive for a couple of years thereafter underscores her desire for motherhood, as did the statement early in her marriage that she cried "inconsolably" about her lack of success. Another piece of evidence confirming her wish for children is found in a letter she wrote as late as 1938 to her friend, Lucienne Bloch, upon learning of the latter's pregnancy:

> Please give my love to Dimi [Stephen Dimitroff, her
> husband], and tonight, after you go to bed, make some nice
> caresses on your belly, thinking I make them myself to my future
> godchild. I am sure it will be a girl, a little nice beautiful girl
> made with the best chosen hormones from Lucy and Dimi, in
> case I fail, and it happens to be a boy, gee! I will be proud of him
> just the same, any way, boy or girl *I will love it as if it were the
> child I was going to have in Detroit.*[43] [italics added]

Perhaps the clearest statement Kahlo made about her inability to have children and what it meant to her came in an interview with her friend Raquel Tibol in 1953, a year before her death. Kahlo affirmed the fact that her reproductive failures left her with a profound emptiness, and that her work as an artist helped to partially overcome the void and give meaning to her existence. "Painting completes my life," she asserted. "I lost three children and another series of things that would have filled my horrible life. Painting is a substitute for all that. I think work is the best thing."[44] From her comment as an adolescent that one of her goals in life was to have a child with Rivera to her later reflection on the importance of painting in lieu of motherhood, it appears that Kahlo truly longed for children. The results of the Thematic Apperception Test (TAT) administered in 1949 by Olga Campos, in which Kahlo told a story of a man and wife who had recently lost a son, also confirm her lifelong concerns. In response to a TAT picture of a man and a woman together, Kahlo stated, "They are father and mother. That is, they are husband and wife, and have had a great sorrow: the loss of a son. They are going to say goodbye, never to see each other again. And they have spent more than twenty-five years together. Something tremendous has happened to them. Their son has died. . . ."[45]

Why she was unable to have children is still unclear. Most scholars have generally assumed that Kahlo's inability to carry a pregnancy to term was directly related to the severe injuries she sustained at age eighteen in the bus accident. But others see it connected to longer-term problems. A medical history taken retrospectively by Dr. Henriette Begun[46] in 1946 states that as a child Kahlo sustained a blow to her right leg from a tree trunk and from then on the leg atrophied "with slight shortening and foot turned outward." Polio was diagnosed by some physicians and a "white tumor" by others. In his provocative study, *Creativity and Disease* (1982), Philip Sandblom, M.D., proposed an alternate explanation, asserting that Kahlo's progressive deterioration was due to spina bifida, a congenital defect in which the lower spine does not close during fetal development. He pointed out that Dr. Eloesser had made the diagnosis when he first evaluated Kahlo in San Francisco in 1930 and that X-rays showed "considerable scoliosis and apparent fusion of third and fourth lumbar vertebrae with disappearance of intervertebral meniscus."[47] According to Sandblom, the trophic ulcers on her legs and feet are frequently associated with spina bifida, and it was the progressive ulceration that led to numerous surgeries, use of pain medication, and ultimately to amputation of her right leg. Sandblom pointed out that the trophic ulcers can be readily observed in her painting, *What the Water Gave Me* (1938), in which the sores between her toes appear to be typical lesions caused by spina bifida.[48] In any case,

Sandblom's study is now given considerable weight by most scholars, but not all agree that this comprises the whole story.

Other factors may have contributed to Kahlo's failure to bring a child to term, although no single explanation is conclusive. From the same medical history (1946) cited above, which includes a brief description of each pregnancy, it was stated that the one which occurred in Mexico during her first year of marriage was terminated by Dr. J. de Jesus Marín because of a "malformed pelvis." Could this have been partially caused by the bus accident? Perhaps, but the connection is not fully apparent. The same is true regarding her miscarriage in Detroit two or three years later. The next pregnancy, her third, was terminated by a Dr. Zollinger in Mexico in 1934, for an entirely different reason—when an exploratory laparotomy showed "undeveloped ovaries." There is also mention of her being tested for syphilis during this period though it is unclear that she had the disease. Even today the causes of miscarriage, or recurrent miscarriage, are frequently ambiguous and may be related to a combination of conditions. It is also possible that Kahlo's pregnancy failures were related in part to factors such as ovarian dysfunction, which occurred in several female members of her family. Indeed, among all of Guillermo Kahlo's daughters, only Frida's younger sister Cristina ever successfully bore children. Her oldest sister was noted to be "sterile," and her next oldest sister had three miscarriages and was described as having "ovarian insufficiency."

Besides another pregnancy loss, life for Frida after her return to Mexico brought other hardships. In 1934, she had the first of many surgical procedures on her right foot, leading to increasing physical pain. But more devastating was the emotional blow she received upon discovering that her husband Diego had initiated an intimate affair with her sister, Cristina, who had often posed for him. To Frida, it was one thing for him to have casual sex with an anonymous model; it was another to seek out her own sister. Deeply angered and distraught by his actions, Kahlo separated from Rivera, moving out of their joint residence. During this period she painted very little. The only two canvases she completed in the following year have been interpreted as reflecting the inner rage she felt toward her husband. One was titled *Self-Portrait* (1935), which shows a teary-eyed Kahlo wearing a man's suit and without the long hair that Rivera liked so much. The other, called *A Few Small Nips* (1935), depicted a stabbed and bloodied woman lying naked on a bed, wearing a high shoe on her right foot (as Kahlo did for her injured limb), with a man standing over her holding a bloody knife. The painting was based on a contemporary newspaper story, but there is the implication that it symbolized how wounded she felt as a result of Rivera's actions. Yet despite the turmoil of her private life, Kahlo survived these difficult years, perhaps coming to realize the limits of her partnership with Rivera, whom she still loved in spite of his failings. She herself began to have affairs with other men, including the sculptor Isamu Noguchi, and then the photographer Nickolas Muray, whom she cared about deeply for a time. She is also alleged to have had a brief relationship with the exiled Russian revolutionary Leon Trotsky, who sought refuge in Mexico in 1937 and stayed for a while at Kahlo's Coyoacán home. But none of these attachments brought her long-term fulfillment, and by the late 1930s, she more or less returned to her old living arrangements with Rivera, though the two of them remained somewhat cool and detached.

Although Kahlo continued to have problems in her personal life and with her health (and never became pregnant again), her artistry now flourished. Some of her most notable canvases were completed during this time, and she began to receive national and then international recognition. In Mexico City, four of her paintings were featured and praised at a major group showing in 1938. The following year, a leading avant-garde art promoter, Julien Levy, who heard about her work, arranged her first solo exhibit at his gallery in New York. In addition, the French surrealist painter André Breton, after visiting Mexico and being impressed with Kahlo's art, agreed to write the preface to the catalog of Kahlo's New York show. Both Breton and Levy saw Kahlo's very imaginative creations as surrealist, and subsequently, she came to be seen by many critics as a surrealist artist. But Kahlo rejected this designation, insisting that she never painted dreams but rather her own reality. "They thought I was a surrealist, but I wasn't," she exclaimed.[49] Bertram Wolfe, her friend and Rivera's biographer, also disagreed with the Surrealism label, and pointed out that Kahlo had never created her art by following the methods of the Surrealist school. In a 1938 article in *Vogue* magazine, Wolfe wrote, "While official Surrealism concerns itself mostly with the stuff of dreams, nightmares, and neurotic symbols, in Madame Rivera's brand of it, wit and humor predominate."[50] Kahlo, who had always painted for herself, without the public in mind, had some difficulty understanding the rising interest in her work. She had experienced a similar reaction when the American actor and art collector, Edward G. Robinson, came and purchased four of her paintings earlier that year. Of course, she was pleased with the money that she obtained from the sale, enabling her to feel more financially independent. She was also happy with the success of the show in New York, and the fact that roughly half of the twenty-five paintings in the exhibition were sold. While certain reviewers seemed shocked by such works as *Henry Ford Hospital*, others saw her genius. The critic from *Time* magazine declared that her creations "had the daintiness of miniatures, the vivid reds and yellows of the Mexican tradition and the playfully bloody fancy of an unsentimental child."[51]

The following year, 1939, brought Kahlo further acclaim as André Breton invited her to display several of her paintings in a show of Mexican art to be held in Paris. The French exhibition attracted much interest from the press and from many renowned European artists. As she wrote to Bert Wolfe, there were "lots of congratulations for the Chicua [her nickname for herself], among them, a big hug from *Juan Miró* and great praises from *Kandinsky* on behalf of my painting; congratulations from *Picasso, Tanguy*, Paalen, and from other 'big shits' of surrealism. Overall, I'd say that it was a success, and considering the quality of the stuff (meaning the bunch of congratulators), I think this whole thing turned out quite well."[52] Indeed, one of Kahlo's paintings, a colorful self-portrait titled *The Frame*, was purchased by the Louvre Museum. The exhibition clearly enhanced her reputation in the international art world, but it was not a great financial success and she had to cancel a follow-up exhibit in London. In addition, Kahlo was ill with abdominal distress for much of the time she spent in Paris and was happy to leave in the late spring.

When Kahlo returned to Mexico after the Paris exhibit, Rivera stunned her by asking for a divorce. There had, of course, been long standing conflicts between the two of them. She had always been critical of his affairs, and he claimed that a legal divorce would be the best solution, saying it "would help each of them to work better." Kahlo, though bitter, reluctantly agreed to the dissolution, and her feelings of dejection can be seen in two of the canvases she produced at this time that are now considered among her most notable works. The first of these, *The Two Fridas*, shows two women sitting side by side, one dressed in European style and with a decaying heart, which Rivera would have disliked, and the other wearing traditional Tehuana clothing over a healthy heart, which he would have adored. The second painting, *Self-Portrait with Cropped Hair*, pictured a masculine Kahlo, clothed in a man's suit, seated in a chair with her long hair, loved by Diego, now cut off and wildly spread about. Rivera also expressed anger toward Kahlo in one of his canvases. But the divorce did not last. Within a year, the couple reconciled and remarried under conditions stipulated by Kahlo, that she would not depend on him financially and they would not resume a sexual relationship. Interestingly, their friends claimed that neither of these conditions persisted over time, especially when Kahlo became increasingly ill and was less able to work and support herself. An additional problem that she now faced was trying to moderate her alcohol consumption, as she had begun to drink more heavily in response to increasing pain.

Amid her personal difficulties and declining health, one positive development in Kahlo's life was the chance to become an art teacher at the new School of Painting and Sculpture established by the Ministry of Education in 1942. The school, nicknamed the Esmeralda, had been created to sustain the resurgence in Mexican art, and many prominent artists agreed to serve on the faculty by the following year. Kahlo truly relished the opportunity to teach the young and did more than communicate the mechanics of painting. Consistent with her independence of thought, her teaching took the form of encouraging her students to develop their own talents without forcing them to adopt any particular mode of artistic expression. Moreover, she hoped to inspire them by offering a new way of thinking, a whole philosophy of life. On Fridays she took the class to the marketplace, singing songs along the way, describing the various items on display, and buying everyone tacos. After a few months, when Kahlo became too ill to travel to the school, she invited the students to come to her home in Coyoacán to continue their studies. Although most were unwilling or unable to make the trip on a regular basis, four of them continued to work with Kahlo over the next three years. This band of budding artists became known as "*Los Fridos*" and remained devoted to their mentor even after the formal lessons stopped.

By the mid-1940s, though Kahlo was still comparatively young (only thirty-seven in 1944), her life course started moving abruptly on a downward slope; her health was deteriorating and she was in almost constant pain. During the next decade, Kahlo underwent several major operations and often had to wear steel, plaster, or leather corsets, one of them requiring her to sit upright for three months. Nevertheless, she continued to work, exclaiming, "I am not sick. I am broken. But I am happy to be alive as long as I can paint." She often painted four to five hours a day before tiring, and in these years produced some of her most profound pieces of art, such as *The Broken Column* (1944), *The Wounded Deer* (1946), and *Tree of Hope, Stand Fast* (1946). Kahlo also began creating an unusual diary in 1944, which combined both words and pictures. In it she often used "the Surrealist technique of making an ink blot on the fold of the page and drawing something from the random, apparently meaningless, mark of ink."[53] Besides being an outlet for her artistry, the diary provides revealing insights regarding her psyche over the course of her decline.

Though at times Kahlo was hopeful that her physical condition might improve, her health only worsened. She attempted suicide in July 1949 with an overdose of barbiturates after Rivera asked for a divorce so that he could marry Emma Hurtado, a lover who also helped to organize his business dealings when Kahlo could no longer do so. In 1950 the woman who once craved activity had to be hospitalized for more than nine months due to recurring spinal problems. By this time she had stopped drinking but was addicted to Demerol. Despite her never-ending pain and spinal infections, her hospital room became a center of activity, with friends visiting, films being shown daily, and Rivera establishing himself in the room next door. When the artist left the hospital in 1951 she was barely able to walk, but once established back home she painted every day for as many hours as she could. She began her *Self-Portrait with the Portrait of Dr. Farill* and also painted a number of still lifes. One of the highlights of Kahlo's last years was a major exhibition of her paintings at the Galería de Arte Contemporaneo in Mexico City in April 1953. This comprised the first and only solo exhibition of her works during her lifetime. There was a question about whether she would attend the show since her health was getting worse and her physicians had recommended that she stay in bed. But on the evening of the opening, Kahlo made a dramatic appearance, arriving by ambulance and entering the gallery on a stretcher. That summer her physical status diminished further, and her right leg had to be amputated below the knee because of gangrene. Whereas Kahlo had always painted people, in her diary she now painted several landscapes that foreshadowed her death. The following spring (1954) she was hospitalized in April and May, and two months later in July she died from bronchial pneumonia, departing from life in the house where she was born. She tried to remain active almost to the very end, appearing just a week before her death at a demonstration against the United States' involvement in Guatemala. Kahlo's funeral was a solemn affair attended by hundreds of mourners, one of whom was Diego Rivera, whose usually cheerful face grew "haggard and gray." One friend, recalling Rivera's demeanor, said that he "became an old man in a few hours, pale and ugly."[54] He passed away three years later.

When Frida Kahlo died in 1954, she had only a limited reputation in the international art world. Many encyclopedias and other reference books on painting published in the 1950s and 1960s contain little or no mention of her and her work. However, in response to the emergence of the Chicano/a art movement, the rise of feminism, and the appearance of several in-depth analyses of her life and creativity, Kahlo eventually became an important cultural phenomenon and major cult figure in Latin America, parts of Europe, and the United States. A precursor to her rising popularity came out of a visit to the recently established Frida Kahlo Museum in Mexico City by an American film-making couple, Karen and David Crommie, in 1965. Karen Crommie strongly identified with Kahlo, relating especially to the feminist, childbirth, and fetal imagery in her paintings. She and her husband decided to make a documentary film, *The Life and Death of Frida Kahlo*,[55] which won second prize at the San Francisco Film Festival in 1967. Although the film was then shelved for a number of years, Daniel del Solar, a member of the Bay Area Chicano/Latino artistic community, presented it on public television in San Francisco in 1975, and again it created a stir. Other Chicano/a artists in the 1970s began exploring Kahlo's work, and the growing interest culminated in a 1978 exhibit called "Homenaje a Frida Kahlo," which opened on the evening of El Dia de Muertos in the Galería de la Raza in San Francisco. While people of many backgrounds embraced Kahlo's image, she specifically provided inspiration for Hispanic women artists. One of them, Yreina Cervantez, said, "I feel very connected to Frida for a lot of very personal and social reasons—among them, the fact that there were no role models for Chicana or Latina artists that we were aware of at the time."[56]

Meanwhile, art historians and scholars in several countries were beginning to do in-depth research into Kahlo's life and creative works. In 1973 Teresa Del Conde, after many attempts, was given permission to spend a morning reading Kahlo's diary, and she published an article on the subject in 1974 in the magazine *Artes Visuales*. Also in 1973, Gloria Orenstein wrote an article titled, "Frida Kahlo: Painting for Miracles," which appeared in the *Feminist Art Journal*. Soon Hayden Herrera began researching Kahlo's life for her doctoral dissertation at the City University of New York under the direction of feminist art historian Linda Nochlin; it was completed in 1981 and emerged as a best-selling book in 1983. Herrera had also organized the first solo exhibit of Kahlo's works in the United States at the Chicago Museum of Contemporary Art in 1978. Raquel Tibol, an Argentinean art historian who had known Kahlo at the end of her life, published a book in 1983 called *Frida Kahlo: Una Vida Abierta*, which was translated in 1993 into English as *Frida Kahlo: An Open Life*. Several more biographies and analyses of her art continued to appear throughout the 1990s and into the early 2000s.[57]

Over time Kahlo became more admired as an artist than her husband Diego Rivera, and the craze known as "Fridolatry," or "Fridomania," manifested itself in many ways. The popular entertainer Madonna declared her love for Kahlo in several interviews, and she purchased the painting, *My Birth*, which she reportedly used as a kind of litmus test for potential friends.[58] Kahlo's paintings, which had previously been bought for small sums, now began to sell for record-breaking figures in the millions. Whereas no major museum in New York City was interested in showing the Kahlo exhibit in 1978 when it toured the country after leaving Chicago, by 1990 the Museum of Modern Art began displaying the Kahlo paintings it already owned. Plays and operas about Kahlo were produced, reproductions and calendars of her art proliferated, and artists and merchandisers paid homage to Kahlo through the creation of postcards and miniature statues. Frida brooches and dress-shop mannequins in her image were seen in Mexico City. Even a cookbook appeared, under the title, *Frida's Fiestas: Recipes and Reminiscences of Life with Frida Kahlo*, put together by Guadelupe Rivera, her stepdaughter, and Marie-Pierre Colle, part memoir and part description of meals that Kahlo had prepared.[59] Then, in 2002, Mexican actress Salma Hayek produced and starred in a major motion picture about Kahlo's life called *Frida*, which won numerous awards and attracted even greater public attention to the artist's many struggles and achievements. Finally, the year 2007, the centennial of her birth, brought about the biggest retrospective of her work ever at the San Francisco Museum of Modern Art.

Sarah Lowe wrote in her introduction to Kahlo's diary, "In time, her self-portraits, though they never cease to shock, have overcome some of the prejudice against women painting their own lives."[60] Kahlo painted aspects of her internal experience and various identities, and reproductive loss is one of the strands of identity she actively engaged with as an artist. Kahlo's generativity is impressive both in terms of the legacy of her work and interpersonal relationships; people embrace Kahlo today through her images as they personally embraced her when she was alive. Much has been written about her self-absorption, her narcissism, and her manipulation of her illnesses. Herrera wrote in her biography, for example, "In Frida's case, of course, there also was an element of narcissism. Indeed, it is possible to argue that invalidism was essential to her self-image, and that if Frida's physical problems had been as grave as she made out, she would never have been able to translate them into art."[61] While physical illness generally leads to an increase in self-focus and concern over the integrity of the body, Kahlo did not live her life from a narcissistic basis. Unlike the narcissistic individual, she was oriented to other people, solicitous of their welfare, and extremely generous. Rather than viewing her illnesses as a manipulation of others, one can acknowledge that she lived as full a life as possible while coping with multiple, severe disabling conditions. That she worked productively in spite of her physical problems underlines her discipline, her intellect, and her active stance toward life. Frida Kahlo created rather than endured, and she utilized posttraumatic imagery to portray her infertility on canvas. In an unfinished portrait that she worked on regularly while hospitalized in 1950, called *Portrait of Frida's Family*, Kahlo painted a second version of her genealogy. She portrays her parents, grandparents, her sisters, her niece and nephew, and an unidentified child. Between Kahlo and her older sister is a fetus, perhaps symbolic of the fetal development of all the Kahlo sisters, or the unborn child that Kahlo herself never delivered.

NOTES

[1] Sarah Lowe, "Essay," in *The Diary of Frida Kahlo: An Intimate Self-Portrait* (New York: Harry N. Abrams, 1995), 25.

[2] Quoted in Andrea Kettenmann, *Frida Kahlo 1907-1954: Pain and Passion* (Cologne, Germany: Benedikt Taschen, 1993), 51.

[3] Salomon Grimberg, *Frida Kahlo: Essay and Catalogue* (Dallas, TX: The Meadows Museum, Southern Methodist University, 1989), 7.

[4] Nancy Frazier, *Penguin Concise Dictionary of Art History* (New York: Penguin Books, 2000), 356.

[5] Hayden Herrera, *Frida: A Biography of Frida Kahlo* (New York: Harper & Row, 1983), 148.

[6] Janis Bergman-Carton, "Like an Artist," *Art in America*, 35-39; Janice Helland, "Aztec Imagery in Frida Kahlo's Paintings," *Woman's Art Journal* 11 (Fall 1990-Winter 1991): 8-13.

[7] Martha Zamora, *Frida Kahlo: The Brush of Anguish* (San Francisco: Chronicle Books, 1990), 91.

[8] Herrera, *Frida*, 18-20.

[9] Herrera, *Frida*, 15.

[10] Herrera, *Frida*, 27.

[11] Herrera, *Frida*, 28.

[12] Interview with Olga Campos, in Salomon Grimberg, *Frida Kahlo: Song of Herself* (New York and London: Merrell Publishers Limited, 2008), 95.

[13] Herrera, *Frida*, 40.

[14] FK to AGA, January 10, 1927, in Martha Zamora, ed., *The Letters of Frida Kahlo: Cartas Apasionadas* (San Francisco: Chronicle Books. 1995), 26.

[15] Letter written from New York City in 1938 from FK to AGA, quoted in Raquel Tibol, *Frida Kahlo: An Open Life* (Albuquerque, NM: University of New Mexico Press), 69. Kahlo is referring to an article about her that appeared in *Vogue* magazine. For the quote below from Gómez Arias, see note 37, p. 237n.

[16] Herrera, *Frida*, 43.

[17] Herrera, *Frida*, 43.

[18] Herrera, *Frida*, 60-61.

[19] Zamora, *Letters*, 24.

[20] Zamora, *Letters*, 110.

[21] Herrera, *Frida*, 88.

[22] Herrera, *Frida*, 107.

[23] Florence Davies, "Wife of the Master Mural Painter Gleefully Dabbles in Works of Art," *The Detroit News* (1933), cited in Herrera, *Frida*, 159.

[24] Quoted in Herrera, *Frida*, 120.

[25] Rebecca Block and Lynda Hoffman-Jeep, "Fashioning National Identity," *Woman's Art Journal* 19 (Fall 1998/Winter 1999): 12.

[26] Quoted in Herrera, *Frida*, 106.

[27] Herrera, *Frida*, 106. The medical abortion and the subsequent painting, *Frida and the Caesarian*, believed by Herrera to have taken place in 1930 and 1931, respectively, is now thought to have occurred in 1929. See Grimberg, *Frida Kahlo: Song of Herself*, 110.

[28] Herrera, *Frida*, 142.

[29] Herrera, *Frida*, 142.

[30] Lesley's account of the interview was never published but the notes are quoted in Herrera, *Frida*, 144.

[31] Dina Comisarenco, "Frida Kahlo, Diego Rivera, and Tlazolteotl," *Woman's Art Journal* 17 (Spring/Summer 1996): 14-21. Comisarenco makes the interesting point that Rivera's parents had experienced three stillbirths before he and his twin brother were born on December 8, 1886. His twin died eighteen months later. His mother then studied obstetrics and became a practicing midwife.

[32] Herrera, *Frida*, 145.

[33] Until the late 1970s, thought disorder was considered to be indicative of schizophrenia. Research has since challenged this belief and has found thought disorder in other diagnostic categories such as bipolar illness

and posttraumatic stress disorder, as well as in creative individuals. For a discussion of the topic, see James H. Kleiger, *Disordered Thinking and the Rorschach: Theory, Research, and Differential Diagnosis* (Mahwah, NJ: The Analytic Press, Inc., 1999).

[34] Kettenmann, *Frida Kahlo*, 35.

[35] For a discussion of Kahlo's link to the retablo tradition, see Victor Fosado, "The Intuition of Retablo Painters and the Passion of Frida," in Erika Billeter, ed., *The Blue House: The World of Frida Kahlo* (Houston, TX: Museum of Fine Arts, 1993), 227-37.

[36] Herrera, *Frida*, 146.

[37] Gannit Ankori, "The Hidden Frida: Covert Jewish Elements in the Art of Frida Kahlo," *Jewish Art* 19/20 (1994): 224-47.

[38] Margaret A. Lindauer, *Devouring Frida: The Art History and Popular Celebrity of Frida Kahlo* (Hanover, NH: University Press of New England, 1999), 89.

[39] Again, some would argue that Herrera is over-interpreting Kahlo's life and art with respect to fertility issues. Peter Glusker, who visited Kahlo in his youth, wrote a letter to the editor of *JAMA, The Journal of the American Medical Association* 271 (April 13, 1994): 1078, arguing that she loved botanical life and grew dramatic and rare flowering plants in her garden. He said the "botanical features in Frida's paintings were, rather, a profound celebration of the richness of botanical life and a symbolic way of closely relating human existence with the rest of the biological world."

[40] Portions of the letters are printed in Herrera, *Frida*, 142-43. Preconception genetic counseling is recommended for women patients with spina bifida because the risk of offspring with spina bifida is increased relative to the general population (approximately 4% as opposed to 0.1-

0.3%). See *European Journal of Obstetrics, Gynecology, & Reproductive Biology* 52 (1993): 63-70.

[41] Quoted in Herrera, *Frida*, 142-43.

[42] Herrera, *Frida*, 147.

[43] Zamora, *Letters*, 90.

[44] Tibol, *Frida Kahlo*, 67.

[45] The analysis of the Thematic Apperception Test appears in James Bridger Harris, "Psychological Assessment of Frida Kahlo," which is included in Grimberg, *Frida Kahlo: Song of Herself*, 138.

[46] Dr. Henriette Begun was a German-born gynecologist who immigrated to Mexico in 1942. Begun's compilation, "Frida Kahlo's Medical History," is reproduced in Grimberg's book, 113-19.

[47] Philip Sandblom, *Creativity and Disease* (Philadelphia: George F. Stickley Company, 1982), 12-13.

[48] Sandblom made other Kahlo writers aware of the possibility of spina bifida as the primary cause of her deterioration when he published a letter in response to an article by Herrera about her health. Philip Sandblom, "Congenital Defect," *The New York Times*, December 23, 1990, 4H.

[49] Lowe, "Essay," 26. In addition, see Lindauer, *Devouring Frida*, for an extensive analysis of the connection between Kahlo's work and surrealism.

[50] Bertram Wolfe, "Rise of Another Rivera," *Vogue* 10 (November 1938). Quoted in Herrera, *Frida*, 262.

[51] Quoted in Herrera, *Frida*, 231.

[52] Zamora, *Letters*, 95-96.

[53] Malka Drucker, *Frida Kahlo: Torment and Triumph in Her Life and Art* (New York: Bantam Books, 1991), 128.

[54] Herrera, *Frida*, 433.

[55]Interview with David Crommie on September 19, 1991, quoted by Ramón Favela, "The Image of Frida Kahlo in Chicano Art," in Blanca Garduno and José Antonio Rodriguez, comp., *Pasión Por Frida* (Mexico: Instituto Nacional de Bellas Artes, 1991), 188.

[56] Interview with Yreina Cervantez on September 19, 1991, in Favela, "The Image of Frida Kahlo in Chicano Art."

[57] Among the important works not already cited are: Hayden Herrera, *Frida Kahlo: The Paintings* (New York: HarperCollins, 1991), and Gannit Ankori, *Imaging Her Selves: Frida Kahlo's Poetics of Identity and Fragmentation* (Westport, CT: Greenwood Press, 2002).

[58] Edward Sullivan, "Frida Kahlo in New York," in *Pasión Por Frida*, 182.

[59] Guadelupe Rivera and Marie-Pierre Colle, *Frida's Fiestas: Recipes and Reminiscences of Life with Frida Kahlo* (New York: Clarkson N. Potter, 1994).

[60] Lowe, "Essay," 26.

[61] Herrera, *Frida*, 346-47.

Emma Goldman, 1910, Courtesy of Library of Congress.

Chapter 6
Revolution and Reform:
"Take Care of My Love-Child"
Emma Goldman (1869-1940)

Emma Goldman was a major revolutionary activist of the late nineteenth and early twentieth centuries. For roughly fifty years on the public stage, she vigorously condemned capitalism and criticized many other aspects of the bourgeois western lifestyle, including conventional marriage and motherhood. At the same time, she used motherhood as a metaphor for her revolutionary activities. Throughout her adult life, Goldman worked relentlessly to establish an alternative way of living based on anarchist principles, which meant the withering away of government and other institutional controls. Her message included the demand for free speech without limits, and, even before Margaret Sanger came on the scene, a clarion call for birth control so as to free women from the burdens and risks of continuous childbearing. Appealing to the working class to overthrow the existing system made her a notorious, even monstrous, individual in the eyes of business leaders and governmental authorities. In fact, "Red Emma," as she was sometimes called, was for many years viewed as the most dangerous person in the United States, one who might by her incendiary words set off a class war between capitalism and labor. Many law enforcement officials believed she was behind the assassination of President McKinley and other acts of violence against the ruling establishment. As a result, she was constantly threatened with arrest and eventually was deported from her adopted homeland. But even among anarchists and other radicals she was not always fully accepted, partly because she was a woman and interested in transforming women's position in society. In resisting change in the relationship between the sexes, the men in charge of the radical movement were often no different from those in mainstream politics. Most of them did not really believe in female equality or question traditional gender roles, and pursued policies that had no special benefits for women. Goldman also faced the contradiction between dedicating herself totally to the radicals' goal of transforming the social structure and at the same time wishing to create a family. Most of those who preached revolution told their followers that personal desires were to be denied or sublimated. As stated in a famous late nineteenth-century revolutionary tract: everything should be absorbed "by a single, exclusive interest, a single thought, a single passion—the revolution. All the tender feelings of family life must be stifled . . . by a single cold passion—the revolutionary cause."[1] For a long time Goldman experienced firsthand the tensions between "the yearning for a personal life and the need of giving all to my ideal."[2] While she would ultimately accept the need to give herself totally to the cause, she did on numerous occasions express feelings of regret about not being able to create a family. Goldman was not alone among female revolutionaries in having these ambivalent feelings. Living in roughly the same period, the Polish-born socialist agitator Rosa Luxemburg made similar remarks. Once, when Luxemburg wrote to her lover and fellow comrade Leo Jogiches, pondering their future, she asked whether it might include "perhaps even a baby, a very little baby? Will this never be allowed?"[3] For both Goldman and Luxemburg, giving up the idea of creating a family was not a simple choice, though in Goldman's case it would have been impossible to include children, except through adoption, since she was almost certainly infertile.

Goldman's feelings about her childlessness are not easy to analyze. For one thing, many (though by no means all) of the comments that she made about yearning for children come from her autobiography, which was written when she was around sixty, and may or may not have reflected how she felt about the subject in her childbearing years. In addition, she was evidently not aware that she was infertile at an early age, and always believed that she was childless by choice and could have, if she had wished, altered her condition so as to become a mother. Yet it is obvious from many sources that she thought a great deal about children, and, long before writing her autobiography, put forth an abundance of statements about the attractions of mothering and motherhood. Indeed, maternal images flowed from her pen more profusely than from any of the other figures discussed in this book.[4] To a greater extent than was true for most public women of her time, issues of sexuality and reproduction were clearly part of her everyday consciousness.

Emma Goldman's attitude toward the question of childbearing was very much tied to the difficult experiences of her own childhood. Goldman was born in the Russian town of Kovno in the year 1869 in a region that would become part of modern-day Lithuania. She was the daughter of Jewish parents, Abraham and Taube Goldman. Also present in the household were her two older half-sisters from her mother's previous marriage and eventually two younger brothers. Emma did not get along very well with her parents, either her mother, a homemaker of middle-class origins, who she perceived as cold and distant, or her fiercely traditional shopkeeper father. The latter frequently beat her and taunted her from her earliest years onward with the fact that he would have preferred a son. "As long as I could think back," Goldman wrote in her autobiography, "I remembered his saying that he had not wanted me. He had wanted a boy, the pig woman had cheated him." Later, in her twenties, when she considered the idea of having children, she said "A cruel hand clutched at my heart. My ghastly childhood stood before me, my hunger for affection, which Mother was unable to satisfy. Father's harshness towards the children, his violent outbreaks, his beating my sisters and me. . . ." One frightening incident she vividly recalled took place when "Father lashed me with a strap so that my little brother Herman, awakened by my cries, came running up and bit Father on the calf. The lashing stopped." Her older sister Helena took Emma to her room, "bathed my bruised back, brought me milk, held me to her heart, her tears mingling with mine," while Father outside was raging: "I'll kill her! I will kill that brat! I will teach her to obey!"[5]

As a young adult, when Emma Goldman debated with herself about whether or not to start a family someday, such negative memories as expressed above were counter-balanced by the fact that from an early age she had always loved children. As Goldman subsequently recalled in her autobiography:

I had loved children madly, ever since I could remember. As a little girl I used to look with envious eyes on the strange little babies our neighbour's daughter played with, dressing them up and putting them to sleep. I was told they were not real babies, they were only dolls, although to me they were living things because they were so beautiful. I longed for dolls but I never had any. . . . When my brother Herman was born, I was only four years old. He replaced the need of dolls in my life. The arrival of little Leibale [known afterwards as Morris] two years later filled me with ecstatic joy. I was always near him, rocking and singing him to sleep. Once when he was about a year old, Mother put him in my bed. After she left, the child began to cry. He must be hungry, I thought. I remembered how Mother gave him the breast. I, too, would give him my breast. I picked him up in my arms and pressed his little mouth close to me, rocking and cooing and urging him to drink. Instead he began to choke, turned blue in the face, and gasped for breath. Mother came running in and demanded to know what I had done to Baby. I explained. She broke out into laughter, then slapped and scolded me. I wept, not from pain, but because my breast had no milk for Leibale. . . . My compassion for our servant Amalia had surely been due to the circumstance that she was going to have *ein Kindchen.* I loved babies passionately and now—now I might have a child of my own and experience for the first time the mystery and wonder of motherhood! I closed my eyes in blissful day-dreaming.[6]

Despite her strong love for children, Goldman made the decision sometime in her early twenties not to have any offspring (at least she believed that she was making such a decision). Since early adolescence she had suffered a great deal from recurring menstrual cramps. She described how on those occasions, "I had to take to bed, in excruciating pain for days." When she finally consulted a physician about her symptoms, she was told that she had an "inverted womb," a catch-all phrase used at the time to describe various menstrual or fertility problems, and that only by corrective surgery could she alter her reproductive system and become capable of bearing a child. From the vantage point of the present, it appears doubtful that the medical procedure prescribed by her doctor in the 1890s could have improved her chances for achieving motherhood. She most likely suffered from severe endometriosis, a condition that was untreatable at the time.[7] But Goldman had made up her mind not to seek treatment in any case. Though faced with the high probability of childlessness and no relief from her menstrual difficulties (she was also told she would never experience "full sexual release"), Goldman categorically rejected any such operation.

As Goldman described the decision-making process in her autobiography, she claimed she had already committed herself to being a revolutionary, living for the cause, and was from here on "determined to serve it completely." This meant saying no to the possibility of children so that she would always remain "unhampered and untied." By making the hard choice of giving up childbearing, she believed that she now had the strength to transform the world. She felt she could surmount any obstacle that stood in her path: "Had I not overcome the strongest and most primitive craving of a woman—the desire for a child."[8] In taking this stance she was surely doing more than denying a maternal urge. Goldman's painful childhood memories—her father's rigidity and her mother's coldness—had made her wonder about her own abilities as a potential parent. Having a child, she thought, might simply add to the already sizable number of ill-treated children in the world. But, as her biographer Alice Wexler has written, "if her decision expressed a realistic choice of public commitments over private satisfactions, she presents it in her autobiography as a sacrifice, almost a form of martyrdom."[9] "Years of pain and of suppressed longing for a child," Goldman declared, "—what were they compared with the price many martyrs had already paid. I, too, would pay the price, I would endure the suffering, I would find an outlet for my mother-need in the love of all children."[10] Perhaps, as Wexler asserts, she had to justify her untraditional choice according to a system of traditional values, "as if it were permissible for a woman to remain childless, only if she perceived it as a sacrifice."[11]

The decision to reject motherhood and affirm her wish to be a dedicated revolutionary occurred around a half dozen years following her emigration to America in 1885. After surviving her own difficult childhood, Goldman had left home at age sixteen for the possibilities of a better life in the United States, rejecting her father's demand that she submit to the Old World custom of an arranged marriage. She had obtained some schooling, starting at age eight, in Königsburg, Prussia, while living with her maternal grandmother, and then in St. Petersburg, where the family had moved when her father opened a grocery store there a few years later. But while she yearned to continue with schooling, her formal education came to an end by the time she was thirteen. Anything more was seen as unnecessary by her father who thought she should marry in the not too distant future. In the meantime, before a marriage could be arranged, she was sent out to do menial labor to help support the family. About education, her father is said to have told her: "Girls do not have to learn much! All a Jewish daughter needs to know is how to prepare gefüllte fish, cut noodles fine, and give the man plenty of children."[12] Emma Goldman clearly desired a more unfettered and worldly kind of existence than this, and refused to follow her father's prescription. "I would not listen to his schemes; I wanted to study, to know life, to travel. Besides, I never would marry for anything but love, I stoutly maintained."[13] While working in a glove factory in St. Petersburg in her early teens she became attracted to some of the radical ideas that were circulating in the Russian capital about the possibility of a new and better world, and an enhanced role for women in creating it. Goldman was particularly influenced by a fictional character she read about, the free-spirited Vera Pavlovna, heroine of Nicolai Chernyshevsky's popular and influential novel, *What Is to Be Done?* (1863). In the book, Pavlovna chooses to sacrifice her middle-class existence in order to work among and help improve the lives of the laboring classes. Goldman was probably also influenced by the exploits of actual women radicals like Vera Zassulich and Sophia Petrovskaya, who were members of radical groups attempting to overthrow the czarist regime at the time.[14]

Leaving Russia in the mid-1880s, Goldman would try to live out these new ideas in the United States, where a few members of her family had already emigrated. She first resided with her half-sisters in the city of Rochester, New York, and started working as a seamstress in a clothing factory. Not finding factory conditions in America much better than in her former homeland strengthened Goldman's belief in the need for major societal change. Her view was reinforced while attending meetings of a local socialist group and upon reading about the trial and execution of the so-called Haymarket rioters in Chicago in 1887—men who had been charged, despite their claims of innocence, with setting off a deadly bomb at a labor protest that had killed several people. Her sympathies toward the accused, who were known as anarchists, led her to study their philosophy and eventually embrace their political cause. Recalling her initial attraction to anarchism, Goldman declared that a whole world, hitherto unknown, had opened to her:

> I had a distinct sensation that something new and wonderful had been born in my soul. A great ideal, a burning faith, a determination to dedicate myself to the memory of my martyred comrades, to make their cause my own, to make known to the world their beautiful lives and heroic deaths.[15]

Around this same time, when Goldman was nearing eighteen, and had not yet become a full-fledged revolutionary, she also began thinking seriously about marriage as a means to greater personal freedom. She was now back living in her parents' household, as they had both immigrated to Rochester, and the old tensions had reemerged. Marriage, she thought, would take her away both from her family and from the grind of sweatshop labor. She had met a fellow immigrant a few years her senior named Jacob Kersner, who toiled in the clothing industry, and like her wished to get away from the restrictive ten-and-a-half-hour day and six-day work week which was common in the factories of that era. The marriage, however, did not prove satisfactory, and within a year the couple divorced, as Kersner failed to provide satisfactory companionship and was allegedly impotent. Goldman moved away and took another factory job for a brief time in New Haven, Connecticut, but when faced with a prolonged illness, came back to Rochester. As a result of the urgings of both her parents and Kersner, who threatened suicide if she did not agree to reconcile, Goldman remarried her ex-husband. But as the relationship fared no better than before she soon divorced him a second and final time. Goldman's parents, horrified by their daughter's behavior in again rejecting her marriage vows, refused to allow her to enter their home and she left her family swearing never to return.[16] By this point Goldman had become more thoroughly entranced by anarchism. She now avidly read the leading anarchist newspaper, *Die Freiheit*, and was determined to turn from words to deeds by committing herself wholeheartedly to the goals of the radical movement.

At age twenty in the summer of 1889 Goldman moved to New York City, the biggest industrial city in the United States as well as the center of radical socialist and anarchist activity. This, she later said, was where her life really began. She soon met and befriended Johann Most, editor of *Die Freiheit* and chief spokesman for the anarchist cause in this country. He quickly recognized her talent and enthusiasm, and helped train her to become a public speaker. A gifted platform performer, she was soon lecturing before groups of immigrant laborers in German and Russian, and eventually in front of English-speaking audiences. Given the subject matter, those who attended her talks were perhaps surprised to find her an attractive young woman, albeit only about five-feet tall. Famed reporter Nellie Bly noted that she had a "saucy turned-up nose and very expressive blue-gray eyes . . . [brown hair] falling loosely over her forehead, full lips, strong white teeth, a mild pleasant voice, with a fetching accent."[17]

Besides her friendship with Most, Goldman formed an even closer bond with Alexander (Sasha) Berkman, like herself, a young, Russian-born immigrant and revolutionary. Having similar goals, the two began an association and collaboration that on and off lasted over four and a half decades. Although their relationship was perhaps more political than romantic, she and Berkman started living together and working toward the creation of an anarchist system in America and elsewhere. Goldman's political outlook was informed by many factors—her rebellious nature, her passion for justice, her experience with the restrictive social order of Russia along with the harsh conditions facing immigrants in the United States. Her ideas also reflected the anarchist visions of Russian social philosopher Peter Kropotkin, who imagined a world where the coercive structures of the state and traditional social hierarchies would be replaced by a society of equals living in small cooperative communities, where harmony, decency, and justice would rule. Freed from oppressive controls by the state, people would work together for the common good, Kropotkin believed.[18] Contemporary writers like Frederick Nietzsche and Henrik Ibsen, who emphasized the importance of a strong sense of individualism, influenced her thinking in that direction as well.

Late in her life, Goldman summarized her anarchist views this way, further emphasizing freedom of the individual: "Anarchism alone stresses the importance of the individual, his possibilities and needs in a free society. Instead of telling him that he must fall down and worship before institutions, live and die for abstractions, break his heart and stunt his life for taboos, Anarchism insists that the center of gravity in society is the individual—that he must think for himself, act freely, and live fully."[19] Goldman, however, never produced lengthy philosophical tracts on the subject of anarchism and was always more of a public activist and popularizer of ideas than she was a behind-the-scenes theoretician. Her major contribution to anarchist theory was to enlarge its scope by insisting on gender as a primary category of oppression. Only when women were free and equal could a society be seen as truly just, she asserted.

Like other radicals, Goldman at first believed that force might be necessary to liberate mankind so as to bring about the new utopia she envisioned, and for some years condoned personal acts of violence against the leaders of capitalism. She aided Alexander Berkman in planning his attempt to assassinate the influential anti-labor steel magnate Henry Clay Frick during the Homestead Strike in 1892 in Pennsylvania. Frick survived the attack but Berkman would spend the next fourteen years in the state penitentiary. As Goldman was not known to have been an actual participant in the event itself, she managed to avoid imprisonment on this occasion. But not too long afterward she was sentenced to a year in jail in New York City for inciting a crowd of unemployed men to riot if their demands for food were not met. (Later on, when she was taken in after a similar incident and struck by a policeman, she told the officer that she might be pregnant, perhaps saving her from a further beating.) Her most notorious arrest occurred in 1901, following the assassination of President William McKinley by a young unemployed laborer named Leon Czolgosz. Czolgosz, who may have been delusional, claimed that he was an anarchist and had listened to Goldman speak harsh words against the ruling class. Hearing the story, many people wanted her locked up for the rest of her life. However, she was eventually released after demonstrating to the authorities that she no longer advocated violence against political and business leaders and that she had no substantive ties to this particular person. Although she continued to favor "direct action" rather than "political action" to bring about revolutionary change, she increasingly defined such efforts in terms of strikes, boycotts, acts of civil disobedience, and propaganda aimed at raising political consciousness.[20]

While Berkman served out his long prison term, Goldman had intimate relations with a number of men, usually individuals tied in one way or another to the radical movement. None of these affairs was long lasting, and none led to marriage. Goldman, in fact, whose philosophy of anarchism emphasized personal freedom, now scorned the concept of marriage as old-fashioned and harmful, one which prevented men and particularly women from truly fulfilling their potential. But if she rejected traditional wedlock and with it the role of traditional wife and mother, Goldman did in these personal relationships display many aspects of strongly nurturing behavior. Her overprotective treatment of Berkman through the years, she once wrote, was done in the belief, "usual with mothers, that they know best what is good for their children."[21] Late in life, she personally admitted to him that her deepest and "most compelling feeling for you is that of the mother."[22] Goldman often found herself in a quasi-mother role even with those men whom she had briefer and more limited attachments. She seems to have enjoyed caring for them when they were sick and advising them on matters of hygiene and other types of personal behavior. With those few men she truly desired she sometimes questioned (at least in hindsight) her decision about not trying to have children. Even with the anarchist leader Johann Most, a much older and unattractive man, who may or may not have been her lover, she said she pondered the idea of motherhood. "I knew I could bring him children if I would have the operation. How wonderful it would be to have a child by this unique personality! I sat lost in the thought."[23]

In her relationship to the Austrian-born anarchist, Edward Brady, in the mid-1890s, these maternal feelings were even more strongly aroused. Brady shared Goldman's belief in the virtues of anarchism, though after languishing in prison for several years, he had become less hopeful about a revolution succeeding in the short run. In addition, in his thoughts about the private domain he had come to prefer a conventional home and family rather than having a string of temporary liaisons. Brady told Goldman that she should give up her career as a public speaker, perhaps do some writing, but in their life together be primarily a wife and mother. Not only did he believe that she would be more safe and secure in this mode but, using ideas later popularized by the famous psychoanalyst Sigmund Freud, he argued that the underlying motive in her devotion to the radical movement was her "unsatisfied motherhood seeking an outlet." "You are a typical mother, my little Emma, by build, by feeling," Brady said to her. "Your tenderness is the greatest proof of it." Goldman admitted to being very moved by these words, as she later wrote in her autobiography, but felt unwilling to give up her activist role and ultimately chose not to yield to his wishes:

> I was profoundly stirred. When I could find words, poor
> inadequate words, to convey what I felt, I could only tell him
> again of my love, of my need of him, of my longing to give him
> much of what he craved. My starved motherhood—was that the
> main reason for my idealism? He had roused the old yearning
> for a child. But I had silenced the voice of the child for the sake
> of the universal, the all-absorbing passion of my life. Men were

consecrated to ideals and yet were fathers of children. But man's physical share in the child is only a moment's; woman's part is for years—years of absorption in one human being to the exclusion of the rest of humanity. I would never give up the one for the other.[24]

Although Goldman rejected Brady's offer with its implication of a more restricted and burdensome existence, she did, partly due to his influence, go abroad to Vienna in 1895 at the age of twenty-six to study nursing and midwifery. During the time she spent in jail the previous year, she had frequently assisted the medical staff in looking after the well being of her fellow inmates and now sought to become a certified health care professional. The skills she learned in the hospital training program were to be extremely helpful, and, among other things, allowed her to earn income at times when other sources of funds were not easily available. In becoming a nurse and midwife, Goldman, whose maternal urges were directed toward improving social conditions for the youth of the world, would now have direct contact with children by assisting in childbirth on numerous occasions. Her experience in this regard was not always rewarding, however, as she often felt depressed about bringing the unwanted offspring of indigent women into a situation of dire poverty. Nevertheless, a few years later after attending an international medical conference on reproductive issues in Paris, Goldman found an aspect of the subject that she felt more positively about and wished to pursue—birth control. As part of her reformist goals she became a strong advocate of contraception to prevent unwanted pregnancy, tying in her knowledge of midwifery when she spoke on the topic. This area allowed her to integrate her desire to nurture with her desire for radical social change. As her biographer Candace Falk notes: "By combining her work as midwife with her interest in birth control, Emma could make a direct contribution to the liberation of women, while performing the supportive functions of a devoted mother. She could return to the speaker's platform to advocate contraception, proclaiming that a revolution in sexual values was now possible. . . ."[25]

In advocating birth control, Goldman was going against the prevailing view of the time, which still saw sizable families as beneficial to society and motherhood as the central purpose in a woman's life. Opponents of birth control insisted that its widespread use would contribute to women's growing individualism and detract from their primary responsibility as mothers. American women who practiced contraception, leaders like Theodore Roosevelt warned, were contributing to "race suicide," as fewer and fewer children of "good stock" would be born.[26] In response, Goldman strongly defended her position, both through the written and the spoken word. One of her essays sought to expose the hypocrisy of her critics' sanctimonious invocation of motherhood, by focusing instead on the reality of the birthing experience of women in many categories, and not just the poor. For these women, as she pointed out, giving birth often brought severe and ongoing pain both to the body and to the soul:

> The woman, physically and mentally unfit to be a mother,
> yet condemned to breed; the woman economically taxed to the
> very last spark of energy, yet forced to breed; the woman, tied to
> the man she loathes, whose very sight fills her with horror, yet
> made to breed; the woman, worn and used-up from the process
> of procreation, yet coerced to breed, more, ever more. What a
> hideous thing this much-lauded motherhood![27]

While Goldman may at times have regretted not becoming a mother, she at no point ever desired to have a big family. Nor did she believe the vast majority of women in the world wanted large numbers of offspring. Later in life, in response to a statement by an anarchist operative about Spain implying women in that country still wished for "broods of children," Goldman emphatically denied the validity of this notion. She discounted the idea that such beliefs were widespread among Spanish women and saw the men who encouraged these views as out of touch with reality in looking upon women as "mere breeding machines as the cavemen did." Regarding female attitudes toward childbearing, she went on, "I wish to say that I have yet to meet the woman who wants to have many children." She did concede that "most women hope to have *a* child, although that, too, has been exaggerated by the male. I have known quite a number of women, feminine to the last degree, who nevertheless lack that supposed-to-be inborn trait of motherhood or longing for the child." Even if for argument's sake one granted that every woman wants to become a mother, she added, "unless she is densely ignorant with an exaggerated trait of passivity, she wants only as many children as she can decide to have."[28]

On the subject of children, though Goldman cared deeply about them and sought to prevent unwanted births, she did not say or write too much about the social and physical welfare of the young. Presumably her concentration on bettering the lives of all people included the needs of children. Her one major essay that focused exclusively on the subject of youth dealt mainly with the way a child should be educated, and the need for parents to allow children enough freedom to grow on their own. In this essay, entitled "The Child and Its Enemies," Goldman criticized the manner in which the family and the state traditionally sought to stifle children's growth as individuals—how every effort was made to cramp human emotion and originality of thought from earliest infancy. She condemned the way those in authority tried to mold a young person into one rigid pattern, "not into a well-rounded individuality but into a patient work slave, professional automaton, taxpaying citizen, or righteous moralist."[29] In a related essay, which dealt with the subject of schools, she cited the words of Spanish reformer Francisco Ferrer: "I like the free spontaneity of a child who knows nothing, better than the world-knowledge and intellectual deformity of a child who has been subjected to our present [system of] education."[30] She even found fault with those radicals who in their role as parents forced their children to mimic their elders and memorize the names of Karl Marx and Thomas Paine rather than permitting them to seek their own direction.[31] Perhaps somewhat naively, Goldman seemed to think that given complete freedom each and every child would somehow find his or her way to lead a fully productive life. She championed the creation of modern alternative schools, what educator John Dewey would soon promote as "progressive schools," where there would be few constraints on learning and students would be able to devote a considerable part of their time to pursuing whatever subjects they wished. In fact, she would assist in creating such a school, the New York Modern School in lower Manhattan.

Regarding the child-rearing process, Goldman believed that much of it should occur away from the parental environment and by persons other than the mother so that she would have the opportunity to pursue a career. In her idealized view, as told to an interviewer, "children would be provided with common homes, big boarding schools, where they would be properly cared for and educated, and in every way given as good, and in most cases better, care than they would receive in their own homes. Very few mothers know how to take proper care of their children anyway. It is a science only a very few have learned."[32] In response to the question about who the expert caregivers would be, Goldman answered that everyone has tastes and qualifications suiting them to some occupation and that there will be those who want to teach and care for children.

Without having children of her own Goldman's theories of child rearing were never fully put to the test. Nevertheless, she thought of herself as a good caregiver, especially when it came to treating and nursing the very young. While engaged in her nurse and midwife training at the General Hospital in Vienna, she claimed she had a better understanding of children than any of her fellow female trainees. The others, she said, were often harsh and domineering in dealing with their young patients. The difficulties of her own childhood, she believed, had made her sympathetic toward the needs of children, especially the sick. "I had much more patience with them than with grown-ups. Their dependence, aggravated by illness, always moved me deeply. I wanted not merely to give them affection but to equip myself for their care."[33] Whether she still showed warmth toward children as she got older is somewhat open to question. When on one occasion youngsters from the anarchist-run day school she had helped to create came to visit her at her workplace, they found her to be rather "cold and formidable."[34] However, a Canadian-born leftist, who remembers in his youth Goldman being present at a nighttime political meeting in his parents' house, claims that she pulled him toward her with fondness though perhaps with a bit too much strength. "Emma crushed me to her ample bosom and held me there in a vice-like embrace," as he tried unsuccessfully to fall asleep amid the discussion going on around him.[35]

Being childless, Goldman, as we have seen, sometimes put her nurturing into other areas such as her relationships with men and toward her nursing efforts. But in addition to these realms she seems to have made a frequent connection to the subject of childbearing or child rearing, whether she was fully conscious of it or not, in writing or speaking on just about any topic. Such references are perhaps most evident in the left-leaning monthly magazine she began to publish in 1906 to disseminate her views, *Mother Earth*. The title, as Candace Falk has written, evoked "an image of regenerative natural powers that could prepare the ground for the growth of a new anarchist world. The name also expressed Emma's own powerful maternal urges, which now had no other structured outlet since the demands of starting the new magazine forced her to drop all her other work. . . ." It is probably no coincidence that this new undertaking occurred when Goldman was moving toward her late thirties, "passing beyond what were then considered the childbearing years." Instead of bearing children, she told herself, "she would give birth to the magazine, nurse it through its infancy, and nurture it to maturity." According to Falk, "frequent allusions in *Mother Earth* to the magazine as 'a child born of love' made it clear that this was a substitute for the baby she would never have."[36] It is worth noting too that Alexander Berkman, who had just been released from jail, became the main editor of the magazine, though the many years they spent apart made it impossible for Goldman to take him back as her lover.

In subsequent years, Goldman continued to make reference to her publications as her children, and sometimes alluded to their arrival in a wry and humorous manner. When she produced a book of some of her previous writings entitled, *Anarchism and Other Essays*, in 1910, she described its initial appearance coming off the press as follows: "Baby arrived three pm, has beautiful body, hope the soul is also worthwhile specimen." Later, upon being sent to jail during the First World War and forced to leave behind the *Mother Earth Bulletin*, the short-lived successor to *Mother Earth*, she told friends to "take care of my love child." On another occasion, when telling about a former lover's completion of his memoirs after a long delay, she wrote: "The baby is born at last. The labor pains were excruciating enough to give birth to a dozen puppies." Finally, upon undertaking the difficult task of writing her own autobiography and compelled to relive often bitter and stressful moments from her past, she referred to the book project as "this child of sorrow."[37] When the two-volume work was finally published, she again used the phrase "The baby is born at last," and explained to a friend, "You see my dear, I had to deny myself a child in the flesh. *Living My Life* has taken its place."[38]

During the *Mother Earth* years, many of her friends and colleagues commented upon Emma Goldman's motherly manner, which the rest of society did not usually get to observe. Leonard Abbott viewed her as "motherly and compassionate;" Roger Baldwin said he was struck by "the warm tenderness of a mother which lay just under that defiant, unyielding public exterior." Mabel Dodge, who had become a fashionable hostess among the avant garde in New York, also witnessed the softer side of the famed anarchist. Attending a gathering at the *Mother Earth* offices, which also served as Goldman's residence, Dodge claimed she was surprised at first not to find her and other anarchists drinking something like "nitroglycerin punch" as "I knew she stood for killing people if necessary." But, she continued, "what a warm, jolly atmosphere, with a homely supper on the table, and Emma herself like a homely, motherly sort of person giving everyone generous platefuls of beefsteak . . . and fried potatoes! She looked to me, from the very first, rather like a severe but warm-hearted schoolteacher and I'm sure that that was essentially what she was. . . ."[39]

Although Goldman had no genetic children of her own, she did have a strong maternal relationship with several of her younger family members. Her younger brother Morris even lived with her briefly during her association with anarchist Edward Brady and she once alluded to the pair of them as "my two children."[40] She established an even closer connection with her niece and nephew, the offspring of her older half-sister Lena. Her nephew Saxe Commins (nee Comminsky) after leaving school worked on *Mother Earth* for a time and later became a noted book editor ultimately employed by the prestigious publishing firm of Alfred Knopf. He often advised his aunt regarding her future publications. The deepest family bond she developed, however, was with her niece, Stella, Saxe's sister. Stella Comminsky (later Ballantine), who, like Saxe, grew up in Rochester, New York, had from a young age come to admire her "Tante Emma." During the early 1900s, when Goldman was having difficulties with the authorities following the McKinley assassination, Stella came to New York City to live and work near her aunt. She often helped her by performing secretarial functions and acting as an intermediary when Goldman was afraid to go out in public. She even shopped and cooked for her at times. As Candace Falk noted, "Emma had always been drawn to her young niece, identifying with Stella as an adventurous spirit in a stifling family. In turn, Emma's fugitive status gave Stella new freedom and expanded her life experiences."[41] Later, she would help out her aunt during the period of her imprisonment at the time of the First World

War, visiting her and acting in her behalf on legal and business matters. (Goldman later described one of the prison visits as time spent with "my beloved child.") Stella was also present at critical junctures in Goldman's final years, accompanying her on her last American speaking tour and being in attendance at the moment of her death.[42]

Almost concurrent with the years of publishing *Mother Earth* came Goldman's most passionate, tumultuous, and ultimately painful personal relationship with the handsome and flamboyant activist Ben Reitman, a man ten years her junior. Trained as a doctor, with a specialty in gynecology, Reitman had spent more time in radical politics than practicing medicine. Contemporarily known as "King of the Hobos" for being a crusader for the unemployed, he first came into Goldman's life as her public relations and lecture tour manager. Their connection, however, soon became much more close and intimate, and Goldman for the first time in her life, at age thirty-eight-and-a-half, began to experience a high level of sexual satisfaction. Reitman, she wrote, brought about "the torrent of an elemental passion [she] had never dreamed any man could arouse in her."[43] Nevertheless, the intense bonding had its lows as well as highs for Goldman as she soon discovered Reitman was a womanizer and simultaneously involved with a number of other lovers. He also had a strong attachment to his mother, consequently forcing her to compete with Mrs. Reitman for his interest and attention. Indeed, in doing so, Goldman began to take on a dual position as mother and lover, even though she felt conflicted by the complexity of her roles. Sometimes when she competed with Mrs. Reitman for her son's time, she facetiously signed her letters to him as "Mummy Reitman." (He in turn often referred to her as "his blue-eyed Mommy.") Rather than distancing herself from this bizarre situation, Goldman, according to Falk, "played out her role as 'his blue-eyed Mommy' with all of its incestuous titillation." This fantasy, Falk states, "helped Emma to reconcile the disparity between the fleeting relationship with a passionate lover she seemed to be having, and the most stable relationship in the world which she craved—that of mother and child."[44] One time when they were apart, Goldman wrote to Reitman:

> I have a great deep mother instinct for you, baby mine; that instinct has been the great redeeming feature in our relation. It has helped me on more than one occasion to overlook your boyish irresponsible pranks.[45]

This last reference to so-called "boyish" behavior refers to his "visiting" other women besides his mother. Falk asserts that on a deep level, "Emma's adoption of the role of mother evinced her secret wish to supplant Ben's mother. She gave morbid expression to this desire in retelling the Yiddish legend of the son who complied with his mistress's request that he prove his love for her by tearing out his mother's heart and bringing it to her."[46] She included the story in a letter to Reitman just prior to his going off to spend the summer with his mother in Chicago in 1908:

> The man adored his mother, she had always been so kind and good to him. But his passion was great, so he killed his mother, tore out her heart and rushed with it to his mistress. On the way he stumbled and fell. And his mother's heart said to him, 'My precious child, have you hurt yourself?' It's that side of my nature, Ben dear, that stretches out to you, that would like to embrace you and soothe you. The mother calls to you, my boy, my precious boy!![47]

A few years later, in connection with another of their separations and the desire to lure him back, Goldman presented Reitman with her version of a Yiddish expression usually aimed at women reluctant to marry, "The man you will marry hasn't been born yet, and his mother died in childbirth." To this she added, "As to my lover, he is still in embryo. Will he ever be born into radiant maturity?" She continued emphasizing the idea of her young lover "in embryo" in several subsequent communications. "You see, my boy. I know you much better than you know yourself. I know that you are strong only in one phase, that's our work. In everything else you are as weak as a newborn babe. That's why I never have faith in your resolutions."[48]

Goldman's attachment to Ben Reitman also brought to the surface for her once again the question of actual motherhood. Although their association began when she was beyond the normal childbearing age for the period, Goldman briefly considered the possibility of offspring. She thought that a child might have a positive effect on her relationship with her lover, by bringing them closer together. Yet even if having a child was possible, the evidence shows she clearly had doubts about whether the situation would work out for the better. The issue of childbearing came up as Goldman observed the deep bond of affection that existed between the acclaimed writer Jack London and his wife Charmian shortly before the birth of their child. "I think, if you loved me as much as Jack loves her," she wrote to Reitman, "I too might yearn [for] a child." But she showed her hesitancy when she added, "And yet I might not. I might enjoy the ecstasy of your love so, I'd hate to share it."[49] Reitman, too, sometimes thought about how their relationship would fare with the addition of a child. In fact, the subject took on a certain degree of reality at least for a little while, for according to his reminiscences, Goldman believed for a time that she might be pregnant. Finding out that it was a false alarm brought her to tears, the only time, Reitman said, he ever saw her cry. Later on, in 1914, when Reitman again mentioned the idea of wanting a home and children, the now forty-five-year-old Goldman responded with less enthusiasm. She asserted that a child at this time would only hamper her work in the radical movement.[50] After this episode, the subject was conveniently dropped. Over the next few years the intimate bond between the two slowly diminished and Reitman eventually found a woman with whom he could have a family.

All through her long and tortured relationship with Reitman, Emma Goldman continued to lecture widely, focusing on the need for radical changes in society. In 1910, for example, Goldman recalled speaking 120 times in thirty-seven cities in twenty-five states, before audiences of thousands of paying and many more non-paying listeners. For someone without much formal education, the range of subject matter she dealt with was impressive, as was her courage in facing potentially hostile crowds and police. As Goldman's early biographer Richard Drinnon has written, "Perhaps the most accomplished, magnetic woman speaker in American history, she crisscrossed the country lecturing on anarchism, the new drama, the revolt of women. Subject to stubborn and sometimes brutal police and vigilante attempts to censor her remarks or to silence her completely, she joyfully waged countless fights for free speech."[51] One of the leading civil libertarians of the twentieth century, Roger Baldwin, asserted that "for the cause of free speech in the United States Emma Goldman fought battles unmatched by the labors of any organization."[52] He later credited her as being the inspiration for the establishment of the American Civil Liberties Union.

In seeking to convey her message of the need for greater individual freedom, Goldman at her speaking engagements often discussed the dramatic works of modern European playwrights such as Henrik Ibsen, August Strindberg, Gerhart Hauptmann, and George Bernard Shaw. She tried to show the relevance of their writings to contemporary social problems, especially in regard to women, and in so doing was very influential in bringing these playwrights' works to the attention of American audiences. As the influential critic Van Wyck Brooks declared: "No one did more to spread the new ideas of literary Europe that influenced so many young people . . . than the Russian-American Emma Goldman. . . ."[53] Goldman's lectures on the subject of these authors and their plays would eventually be published in 1914 as *The Social Significance of the Modern Drama*. Using the works of these dramatists as a means to explore controversial subject matter also enabled Goldman to appear less menacing to her listeners and to the authorities in some of the places where she spoke.

In her years as a lecturer Goldman often dealt with many controversial topics but perhaps none more so than "free love." Her tortuous association with Ben Reitman often made it painful to defend this concept but she did. To her the term did not imply promiscuity, as some critics charged; rather it referred to the idea that relationships between men and women should be based not on some form of economic coercion but on unforced mutual affection for each other. In her eyes, marriage for women, as it then existed, was nothing more than a financial arrangement, "an insurance pact." It had little to do with love. "Whatever she gains she pays for with her name, her privacy, her self-respect, her very life 'until death doth part.'"[54] It leads, she said, to the "complete surrender of all faculties," and "absolutely incapacitates the average woman for the outside world." Children, she felt, were not protected by the institution of marriage any more than women were. As she wrote: "Marriage protecting the child, yet orphan asylums and reformatories overcrowded, the Society for the Prevention of Cruelty to Children keeping busy in rescuing the little victims from 'loving' parents. . . . Oh, the mockery of it."[55] Instead, Goldman advocated "free motherhood," where women would not be under such legal constraints. "If motherhood is the highest fulfillment of woman's nature, what other protection does it need, save love and freedom."[56] She apparently believed that the single mother would do just as well as the married one, though she never brought up the issue of affordable child care or other problems faced by a woman raising a child on her own.

Regarding free love, Goldman, like most feminists of the time such as Charlotte Perkins Gilman, firmly believed that women should be more than a "sex commodity." However, Goldman disagreed with those who had what she called a "narrow, Puritan vision," and wished to eliminate men completely from their personal lives. In her essay, "The Tragedy of Woman's Emancipation," Goldman took a dim view of women's rights activists who would banish man "as a disturber and doubtful character." These individuals, she asserted, were diverting women away from "true" emancipation and male partnership. According to them, Goldman declared, "Man was not to be tolerated at any price, except perhaps as the father of a child, since a child could not very well come to life without a father." "Fortunately," she added, "the most rigid Puritans never will be strong enough to kill the innate craving for motherhood."[57] Goldman called upon each woman to listen to the voice of her true nature, "whether it call for life's greatest treasure, love for a man, or her most glorious privilege, the right to give birth to a child."[58] Until then, she said, a woman cannot call herself emancipated. It is, of course, somewhat ironic that Goldman, while praising motherhood, lived a childless existence, yet criticized others for following the same path.

Some feminist critics would later take Goldman to task for her severity toward women who rejected both men and motherhood.[59] Though she defended the right of women to have relationships with other women, she never promoted gender separatism, and the question of lesbian rights was never really a major concern for her. A number of the same critics have also faulted the famous anarchist for dismissing the importance of woman suffrage, an issue then undergoing serious debate in much of western society. While most advocates of sexual equality in the early twentieth century looked upon the acquisition of voting rights as a major milestone in the long struggle, Goldman saw it as having little bearing on women's lives. She did not argue, as some did, on political grounds—that women would end up losing their power as moral critics by being drawn into the partisan fray and co-opted by men—but rather on a personal basis. Real equality for women, she believed, would have to come from within. In her essay, "Woman Suffrage," she wrote:

> Her development, her freedom, her independence, must
> come from and through herself. First, by asserting herself as a
> personality, and not as a sex commodity. Second, by refusing the
> right to anyone over her body; by refusing to bear children, unless
> she wants them; by refusing to be a servant to God, the State,

society, the husband, the family, etc. . . . Only that, and not the ballot, will set women free.[60]

Not only did Goldman understand the limits to the value of equal suffrage, she also saw more clearly than many others the obstacles facing women in the workplace, even if by chance they achieved a modicum of success. She observed that few women in the workforce ever ascended to high-level positions and that all the upward striving would take its toll, especially in their personal lives. In her essay, "The Tragedy of Woman's Emancipation," she noted that while an educated woman in the early twentieth century may now choose a profession, "she is often compelled to exhaust all her energy, use up her vitality, and strain every nerve in order to reach the market value."[61] Goldman evidently realized that for a woman to make it to the top ranks in the professional world she might have to give up the idea of having children. She was also aware of one of the major problems that would burden later generations of working women—trying to have a successful career and also be a good mother. She knew that an ambitious career woman would probably lose some of her desire to achieve motherhood, though she connected it to a loss or sublimation of natural "instinct." "Our highly praised independence," she added, "is after all, but a slow process of dulling and stifling woman's nature, her love instinct, and her mother instinct." "The horror that love or the joy of motherhood will only hinder her in the full exercise of her profession" helps make of the emancipated modern woman "a compulsory vestal, before whom life, with its great clarifying sorrows and its deep entrancing joys, rolls on without touching or gripping her soul."[62]

In advocating women's equality, birth control, free speech, and other individual rights, Goldman endeared herself to the emerging group of avant-garde writers and other intellectuals in the era before the First World War such as Eugene O'Neill, John Reed, and Floyd Dell. She and her ideas criticizing traditional social mores were much talked about in the fashionable salons of Mabel Dodge and other well-known "new age" hostesses in New York's Greenwich Village. But with few exceptions, most of the era's leading bohemians were probably less than enthusiastic about her calls for the overthrow of capitalism. To them anarchism represented personal rebellion, not class revolution. Indeed, even among the working class Goldman found little support for anarchism among mainstream English-speaking trade unionists. Only among the more extreme members of the Industrial Workers of the World (I.W.W.) and a small number of immigrant laborers from Central, Southern, and Eastern Europe did she and her fellow anarchists attract much of a following. While the majority of workers may have agreed with her regarding the need to correct the inequities of the existing economic system with its long hours and low wages, the philosophy of anarchism, which called for total revolution, probably seemed too abstract or fanciful to be taken seriously.

By the second decade of the twentieth century, even though she was no longer associated with acts of revolutionary violence, Goldman's radical views on many subjects could still get her caught up in brushes with the law. One occasion took place after a speech she delivered in 1916, where she explained the use of contraceptive devices and handed out birth control information, leading to her arrest. Goldman had been speaking and writing on the subject of birth control since 1900. She saw the legal prohibitions on the manufacture, sale, and distribution of birth control devices as harmful to women's health, an obstacle to family limitation, and a restriction upon women's personal freedom. But before 1915 she carefully avoided mentioning anything about the methods of contraception so as not to wind up in jail under the so-called Comstock laws. Such open discussion of methods, however, had recently become the main focus of Margaret Sanger, a trained nurse and leftist sympathizer, who in 1914 had begun publishing *The Woman Rebel*, which contained explicit material on the topic. When Sanger's paper was censored and she herself indicted, Goldman felt that she too had to speak openly about contraceptive methods, regardless of the consequences, and it was this

decision that led to her arrest in New York City. Goldman's trial became
something of a spectacle where she lectured the court for an hour about
how legalized birth control would lead to "healthy motherhood and
happy childlife." But the judge rejected her arguments and sentenced the
publisher of *Mother Earth* to fifteen days in jail. Goldman's efforts over
the years clearly contributed to the eventual legalization of birth control
in subsequent times, but it was Margaret Sanger, the most active and
outspoken member of the movement, who received the bulk of the credit.
Long before that happened, Goldman had moved on to what she perceived
as more immediate and pressing issues.

Most on her mind at this point was the need to oppose U.S. intervention
during the First World War, seeing it as a capitalist war in which the
common people had little at stake and therefore should avoid taking part.
When Congress in April 1917 approved President Woodrow Wilson's
decision to have the country enter the European conflict, Goldman spoke
out strongly in condemnation. She also led public demonstrations against
military conscription. Her obstructionist tactics were soon ruled illegal by
the authorities and resulted in her being sentenced to a two-year prison
term at a women's detention facility in Missouri. Unable to do much about
disrupting the war effort while behind bars, the famed anarchist tried to
do what she could to help her fellow prisoners handle various health and
personal matters. During the devastating influenza epidemic of 1918, for
example, she engaged in informal nursing, which was clearly appreciated
by the recipients of her care. Kate Richards O'Hare, another imprisoned
leftist agitator, who befriended Goldman and saw this work first hand,
said she was a "loyal comrade and cosmic mother," who possessed "a
passionate maternal spirit" that appealed to the other inmates.[63] Besides
O'Hare, Goldman formed a close friendship with a young radical named
Ella Antolini, who, she later wrote, had "grown into my heart as my own
child."[64] One difficult moment for Goldman during her prison stay was
learning the news from her former lover Ben Reitman, who had just

recently married, that he was also about to become a father. "Whether it was the defeat of my own motherhood or the pain that another should have given Ben what I would not, his rhapsodies about impending fatherhood increased my resentment toward him and everyone connected with him," she wrote.[65] Later in life she would forgive his past behavior toward her to some degree, realizing that he was one of the only men she ever knew who had dedicated many years to serving her interests.

When Goldman was released from prison in 1919 shortly after the war, America faced growing labor strife and other forms of domestic conflict, including an upsurge of radical—socialist, communist, and anarchist— political agitation. The alleged danger to the republic caused by the chief perpetrators of these acts, many of whom were foreign born, led federal officials to take harsh disciplinary action against them. The widespread government crackdown following this so called "Red Scare" eventually led to the arrest and deportation of almost 250 persons considered "subversive aliens," including Goldman, who, because of her notoriety, must have been close to the top of the list. Stripped of her U.S. citizenship, she was confined on Ellis Island and then put on a ship, the *Buford*, along with many of her comrades, including Alexander Berkman, and sent back to her Russian homeland.

Although naturally angered at being forced into exile, Goldman in part looked forward to residing in the new Soviet Union and participating in the ongoing Bolshevik-led revolution. She hoped that anarchist principles, most notably the idea of individual rights, might find some acceptance there in the changed political climate. But as time passed what she wished for failed to happen. Over the next few years the banished American radical became increasingly dissatisfied with the policies of the new Soviet government, and especially its continued suppression of civil liberties. To her, the Bolsheviks, after taking power, had simply substituted one kind of state control for another. In addition, the new Russian leaders showed little interest in responding to her constant complaints about these matters. Goldman's criticisms of Soviet policy soon made it impossible for her to remain in her country of origin and she found herself once again on the road to exile. Subsequent to her departure she wrote a book detailing the frustrations she experienced during her stay there entitled *My Disillusionment in Russia* (1923).[66] The message, however, was not well received by most communists and other left-leaning individuals around the world, who did not want hear anything negative about the revolutionary struggle going on in the USSR. Yet despite the book's anti-totalitarian stance, it did little to endear her to governing officials in non-communist nations either. Seen still as a troublemaker wherever she traveled, the longtime advocate of anarchism, seeking to move on with her life, would have trouble finding a suitable home.

Goldman drifted from place to place over the next few years, living for a time in Berlin, London, and Toronto, trying to establish a new niche and maintain an impact upon world events. As part of this plan, she entered into a fictitious marriage with a Welsh laborer named James Colton in 1925, in order to obtain British citizenship and permanent residence rights. But as she now approached her late fifties she was not very happy, feeling frustrated both in the political and the personal realm. She brooded over the shortcomings of the Russian Revolution and the failure of anarchism to take hold there or anywhere. She also dwelled upon her inability to return to America, the country she still considered her home, as well as what was missing in her own personal life. Despite all she had done for others, she felt "quite alone," without love and affection, longing "for some human being of my own." Lacking an ongoing relationship with a man, she began reflecting bitterly on the "tragedy of the emancipated woman" in general, who found herself "getting on in age without anything worth while to make life warm and beautiful, without a purpose." Wherever she went she noted how older men could usually obtain the company of younger women, whereas society still frowned upon relationships between older women and younger men. Writing to her old comrade Alexander

Berkman, who after being expelled from Russia had settled in France and found a younger woman named Emmy Eckstein to live with, Goldman expounded on this and related themes. She claimed that the aging single woman, no matter how "modern" she was, would always feel a certain degree of emptiness in her existence owing to the absence of a mate and any children. However, she insisted that regardless of how she felt at this moment she not implying she would have lived life differently if she had the chance to do it over again. Instead, she concluded in a somewhat fatalistic but determined manner, saying, "Ah well, life is one huge failure to most of us. The only way to endure is to keep a stiff upper lip and drink to the next experience."[67]

Goldman, in fact, did have a few intimate relationships with men in her later years. All were much younger, all were anarchists, and all idolized her. Indeed, they all may have been more in love with the image of the fiery revolutionary than with the actual person. In each case at the outset, Goldman realized the improbability of success in going ahead with the pairing, but somehow allowed herself to get carried away by her fantasies, imposing her romantic vision of reality on these involvements as she sometimes did with her political ideals. But it must have been more than a youthful lover that she was seeking, as she referred to each one at times as her child. Perhaps having someone to mother was part of the attraction in addition to having a shield against loneliness and advancing age. In any event, in each instance the period of high passion was usually brief after which a cold reality began to set in. The first of these relationships was with a Swede, Arthur Svenson, who helped Goldman deal with the immigration authorities in Stockholm immediately after she left Russia. They subsequently lived together for six months in Berlin before he began losing interest and she broke it off.[68] Another man who touched her heart for a time was Leon Malmed, an Albany, New York, delicatessen owner, with whom she had corresponded for several years. He had helped Goldman financially while she languished in prison and had sent her packages of food. When they became intimate during one of her stays in Canada, Goldman saw it as a "miracle"—"a child and lover have come to me and life has new meaning." She said she felt like the biblical Sarah "to whom a son came in old age."[69] (One can perhaps see this reference as an affirmation of her infertility as well as a temporary wish fulfillment.) But being in close physical proximity to Malmed soon revealed the many differences between them and their ardor quickly cooled. Goldman's last affair (around age sixty-five) was with Frank Heiner, an intellectual Chicagoan almost thirty years her junior, who she met on her speaking tour of America in 1934. Despite being blind, Heiner had become a charismatic spokesman for the anarchist cause and pursued Goldman intensely until she realized the possibility of a future together between them was doomed. Like Malmed, Heiner was married and ultimately unwilling to leave his wife and family.[70]

Although Goldman's connections with men in her later years brought little lasting satisfaction, she did derive longer-term pleasure from her associations with some of the younger members of the anarchist movement. These too had maternal overtones for her. The two most important people to her in this regard were Mollie Steimer and her male companion Senya Flechine. Steimer was a Russian-born radical who, like Goldman, had emigrated to America, was imprisoned for opposing the First World War, deported to the USSR, and then expelled. In subsequent years in Western Europe, the two women, despite their considerable age difference, became close. Senya Flechine, also Russian-born, had briefly worked in the *Mother Earth* office in New York before the war. Returning to the European continent, he became Steimer's collaborator and lover starting in the 1920s. When the three were together, Goldman frequently called them "my children" and had a nurturing relationship with them both. While arguments over anarchist doctrine sometimes developed between the younger idealistic Steimer and her older more experienced female mentor, the two retained a high degree of respect for one another. Steimer, who lived until 1980, always spoke about Goldman in reverential terms in the years after her death.[71] In addition to nurturing young anarchists, Goldman also had friendships with two young female expatriate writers, Evelyn Scott and Emily Coleman. Scott, a Tennessean, who had lived in New York's Greenwich Village and written an experimental novel, met Goldman in Europe in the mid-1920s. Although not very political, Scott admired Goldman's radical stance, and continued to see her as a wonderful role model, a strong female rebel and provocative writer in a world that provided little support for either. Coleman, born to a well-to-do family and a graduate of Wellesley, became an admirer of the famous anarchist through Emma's nephew Saxe Commins. After corresponding, the two met in Paris and Goldman encouraged the young woman's writing efforts, leading to the completion of her only novel. Coleman, in turn, became Goldman's literary assistant for a time and helped her in organizing ideas and materials for her autobiography.[72]

Goldman had long wished to write an autobiography but with a limited source of income from her lectures and writings she had found it difficult to establish a time and place to do so. Eventually, through the help of wealthy art collector Peggy Guggenheim and a few other benefactors, Goldman was able to obtain a small villa outside Saint-Tropez in southern France. It was here that she spent a good part of her existence in the late 1920s reviewing her past and writing her autobiography, *Living My Life*, which was published in two volumes in 1931. In many ways her autobiography was a pathbreaking work. It revealed for the first time many details of her anarchist-driven activism, such as her involvement in the effort by Berkman to assassinate business tycoon Henry Frick back in 1892. Yet in telling her story Goldman to a degree played down certain aspects of her extreme radicalism and tried to portray herself as being more like a progressive American reformer than a dangerous European revolutionary. What she wrote also revealed a great deal about her personal life—her complex relationships with Berkman and Reitman, including intimate details of the kind rarely put forth in print by a public figure before this time. Overall, the book showed Goldman's frustrations with her lifelong attempt to establish anarchism, but it also demonstrated that in spite of the many obstacles she faced she never gave up her quest in more than four decades of vigorous effort. Although Goldman was unable to transform the world into the kind of peaceful and harmonious place she had envisioned, her life's work, as she described it in her autobiography, probably served as an inspiration to many readers, particularly women, with an idealistic and reformist outlook. Unfortunately for Goldman, who had hoped to live on the royalties, the book did not meet sales expectations, which meant that she would have to continue lecturing in order to survive.

In the years following the publication of *Living My Life*, Emma Goldman, aided by friends, again sought to return to America. Since most high government officials still considered her an "undesirable alien," Goldman's wish to live in the United States remained an impossibility. However, under the new, more liberal administration of Franklin Roosevelt in the 1930s, a brief lecture tour in the U.S. was deemed acceptable as long as she agreed not to speak at partisan rallies, discuss "immediate political issues," and accept certain other limitations on what she could say. After many months of negotiation, she was finally granted a three-month visa. A sixteen-city tour was arranged in the winter of 1934 but it proved to be disappointing both to Goldman and her sponsors. Audiences were usually not very large outside New York City and Chicago, and those that came to hear her were mostly older prewar liberals—middle aged and middle class—not the younger members of the working class she wanted to reach. But she must have been heartened by the fact that at least some people remembered her and applauded her words and achievements.[73]

Back in Europe at the time of the Spanish Civil War in the mid-to-late 1930s, Goldman briefly saw a successful anarchist revolt in parts of Spain as workers' collectives were formed in Barcelona and a few other locales. She was appointed by the anarcho-syndicalist organization Confederacion

Nacional del Trabajo Federation Anarquista Iberica (CNT-FAI) to go to England to be a publicist and fund raiser for their cause. In these years she made three trips to Spain to survey the situation. But following the defeat of the Republic in 1939 and the establishment of the dictatorial Franco regime throughout Spain, this advocacy effort came to an end. Goldman, shifting gears, next traveled to Canada at the start of World War II to work on behalf of refugees from European fascism but she died of a heart attack in Toronto the next year at the age of seventy. Although she had not been allowed to live in the United States since the First World War, the government consented to her prior wish to be buried in the country she thought of as home. She was interred in Chicago's Waldheim Cemetery not far from the graves of the Haymarket martyrs who first inspired her commitment to activism.[74]

Emma Goldman's image has undergone abrupt shifts in the seven decades since her death. During the first twenty-five years (1940-1965), as radicalism was in retreat in the United States and elsewhere in the western world, few people read her books or even knew her name. However, starting in the late 1960s, with the resurgence of radical thinking and activity, and especially through the rise of the feminist movement, Goldman's name and what she stood for began to be lifted from oblivion and increasingly spoken about. Within a few years, she became a heroic figure to advocates of women's liberation. Her views on birth control and woman's need to take responsibility for their own lives and not depend on men coincided with the aims of many in the new generation of women, and their understanding that "the personal is political." To young feminists, she was the model "woman warrior," willing to face punishment, exile, even death, in attempting to change society. As a result of her new notoriety, her ideas were now taken more seriously and debated in women's studies courses. Her books began to be reissued and new biographies and compilations of her writings began to be published. Her picture appeared on T-shirts and posters. An Emma Goldman Clinic for Women was established in Iowa

City, and an Emma Goldman Brigade was founded in Chicago. Novels, movies and plays, focusing on various dramatic moments of her existence, became popular. She was a featured personage in E. L. Doctorow's acclaimed best-selling novel of the early twentieth century, *Ragtime.* She was also a leading character in the major Hollywood production *Reds,* and actress Maureen Stapleton won an Academy Award for portraying the strong-willed radical in the 1981 film. However, by the end of the century, Goldman's image as a dangerous militant had softened somewhat and she came to be seen as a less threatening and more beloved figure, emphasizing reform rather than revolution. Some writings even portrayed her as a kind of wise and knowledgeable Jewish mother or grandmother.[75]

Emma Goldman's legacy would remain controversial. Her half century crusade in behalf of anarchism would never get very far. Her efforts may have further divided the left. Capitalism and the state did not wither away. The masses did not rise up and create an alternative system. She herself can be criticized as being too domineering and dictatorial. As time went on, she became more isolated culturally as well as politically, less at home with the avant garde. Yet her ideas and actions did influence the trade union movement and radical groups such as the I.W.W. She also had profound effects on the movements for free speech and for birth control. What stands out especially, says Alice Wexler, "is her extraordinary tenacity in the face of persecution, isolation, and loneliness." No other figure, she asserts, "so skillfully dramatized the rebellious social and cultural currents of Gilded Age and Progressive America. Certainly no other woman of her generation used her public persona so effectively to flout bourgeois conventions and taboos, using her own body on stage as a lightning rod for rebellion."[76] Goldman's generativity embraced her colleagues, her lovers, and her vision of revolutionary change. She advocated a new relationship between women and their bodies, based on women's autonomy and free choice. In her ideal world, children would be conceived from free will and born into a family where they were wanted and could be adequately cared for.

NOTES

[1] Bakunin and Nachaev, *The Catechism of a Revolutionary* (1896), quoted in Elzbieta Ettinger, *Rosa Luxemburg: A Life* (Boston: Beacon Press, 1986), 53.

[2] Emma Goldman, *Living My Life*, 2 vols. (New York: Alfred Knopf, 1931), 1:53. Hereafter cited LML

[3] Quoted in Ettinger, *Rosa Luxemburg*, 60.

[4] Richard Drinnon, "Emma Goldman," in Edward T. James et al., eds., *Notable American Women, 1607-1950*, 3 vols. (Cambridge, MA: Harvard University Press, 1971), 2:58. Drinnon's early biography *Rebel in Paradise: A Biography of Emma Goldman* (Chicago: University of Chicago Press, 1961), was for a long time considered the standard work on Goldman's life.

[5] LML, 1:59.

[6] LML, 1:58-59.

[7] LML, 1:57, 61; Alice Wexler, *Emma Goldman in America* (Boston: Beacon Press, 1984), 73.

[8] LML, 1:61; Wexler, *Emma Goldman in America*, 73.

[9] Wexler, *Emma Goldman in America*, 73.

[10] LML, 1:61.

[11] Wexler, *Emma Goldman in America*, 73.

[12] LML, 1:12.

[13] LML, 1:12.

[14] Candace S. Falk, *Love, Anarchy and Emma Goldman* (New Brunswick, NJ: Rutgers University Press, 1990), 13. (Falk is the editor of the Emma Goldman Papers, Berkeley, California).

[15] LML, 1:10.

[16] Falk, *Love*, 15-19.

[17] Quoted in Drinnon, *Rebel in Paradise*, 55.

[18] For a full statement of his ideas, see Peter Kropotkin, *Memoirs of a Revolutionist* (Boston: Houghton Mifflin, 1899). For Goldman's view of Anarchism, see "Anarchism: What It Really Stands For," in Alix Kates Shulman, ed., *Red Emma Speaks: An Emma Goldman Reader*, 3rd ed. (New Brunswick, NJ: Humanities Press, 1996), 61-77.

[19] Emma Goldman, "Was My Life Worth Living?" *Harper's Magazine*, CLXX (December 1934): 52-58.

[20] Falk, *Love*, 39.

[21] LML, 541.

[22] Quoted in Theresa Moritz and Albert Moritz, *The World's Most Dangerous Woman* (Toronto: University of Toronto Press), 153.

[23] LML, 1:77.

[24] LML, 1:153-54.

[25] Falk, *Love*, 32-33.

[26] On this subject, see Thomas G. Dyer, *Theodore Roosevelt and the Idea of Race* (Baton Rouge, LA: Louisiana State University Press, 1980), chap. 7.

[27] "Victims of Morality," in Shulman, ed., *Red Emma Speaks*, 173.

[28] Emma Goldman to Max Nettlau, February 5, 1935, in Richard and Anna Maria Drinnon, eds., *Nowhere at Home: Letters from Exile of Emma Goldman and Alexander Berkman* (New York: Schocken Books, 1975), 185-87.

[29] "The Child and Its Enemies," in Shulman, *Red Emma Speaks*, 132. In the same volume, see Goldman's essay, "The Social Importance of the Modern School," 140-49, and also Paul Avrich, *The Modern School Movement* (Princeton, NJ: Princeton University Press, 1980).

[30] "Francisco Ferrer: The Modern School," in Emma Goldman, *Anarchism and Other Essays* (New York: Dover Publications, 1969), 167.

[31] "The Child and Its Enemies," 137-38.

[32] "What is There in Anarchy for Woman?" in Candace Falk et al., eds., *Emma Goldman: A Documentary History of the American Years*, vol. 1 (Berkeley, CA: University of California Press, 2003), 291.

[33] LML, 1:170.

[34] Peter Glassgold, *Anarchy! An Anthology of Emma Goldman's MOTHER EARTH* (Washington DC: Counterpoint, 2001), xxx.

[35] Cyril Greenland, "Dangerous Women—Dangerous Ideas," *Canadian Journal of Human Sexuality* 11 (Fall-Winter, 2002).

[36] Falk, *Love*, 37.

[37] Falk, *Love*, 92, 134, 169, 199, 240; Drinnon, *Nowhere at Home*, 145.

[38] Quoted in Alice Wexler, *Emma Goldman in Exile* (Boston: Beacon Press, 1989), 153.

[39] Drinnon, *Rebel in Paradise*, 148, 150.

[40] LML, 1:212, 291.

[41] Falk, *Love*, 34, 36, LML, 2:663.

[42] Falk, *Love*, 171, 173-74, 240, 317.

[43] For Goldman's relationship with Reitman, see Falk, *Love*, chaps. 3-11; Suzanne Poirier, "Emma Goldman, Ben Reitman, and Reitman's Wives: A Study in Relationships," *Women's Studies* 14 (1988): 277-97. The quotation is taken from LML, 1:420.

[44] Falk, *Love*, 54.

[45] Quoted in Falk, *Love*, 54.

[46] Falk, *Love*, 55.

[47] Quoted in Falk, *Love*, 55.

[48] Falk, *Love*, 96.

[49] Falk, *Love*, 86.

[50] Falk, *Love*, 93-94, 133.

[51] Drinnon, "Emma Goldman," 58.

[52] Quoted in Drinnon, "Emma Goldman," 58.

[53] Quoted in Drinnon, *Rebel in Paradise*, 164.

[54] "Marriage and Love," in Shulman, ed., *Red Emma Speaks*, 205.

[55] "Marriage and Love," 210.

[56] "Marriage and Love," 211.

[57] "The Tragedy of Woman's Emancipation," in Shulman, ed., *Red Emma Speaks*, 163.

[58] "The Tragedy of Woman's Emancipation," 165.

[59] See, for example, Bonnie Haaland, *Sexuality and the Impurity of the State* (Montreal: Black Rose Books, 1993), chap. 6.

[60] "Woman Suffrage," in Shulman, ed., *Red Emma Speaks*, 202.

[61] "Tragedy of Woman's Emancipation," 160.

[62] "Tragedy of Woman's Emancipation," 161.

[63] Falk, *Love*, 175; LML, 2:668.

[64] LML, 2:692.

[65] LML, 2:659.

[66] Emma Goldman, *My Disillusionment in Russia* (Garden City, NY: Doubleday, Page and Co., 1923).

[67] Drinnon and Drinnon, *Nowhere at Home*, 133; Wexler, *Emma Goldman in Exile*, 112-13.

[68] On Svenson, see Wexler, *Emma Goldman in Exile*, 61-62.

[69] On Malmed, see Wexler, *Emma Goldman in Exile*, 124-28; the quotation is on page 124.

[70] On Heiner, see Wexler, *Emma Goldman in Exile*, 170-78.

[71] Wexler, *Emma Goldman in Exile*, 86-87.

[72] Wexler, *Emma Goldman in Exile*, 118-19, 133-35.

[73] For a description of her American tour, see Oz Frankel, "Whatever Happened to 'Red Emma'? Emma Goldman, from Alien Rebel to American Icon," *Journal of American History* 83 (December 1996): 903-42, esp. 909-18.

[74] For Goldman's last years, especially her activities on behalf of Spain, see Wexler, *Emma Goldman in Exile*, chaps. 9-10.

[75] For a good discussion of her changing image in recent decades, see Frankel, "Whatever Happened to 'Red Emma'?" Although Goldman often sought to distance herself from the Jewish religion and its patriarchal tradition, she also addressed Jewish audiences in the Yiddish language, filled *Mother Earth* with Yiddish stories and items from the Talmud, and showed a love for Jewish food.

[76] Alice Wexler, "Emma Goldman," in John A. Garraty and Marc C. Carnes, eds., *American National Biography*, vol. 9 (New York: Oxford University Press, 1999), 193.

Ruth Benedict, 1937, Courtesy of Library of Congress.

Chapter 7
Reflection: "So I Might as Well Have Hottentots"
Ruth Benedict (1887-1948)

Toward the end of her acclaimed autobiography *Blackberry Winter*, the famous anthropologist Margaret Mead wrote the following: "Something very special sometimes happen to women when they know they will not have a child—or any more children. It can happen to women who have never married, when they reach the menopause. . . . It can happen to young wives who discover they never can bear a child. Suddenly, their whole creativity is released—they paint or write as never before or they throw themselves into academic work with enthusiasm, where before they had only half a mind to spare for it. . . ."[1] While Mead mentioned no one specific here, her close friend and longtime colleague, Ruth Benedict, most definitely fit the description. After finding out at age thirty-two that she was infertile, Benedict, who since college had ventured forth creatively in a number of directions without real success, now became a serious student of anthropology. She soon obtained a Ph.D., and, through hard work and dedication over the next quarter century, rose to the very top of her field. Perhaps her scholarly achievements would have come about anyway, but it seems likely that she grew freer to focus whole-heartedly on her professional work only when she knew she would not have children.

Far more than most women coming of age in the early 1900s, Ruth Benedict reflected long and hard over the question of having children, time and again debating the positive and negative aspects of becoming a mother. Then, five years into her marriage, after finally convincing herself that she should try to become pregnant, she was diagnosed as infertile. Benedict was unusual in that she left considerable written evidence about her ambivalence regarding motherhood, as well as her sad feelings upon learning she would never bear a child. She expressed her grief in journal entries, through poetry, and also in talking about it with intimate friends like Margaret Mead. It was also a subject that never fully disappeared from her mind.

Being infertile was not Benedict's first experience of finding herself outside of conventional role expectations. A highly gifted professional woman in the first half of the twentieth century, she, like most of our other subjects, did not lead a traditional life, a fact she recognized in describing herself as an outsider. Indeed, Margaret M. Caffrey underscored this point by using "Stranger in This Land" as the subtitle for her in-depth biography of the renowned anthropologist.[2] Fellow scholars Abram Kardiner and Edward Preble, who included Benedict as the only woman profiled in their book, *They Studied Man* (1961), began their essay: "A sense of estrangement moved with Ruth Benedict all her life. Although intensely sympathetic and kindly she always gave the impression of standing apart from the world she lived in."[3] As an academic who spent her life studying a variety of cultures and stood on the forefront of new developments in psychology and psychiatry, Benedict probably understood better than most people the concept of marginality. From an early stage, she realized that she was not at ease with the culture of mainstream America. In a country that emphasized the material, her mind generally dwelled on the spiritual and artistic. In addition, she grew up having lost a father when she was very young, and as a child suffered from a number of physical problems including partial deafness.

Later, upon reaching adulthood, Benedict felt uncomfortable operating in women's customary subordinate realm. Besides pursuing a high-level career, she also left an unhappy marriage and formed domestic partnerships with women, although to the public she remained "Mrs. Ruth Benedict," placing those words on the title page of her most famous book. Marginality became a major theme of her work as a cultural anthropologist as well. Having always felt different from others, she tended to be tolerant of diversity and actively promoted it. Her writings influenced Western thinking to accept a more relativistic view of cultural values and to understand that culturally learned behavior could be changed. Most notably, she criticized the idea of homosexuality as a psychiatric condition nearly forty years before it was removed from the diagnostic manual of the American Psychiatric Association, and in the 1940s helped introduce the term "racism" and its negative implications to the American public.[4]

Benedict was born in New York City in 1887, though she grew up mostly in central and upstate New York, spending summers on her grandparents' farm near Norwich, along with living for brief periods in the Midwest. Born Ruth Fulton, she was the first child of Frederick S. Fulton, an early cancer researcher and homeopathic physician, and Bertrice Shattuck Fulton, who had graduated Phi Beta Kappa from Vassar College two years earlier. Due to an undiagnosed illness, her father gave up his medical practice in New York City and returned to the Fulton family farm; he then died prematurely when Benedict was just twenty-one months old. In an autobiographical statement she wrote years later, she said that she idealized and identified with her late father and objected to the prolonged grief of her mother, who had trouble coping with early widowhood. In an oft-quoted passage from this essay, Benedict stated that she recognized two worlds in her youth—"the world of my father, which was the world of death and which was beautiful, and the world of confusion and explosive weeping which I repudiated. I did not love my mother; I resented her cult of grief, and her worry and concern about little things."[5] As a child Benedict seems to have ruminated a great deal about death, spending time in an imaginary world inhabited by "people of a strange dignity and grace" who moved by "skimming the ground in one unbroken line. . . ."[6] She used to lie alone in a hiding place in the barn amidst the hay, considering this her "grave." Outside the family the only friend she claimed she had until about age five was an imaginary playmate. She wrote, "Happiness was in a world I lived in all by myself, and for precious moments."[7] Relatives considered her younger sister Margery to be the more attractive and well-adjusted of the two girls; even Benedict described her sister as "a cherubically beautiful child with no behavior problems," obviously in contrast to herself.[8]

Psychologists recognize that an autobiographical essay is the product of a moment in time, influenced by situation and mood. Had Benedict created a similar document ten years later, she might have emphasized other early memories and life themes, and she might have portrayed family members in a different light. While Benedict wrote that her sister played only a small part in her "real life" despite the fact that they were almost always together, Margery viewed their relationship as profoundly close. She later wrote to Margaret Mead, "In the early days we were inseparable, going through all the experiences of life together, and discussing the significance of each, endlessly. I never understood her, but I understood her so much better than did our Mother, that it bound us close together in an intimate fashion not true of many sisters."[9]

While Benedict's repudiation of her mother's grief has been frequently quoted, less has been said about her mother as a role model for a professional woman in the late nineteenth and early twentieth centuries. When her mother graduated from Vassar in 1885, less than one percent of women in the United States attended college and few had careers. Despite the grief she outwardly displayed over the premature death of her husband,

Bertrice Shattuck Fulton managed to support herself and her two young children through teaching and library work, which were among the only professional fields open to women of her generation. She had been employed as a secondary school English teacher before she married, and took up a similar position when her youngest daughter was three and a half. The annual expression of grieving that Fulton experienced is known as an "anniversary reaction," a not uncommon response to a major loss. As others have pointed out, demonstrative grieving, such as crying in church and in bed at night during the month of her husband's death, was also looked upon as a cultural norm in the late Victorian era. Despite her grief, Bertrice Fulton showed strength and courage in moving to faraway places to take advantage of job opportunities that would allow her to provide for her family. Although Benedict never wrote about it, the fact that her mother had been a Vassar graduate and successful professional woman likely opened this pathway for her as well.

Besides dealing with her father's premature death and its effect on others, Benedict faced various physical disabilities, including partial deafness resulting from an early case of measles. Her deafness was not diagnosed until age five when she started attending school; previously her mother had thought that she purposely refused to answer when called, which often created conflict in the household. In addition to her hearing impairment, Benedict had frequent behavioral tantrums, which she described as follows:

> The family were constantly exercised about my ungovernable tantrums. They came on for no reason the family could fathom, and they swept on thereafter without my feeling that I had any participation in them. I was violent either to myself or to anyone else within reach.[10]

> They were outside invasions of my person, and it seemed to me that devils swept down upon me.[11]

As Judith Modell pointed out in her biography of the future scholar, tantrums are not an unusual consequence of the interpersonal frustration experienced by children whose hearing and communication abilities are impaired. In an attempt to de-pathologize Benedict's portrayal of her childhood as highly abnormal, Modell focused on other aspects of her growing up that were more normative, such as having imaginary playmates.[12] Benedict's tantrums continued to around age eleven at which time her mother extracted a solemn promise from her never to have another such outburst. The tantrums ceased to occur but starting with the onset of menstruation over the following year, she began suffering from intermittent but ongoing "depressions," another manifestation of her "devils." Given her subsequent struggle with depression over the next several decades, mood disorder may also have been a contributor to her earlier experience of tantrums as a young girl.

Benedict was also plagued throughout her childhood by "bilious attacks," in which she lay in bed vomiting for two days. She dated the onset of these episodes to age two or three, but she felt certain that by age seven or eight they occurred rhythmically every six weeks. After she reached puberty, her menstrual periods followed the same six-week pattern, accompanied by severe pain but no longer by nausea and vomiting.[13] She subsequently affirmed that she "had a great deal of menstrual pain as a child."[14] Although not known at the time, later developments in endocrinology have shown that hormonal reorganization occurs as early as age six in girls and that hormonal cycling can begin at that young age and be manifested as headache or nausea. An alternative explanation for her symptoms would be the existence of an imperforate hymen, meaning a hymen without an opening, leading to abdominal pain, nausea, and retrograde menstruation, consistent with fallopian tube scarring. Equally speculative, the presence of severe menstrual pain, in conjunction with her later diagnosis of blocked fallopian tubes, would be consistent with a diagnosis of endometriosis.

While feeling estranged from others and suffering from these various health problems, Benedict early on used her verbal giftedness to express herself in a creative fashion. By adolescence she was already engaged in serious writing, both prose and poetry. She also read a great deal of literature, most admiring "—Dickens, especially David Copperfield, and Scott, especially Ivanhoe," and episodes from the Bible such as the life of Jesus, which she claimed she knew better by age ten than did the local ministers. Indeed, for her, no book she read as a child could compete with the Bible. "The story of Ruth was better than *Ramona*, and the poetry of Job was better than Longfellow," she later wrote.[15] It was, she said, "this habit of Bible learning that gave me the idea of learning poems." As a young girl she made a cloth-covered rack to set up over the dish drain to hold poems she had copied so that she and Margery could learn them while they washed the dishes. In the realm of formal education, Benedict always did very well, gaining admission to a prestigious Episcopalian preparatory school in Buffalo, and then winning a scholarship to Vassar College, one of the top-rated institutions of higher learning for women. During her four years at Vassar, which she attended along with her sister, Benedict's intellectual horizons widened. She abandoned some of her strict religious beliefs and developed a more humanistic view of culture. Majoring in English and excelling academically overall, she graduated Phi Beta Kappa (as her mother had) in 1909.

Though her undergraduate education emphasizing the humanities did not directly prepare her for a career as a social scientist, Benedict's extensive reading in literature and related subjects provided a strong background from which to engage in further study. Not that she was thinking about the pursuit of graduate education at this time; nor did she consider becoming a social activist. Admittedly, Benedict, like many other members of her college generation wished to do something to improve society. (Dr. Henry MacCracken, the Vassar College president, described the years from 1890 to 1915 as "the period of the crusader.") However, as her biographer Caffrey has stated, "her response was indirect rather than direct, intellectual rather than social."[16] Unlike her charismatic classmate, Inez Milholland, who subsequently earned a law degree and achieved acclaim as an outspoken suffragist and advocate of reform, Benedict was a shy, private person who would have felt uncomfortable making speeches from a public platform. Neither did she have a great desire to live and work at a settlement house, as Jane Addams and her colleagues were doing at Hull House in Chicago at the time in order to help the disadvantaged.

Upon completing college, Benedict was still undecided about her future—whether to embark upon a career or immediately seek marriage. Her sister Margery chose the latter course, having wed a young minister with a degree from the Princeton Theological Seminary following graduation. Ruth, on the other hand, traveled in Europe for several months with two classmates through a fellowship provided for the class's top graduates by a Vassar trustee. Following the trip, she returned home to live with her mother in Buffalo, and did social work for a year at the Charity Organization Society. She then moved to Pasadena, California, to be with her sister and her expanding family. For the academic year 1911-1912, Benedict taught English at the Westlake School for Girls in Los Angeles and for the next two years at the Orton School for Girls in Pasadena.[17] Although teaching brought some satisfaction, Benedict asked herself whether this was what she really wanted to do on a permanent basis. She began a period of deep introspection, in which she frequently wrote in her journal, debating the roles of work, marriage, and children in women's lives. In doing so, she sometimes reflected on her lack of fulfillment and what seemed like the "episodical" nature of happiness:

A morning in the library, an afternoon with someone I really care about, a day in the mountains, a good-night-time with the babies [Margery's children] can almost frighten me with happiness. But then it is gone and I cannot see what holds it all together. What is worth while? What is the purpose? What do I want?[18]

Benedict saw the limited possibilities available for women in that era as the essence of her problem about what life course to follow. In the early twentieth century, women had few professional options, and if one decided, for example, to be a teacher, librarian, or social worker, it usually meant remaining single. The idea of a woman combining a career with marriage was still a rarity, not normally sanctioned by society, especially if she had children. Role models were important to Benedict, and she perceived the lives of the older, unmarried teachers at Orton as mostly sad and empty. Nevertheless, she was not sure she wanted to follow in her sister's path as a full-time housewife. As Benedict struggled with the narrow choices she saw as open to her, she wrote: "So much of the trouble is because I am a woman. To me it seems a very terrible thing to be a woman." Yet an idealized vision of marriage and motherhood plus the willingness to sacrifice certain ambitions was evidently taking hold of her thinking, as she added:

> There is one crown which perhaps is worth it all—a great
> love, a quiet home, and children. We all know that is all that is
> worth while, and yet we must peg away, showing off our wares
> on the market if we have money, or manufacturing careers
> for ourselves if we haven't. We have not the motive to prepare
> ourselves for a 'life-work' of teaching, of social work—we know
> that we would lay it down with hallelujah in the height of our
> success, to make a home for the right man.[19]

Benedict's use of quotation marks around "life-work" suggests that she knew that school teaching or social work would not constitute an enduring career for her. As she pondered the alternatives available at that moment, marriage and motherhood appeared to offer the best solution for finding happiness. She was now past twenty-five, and, atypically for the time, still single and childless. Benedict frequently complained of unbearable loneliness and when she asked herself what her hard-won experience was preparing her for, she concluded, "The great instinctive answer is for Motherhood—yes, I think I could accept that with heart and soul—so much do our instincts help us out in our problems—but no girl dares count on Motherhood. Ethically, if Motherhood is worth while, it ought to be also worthy to have a hand in the growth of a child or a woman. The difference is just a question of instinct."[20] Perhaps seeking justification for taking this course, Benedict began to read the works of feminist writers such as Charlotte Perkins Gilman, Ellen Key, and Olive Schreiner on the subject. Each of them, though praising motherhood in its ideal form, argued that not all women were suited for the role and that those individuals who felt they were lacking the necessary qualifications should be encouraged to seek alternatives. Through her extensive reading and deep soul-searching, Benedict was hoping to find an understanding of the role of women in society that would help her resolve her own dilemmas.

Ruth soon reaffirmed her belief that marriage would provide a good part of the answer, as she became engaged to and subsequently wed (at twenty-seven) Stanley Benedict, a successful biochemist at Cornell University Medical College and a pioneering researcher in chemotherapy. Stanley possessed some of the same qualities that her father had—he was serious, solid, and career-minded. At this point she seemed willing to give up some of her worldly ambitions and focus on being a loving and supportive housewife. As she explained in her journal: "In the quiet self-fulfilling love of Wordsworth's home, do we ask that Mary Wordsworth should have achieved individual self-expression? In general,—a woman has one supreme power—to love. If we are to arrive at any blythness [sic] in facing life, we must have faith to believe that it is in exercising this gift, in living it out to its fullest that she achieves herself, that she 'justifies her existence.'"[21] During her first year of marriage she seems to have been relatively happy, establishing herself as a housewife in the Long Island suburb of Douglas Manor outside New York City. But Benedict eventually began to re-experience her old anxiety about how she was spending her time and whether she had any worthwhile achievements to show for her efforts. She had started a number of projects, including writing detective stories, but none felt very satisfying. Though hoping to become pregnant in the near future, she used her journal writing to articulate her continuing ambivalence about motherhood. Part of her, like most women of her time, wanted very much to become a mother. Like them, she had a "passionate belief in the superior worth-whileness of our children. It is stored up in us as a great battery charged by the accumulated instincts of uncounted generations."[22] Employing the instinct model of motherhood of her day, she added: "When there are no children, unless the instinct is somehow employed, the battery either becomes an explosive danger or at best the current rapidly falls off, with its consequent loss of power."[23]

On the other hand, Benedict utilized her journal writing to ask herself whether the benefits of motherhood outweighed the sacrifices that a woman of her talents would have to make in choosing that course and the impact of that decision on her children. Paraphrasing the philosopher George Santayana, she discussed the "radiant faith" people have in their children, "planted and reared in us by a mocking Master of the Revels." "The dreams that slipped from us like sand in the hour glass, the task we laid aside to give them birth and rearing,—all this they shall carve in the enduring stone of their achievements—The master stroke of the irony, the stabbing hurt of it, is that it is all so noble and self-less a dream; it is truly, 'that last infirmity of noble minds.'"[24] Using a literary format to explicate her view of the central conflict in choosing to mother, she wrote a tale about an advice-giving "Woman-Christ" figure, who had herself born children. In the story, a mother leading her young son approaches the Christ lady. She presents the boy to her, stating, "He is my work, my creation, my immortality. Show me how I shall fashion him that he may bring to pass the dreams I dreamed and could not realize for the strength

I lavished upon his rearing." The Woman-Christ says to the woman: "You cannot fashion him to bring to pass those dreams you dreamed. In your womb you bore the life, and lo! already it was no longer yours. Life is not projected onward like a shadow. The boy, your son, he is *himself*." "These dreams you dreamed," the Woman-Christ continues, "he may denounce as hollow and false: no matter! you gave him breath that he might seek *his* dream." Furthermore, the speaker goes on, "Those visions which you saw, they were given for the guidance of *your own* life; you had no other, nor can attain one. Go! Live the life you covet for your child: —not vicariously; in your own person shall you attain unto it."[25]

Benedict's ambivalence about becoming a mother focused in part on the consequences of a woman living primarily through her children. For the individual woman, dreams had to be laid aside, and unique aspects of the self might never be realized due to the abandonment of her own goals in favor of time and energy invested in child rearing. For the child, in turn, a woman's dreams and hopes were inherited as expectations, regardless of the fit between the child and those expectations. In delineating this conflict, Benedict outlined psychological issues that were later developed at greater length by psychoanalyst Alice Miller in *The Drama of the Gifted Child*.[26] Benedict wrote in her journal during the early years of her marriage, "I must have my world too, my outlet, my chance to put forth my effort. . . . If I had children or were expecting one, it would call a truce to these promptings, I suppose. But surely it would be only a truce—it would sign no permanent terms of peace with them. . . ."[27] Benedict concluded:

> There is no misreading of life that avenges itself so piteously
> on men and women as the notion that in their children they
> can bring to fruition their own seedling dreams. And it is just as
> unjust to the child, to be born and reared as the "creation" of his
> parents. He is *himself*, and it is within reason that he may be the
> very antithesis of the both.—No, it is wisdom in motherhood

as in wifehood to have one's own individual world of effort and creation.[28]

A woman debating the meaning of her existence and the role of children in her life was unusual for the time, and for the Benedicts this appears to have caused friction in the marriage. Combined with this was the larger problem of Ruth's unwillingness to subordinate herself totally to her husband's needs, as was generally expected and as Stanley evidently wished. He clearly objected to the idea of her having career aspirations, and when she subsequently became a professional anthropologist, he refused to meet personally with her colleagues. The closeness that had first existed between the two of them began to diminish, and he spent more and more time absorbed in his work and his hobbies. On one occasion he chided her, saying that just as she had lost enthusiasm for teaching and social work, even having children would only hold her interest for a year or two.[29] Others like her biographer Judith Modell agree that Benedict was a woman who felt uncomfortable with absolutes and perhaps would never have been satisfied being just a housewife and mother.[30]

While the issue of children remained unresolved, Benedict, looking for a purpose and seeking to prove that she was capable of undertaking a serious project, started intensive work on a scholarly book. She planned on creating a multiple biography of significant women, bold and outspoken figures who challenged the boundaries of women's roles in their time. As she stated, "my pet scheme is to steep myself in the lives of restless and highly enslaved women of past generations and write a series of biographical papers from the standpoint of the 'new woman.'"[31] Benedict wanted to show that the contemporary ferment for women's rights was "nothing new," indeed, "the restlessness and groping are inherent in the nature of women. . . ." Eventually, the three individuals she chose to write about were the English writer, Mary Wollstonecraft (1759-1797), the American writer, Margaret Fuller (1810-1850), and British reformer, Olive Schreiner (1855-1920). All three of these unconventional women, especially Wollstonecraft, would later provide models for Benedict in terms of intellectual courage and self-reliance. Interestingly, though it is not clear Benedict ever considered the matter, each of her subjects, after bearing children, saw their experience of motherhood end in tragedy: Wollstonecraft died while giving birth to her second child, Fuller and her young son drowned together after a shipwreck, and Schreiner's only child died in infancy.[32] Benedict completed the Wollstonecraft section and submitted the manuscript to Houghton Mifflin. But its rejection by the publisher apparently had a strong negative effect on her and she soon gave up the entire project.[33]

Around the time of America's entrance into the First World War (1917), as she sought out other activities to help her "get through the days,"[34] Benedict turned to volunteer social work at the State Charities Aid Association. She spent the year coordinating a project that organized day nurseries for working women. During this time she debated in her journal about her "worker's self" versus her "writer's self," and concluded that the best in her seemed to die when she gave up her writing.[35] She stated that it was the writing self that she loved, not her "efficient, philanthropic self."[36] Up to this point, Benedict had tried to express her "writer's self" as much through poetry as she did through prose. In fact, over the next decade she would eventually publish a number of poems, often using the pseudonym Anne Singleton. But evidently writing some verses and occasionally seeing them in print did not provide enough of a benefit at that juncture to fully satisfy her "writer's self."

Still searching for the proper means to express herself and perhaps launch a career, Benedict in 1918 at the age of thirty-one went back to school at Columbia University to study with the famed educator John Dewey. Her goal was to become an educational philosopher and to use education as a means to promote social change. When Dewey went on sabbatical in the fall of 1919, she enrolled instead in a class in "Sex in Ethnology" taught by Elsie Clews Parsons, an independently wealthy folklorist and feminist at the New School for Social Research. It was here that Benedict discovered anthropology, an approach to the study of life that made more sense to her than any she had previously encountered. The course was the only one that Parsons taught at the New School, but Benedict continued to take classes at this institution with another notable figure in the field, Alexander Goldenweiser. After two years of course work, Benedict, feeling she was now on the right track, went on to further study in anthropology at Columbia University in 1921 under the tutelage of the legendary German-born professor Franz Boas. Boas appreciated her imaginative mind and quickly supported her through the requirements for the Ph.D., which she received in 1923. Her dissertation, dealing with a well-recognized cultural aspect of Native American religion, was published as *The Concept of the Guardian Spirit in North America* and was well received within the discipline. Her dissertation research was library-based, as was typical for that era, when anthropologists generally undertook fieldwork only after receiving their doctorates. At Columbia she now stood among anthropologists, like Boas, who were concerned with making anthropology useful to society. With their encouragement Benedict was ultimately able to meet her goal of using her scholarly endeavors for social change, although it would be in the fields of anthropology and psychiatry and not educational philosophy.

Although Benedict had finally found a calling which gave her professional satisfaction, her thoughts about children did not disappear or become fully resolved. In 1920, a year after being informed of her tubal infertility, she was apparently still thinking about motherhood and her failure to achieve it. Writing in her journal that October, she noted that in the presence of her husband she had trouble suppressing thoughts about "subjects which disrupt the quiet—my own ambitions, my sense of futility; children—chiefly children."[37] That children remained so sensitive an issue between them may be related to the fact that Stanley had vetoed the idea of her having an operation to unblock her fallopian tubes, claiming that it was too dangerous. (Whether the couple ever considered the alternative of adoption is apparently unknown.) Three years later, in 1923, when Benedict was approaching the age of thirty-six, the tragic death of a female graduate student prompted her to speculate about the gift of life and whether it was truly appreciated. "I know it's all wrapped up with my wish for children—and dread that they might not want the gift."[38] A few years afterward, having reached forty, she wrote a poem, published in *Poetry* magazine in 1928, which vividly expressed her grief over not having children.

Be desperate in that hour. Lift up your heart

As any cup and drink it desolate—

A drained and ruinous vessel that no fate

Shall fill again in pity, and no art

Make brim quick-passionate.

Leave not one drop for heart-broke artifice

Against the stricken years. You shall know now

The quiet breathing of the apple bough

Past blossoming, peace of the Chrysalis,

The rain upon your brow.[39]

The poem appears to reflect her acceptance of the fact that she would not experience the "quickening" of a growing fetus and that she, like the apple bough, was past blossoming. Interestingly, the appearance of the poem coincided with the publication of a significant paper she wrote in the field of anthropology, "Psychological Types in the Cultures of the Southwest." As Margaret Mead later asserted, prior to this time Benedict's "commitment to anthropology as a career was not yet very deep." Indeed, "It was not until the medical evidence was definite that she would never have children, that she began to consider a greater commitment to anthropology; and not until her field trip to the Pima in 1927, when she suddenly saw the possibilities of viewing culture . . . like a personality writ large. . . ."[40] A short time earlier, Benedict perhaps best summed up the shift in her personal situation, telling fellow anthropologist Esther Goldfrank: "I don't have children, so I might as well have Hottentots."[41]

Certainly this time period marked a major turning point in Benedict's life. The goals she had mapped out a decade and a half earlier, especially marriage and motherhood, had not turned out as planned. She began to drift away from her husband—eventually renting a small apartment near Columbia University to use mid-week. As Benedict later exclaimed: "I've wanted three things: Stanley, and I never could build up any companionship with him; children, and I never had a chance to daydream about them, never having had even an illusion of pregnancy. . . ."[42] The third item she listed was poetry, which she once hoped would provide a creative outlet and which she pursued concurrently with her anthropological studies. However, in 1928, Harcourt Brace rejected a manuscript of her poetry, which according to Mead, "really ended her aspirations as a poet."[43] It is hard to know which of these three Benedict considered the greatest loss but the subject of children was the one she most commented upon in her published writings. The issue of motherhood may have receded further and further as time passed but as she revealed to Mead at one point, it never entirely disappeared. In *Blackberry Winter*, Mead herself remarked about how as a young woman she truly wanted children, but added that she "did not feel, as Ruth had felt, that there was no possible compensation for not having a child."[44] It is clear that for Ruth Benedict her work, no matter how fulfilling, was never experienced as a substitute for children. In 1934, she wrote that "work even when I'm satisfied with it is never my child I love nor my servant I've brought to heel."[45] Benedict never got to be a full-time mother though she did get to display her motherly qualities on visits to see her sister's children in California. Later, when Mead gave birth to a daughter in 1939, she made Benedict the godmother and instructed that she be responsible for raising the child if anything happened to the parents.[46] During World War II, when Mead and Benedict were both working in Washington, D.C., and individually came to New York on certain weekends to spend some time with young Mary, a friend remarked that Ruth seemed "a lot more motherly, by nature, than Margaret was."[47]

Through her new career in academia, starting in the mid-1920s, Benedict was for the first time able to find friends and colleagues with whom she could share an intellectual communion and some emotional intimacy. One of the most important of these was Edward Sapir, a leading linguistic anthropologist and former Boas student who lived and worked in Ottawa, Canada. Benedict found a kindred spirit in Sapir, like herself an aspiring poet and confined in an unhappy marriage, and the two regularly wrote long letters to one another and exchanged their poems. Sapir believed Benedict had greater talent as a poet than as an anthropologist, and spent much time analyzing and encouraging her poetic efforts. Another pleasurable aspect of their connection for her was the development of a relationship with his children. When Sapir brought his ailing wife to New York to seek medical help from time to time, he often brought along one or more of his three children, whom Benedict gladly cared for. As she wrote in her diary on one of these occasions, "Helen Sapir's day—paper dolls in my room, lunch from 'printed menu'; wardrobe of dolls; swimming pool; and typewriter. E.S. in seminar at 4, and ice cream across the street."[48] All three of Sapir's children, according to Sapir biographer Regna Darnell, remember Benedict as a "familiar presence throughout their childhoods."[49] Her relationship with Edward Sapir, however, remained platonic. After his wife's death he moved to the University of Chicago and remarried a short time later. Although Sapir and Benedict remained professional colleagues, their subsequent correspondence became less intense and gradually less frequent.

During this time Benedict also formed a close working relationship, one which would last for the rest of her life, with Margaret Mead, who would go on to become an equally famous author and public intellectual. In fact, it was Benedict who first encouraged Mead to go into anthropology instead of school psychology, having introduced her to the subject in a course she taught as a teaching assistant at Barnard College, where Mead was an undergraduate.[50] The two women were almost fifteen years apart in age and very different in temperament—Mead open and mercurial, Benedict more reserved and deliberate—yet they shared much beside their professional interests. Both struggled a great deal with how to shape their personal lives, and they soon developed an intimate bond with one another. Mead's daughter, Mary Catherine Bateson, later revealed that the two women had become lovers sometime around 1923 or 1924 and continued their relationship through Mead's marriages, although with less frequent contact. Bateson and others have noted that Mead in early adulthood at times sought an intimate attachment with both a man and a woman and felt that the two kinds of relationships complemented one another, whereas Benedict eventually drifted away from intimacy with men.[51] Benedict developed a lesbian orientation over the next several years, though most of her friends and subsequent partners tended to be silent on this issue, not wishing to betray her privacy.[52]

In Benedict's association with Mead, there seems to have been a strong mother-daughter component, and indeed, scholars have pointed out that mother-daughter features of such relationships were often more meaningful to lesbian women at that time than were different gender roles.[53] Clearly, the older and more introverted Benedict delighted in Mead's buoyancy and youthful exuberance. Mead herself in later life confirmed the mother-daughter theme of their early friendship, telling writer Jean Houston: "Ruth Benedict's attitude to me was that I was the child she hadn't had. . . . I had all the things she would have wanted in a child. The joy in living which she didn't have. The positive assumption [about] life which she never had."[54] During the next quarter century, though their personal intimacy may have diminished somewhat as they became more attached to others, their professional collaboration remained strong. Benedict and Mead read virtually everything the other wrote, closely monitoring each other's work and discussing the latest developments in anthropology and related subjects with one another.

From 1923 to 1931, Benedict held a series of one-year appointments as lecturer in anthropology at Columbia. Because she was still legally married and financially supported by her husband, Franz Boas, as head of the department, felt her less deserving of a full-time appointment than a single woman. When an opening in anthropology occurred at neighboring Barnard during this period he recommended another student of his, Gladys Reichard, for the spot. Yet despite Benedict's limited status at the university, Boas recognized her capability and had her appointed editor of the *Journal of American Folk-Lore* in 1925, a post she continued to hold until 1939. According to anthropologist Barbara Babcock, she did much in this position "to professionalize the field of folklore and move it beyond motif collections and folk-narratives distributions."[55] In 1927 Benedict became president of the American Ethnological Association and a member of the executive group of the American Anthropological Association. In addition, she became indispensable as an assistant to the revered but somewhat distant Boas, helping with his classes and acting as a mediator between him and his graduate students. In fact, some of these students would ask Benedict to interpret what Boas meant when he gave out advice and direction. As Margaret Mead later asserted, "The excitement which she felt about his mind broke through the austerity of his fundamentally paternal relationship to his students, and the rest of us became grandchildren to a professor whom . . . we began to call 'Papa Franz.'"[56]

Benedict continued to exert a nurturing influence on anthropology students at Columbia over the years, always willing to lend an ear to those having difficulties and to provide various kinds of assistance. As one former student put it: "She not only teaches them; she advises them, encourages them, hashes over their personal problems with them and constantly lends them money—which she usually forgets about . . . and maintains a steady loyalty toward them."[57] Mead noted that "her gentle, faraway accessibility provided a kind of center in a department in which the professor [Boas] was harried, shy, and abrupt in first contacts."[58] Throughout her teaching career Benedict offered financial aid to her students, either by assisting them in obtaining grants or by financing their work herself. For example, when Mead completed Barnard College in 1923 and needed funds for graduate tuition at Columbia, Benedict gave her a "fellowship" of $300 out of her own pocket for that purpose. This kind of "funding" persisted over the next two decades with others, culminating in 1946 when she funneled a $2,500 award from the American Association for University Women into small stipends to help graduate students continue their research and field work.[59] Her concern did not merely arise from personal generosity; she wanted to keep the best students in anthropology in order to advance the discipline she found so meaningful.

In her prodigious correspondence, one can see that Benedict also aided colleagues and former students such as Oscar Lewis and Zora Neale Hurston by writing letters of recommendation for their research projects, composing advance reviews, and sending words of encouragement. Typical of the many grateful responses Benedict received from those she had helped over the years was a letter from Hurston, then an aspiring African-American writer and folklorist, saying, "You have no idea how your kindly letter touched me. Things looked pretty dark just then. My task is harder at times than I had anticipated."[60] Recognition of Benedict's nurturing style is also illustrated by a letter from a student fieldworker on a Cherokee reservation in 1926, which stated, "The way this short note was written made me feel that, after all, the nickname of '*Mother Ruth*' we gave you last year is very well deserved."[61] Benedict occasionally referred to her graduate students as "the children," part of a larger kinship system that she and Mead worked out to describe the functioning of the anthropology department. Years later, sociologist Jessie Bernard referred critically to Benedict's nurturing relationships with students as a kind of "exalted Momism" with its associated excessive dependence of students on academic women, yet added that Benedict turned out a good product in spite of or perhaps because of her "Momism."[62]

Benedict's warmth toward students and colleagues also extended to her published reviews of the works of poets, psychologists, psychiatrists, and anthropologists, including such major authors as Robinson Jeffers, Erich Fromm, Karen Horney, Gregory Bateson, Bronislaw Malinowski, and Joseph Campbell. These reviews generally began with a positive, concise statement about how the particular work would meet some important need, followed by a careful analysis of the work and brief description of its shortcomings.[63] The poet Robinson Jeffers, in gratitude, wrote to Benedict (as Anne Singleton) in January 1929, "Aside from being one of the kindest [reviews] that I am ever likely to meet, it seems to me to express simply and accurately the intentions of my verses."[64]

Although her interpersonal relationships with students were strong, classroom teaching did not prove to be an easy task for Benedict. Her hearing impairment made interaction with students difficult and there was always the possibility of annoying distractions. As Caffrey has stated: "Some days conditions would be optimal and leading discussions and answering questions went well. At other times she would be totally at sea, operating on guesswork, as students' voices became unintelligible mumbles and she missed their lip movements."[65] The close concentration she needed to conduct every class session was always a strain. Benedict did buy a Western Electric "earphone" but wrote in her journal that she "didn't have nerve to take it out in class!"[66] Lecturing also turned out to be problematic in that she never felt certain whether her voice was loud enough, and her shyness and anxiety often led to stuttering and a choppy speaking pattern. As Margaret Mead later noted: "It was years before she conquered this shyness and could speak with fluency and authority."[67] Eventually too she learned to stand among her students when speaking instead of remaining behind a rostrum, which made it less of a problem to hear, lip-read, and be heard.

While Benedict's partial deafness also stood in the way of her doing much pathbreaking anthropological fieldwork, she did make some notable contributions in this area. Over the course of the 1920s, Benedict did considerable research among indigenous peoples of the American Southwest, studying the Serrano in California (1922), then the Zuni (1924-1925), the Cochiti (1925), and the Pima (1927). In the 1930s, Benedict led a teaching field trip to the Mescalero Apache in the Southwest and another to the Blackfoot and Blood in the Northwest. Recording and understanding material first hand proved challenging, but through the use of interpreters she eventually collected an abundance of stories, which were published as *Tales of the Cochiti Indians* (1931), followed by two volumes of *Zuni Mythology* (1935). While the extent of her fieldwork was limited in time, and hampered by her hearing impairment and minimal knowledge of native languages, the research she did was crucial for laying the groundwork for her later interpretive studies of different cultures.

During Benedict's first decade at Columbia, she felt somewhat conflicted and uncertain about her personal life. She brooded and often felt depressed over her distant but continuing relationship with her husband Stanley. Though they saw each other only on weekends and vacations, the couple did not separate entirely until 1930. They never divorced and, when Stanley died six years later, he left her his entire estate. Only in the decade of the 1930s did Ruth Benedict begin to resolve some of her internal conflicts and experience some relief from depression. After an affair in 1931 with a businessman turned novelist failed to develop, she turned completely away from men as potential lovers. Soon afterward, she developed an intimate, long-term relationship with a woman scientist named Natalie Raymond, who was even younger than Mead. Benedict had met Raymond some time earlier in California, and then got to know her when she came east to study medicine.[68] The two wound up sharing an apartment for several years while Raymond attended Cornell University Medical College in downtown New York. Benedict referred to her as a "gay young soul." She stated in her diary that "loving Nat and taking such delight in her I have the happiest conditions for living that I've every known."[69] But while their relationship remained strong for a while, it eventually grew less intimate and came to an end entirely in 1938 due to Raymond's difficulty in carrying through with any long-term plans (she never finished medical school), as well as her developing intimate friendships with other women.

But even her breakup with Raymond did not stop Benedict from making progress toward ultimately overcoming her long-term depression. By her own report, she had experienced serious depression from early adolescence down through her forties. She always conceptualized these bad feelings as her "blue devils" and tried hard to find ways to keep them from possessing her. Essentially turning inward to deal with this ongoing problem, Benedict used her internal strength and intellect to manage her demons. Her early description of Mary Wollstonecraft can be applied to herself as well: "a passionately intellectual attitude toward living was her essential tool."[70] Noted psychologist Abraham Maslow once humorously named her reserved interpersonal style "the Benedictine enigma."[71] Her voluminous professional correspondence suggests that she remained constantly busy with both the intellectual and practical aspects of her work as an anthropologist and teacher. She once wrote that doing a chore was more effective at keeping her depression away than taking a holiday, though wondering if this approach made her a "masochist." A major aspect of Benedict's ongoing success in managing the blue devils was her ability to discover excitement and challenge in the field of anthropology.[72] In addition to her deep involvement with her work, she developed internal mechanisms to distance herself from depression, saying, "I have always used the world of make-believe with a certain desperation." She created a pair of mental spectacles whereby she imagined that she was doing something for the very last time because the next day she would be dead. She wrote, "Days, weeks, almost years, I wore those spectacles. They are inimitable for producing an illusion of vivacity and even gusto in the most melancholic."[73] Eventually she replaced the fantasy of being dead the next day with a vision of living the life of her imaginary daughter. As she described this new image, it was a mechanism for distancing herself from depression by imagining that she was living someone else's existence, and not primarily a fantasy about having a daughter.

In spite of the severity of her depression, Benedict maintained a strong belief in her "essential self." In an undated journal fragment, she wrote, "I didn't see any place in the real world for a self I recognized."[74] Her faith in herself, a self she called her essential self and her writing self, endured despite rejection of many kinds. A major instance of rejection was the failure of her marriage, of course, which "cut the roots of my life at their source."[75] But there were many others as well: the countless rejections received from poetry magazines for the verses she submitted; the teaching post that she felt she deserved which went to a less qualified colleague; a National Research Council fellowship that was denied her on the grounds that she was too old. When working conditions were less than favorable, she somehow managed to rise above it, doing what was necessary to be done. This enduring strand of belief in her essential self may have been the quality that allowed her to resist suicide and eventually overcome depression. She also at times evidenced a deep capacity for joy. In the early phases of her marriage she claimed she achieved "ecstasy" with her husband—she told of receiving great pleasure in the sensual aspects of canoeing and swimming, and then expressing her feelings in poetry by writing a psalm to canoeing, done in the style of the "23rd Psalm." As she herself would point out, she succeeded, unlike many people, in growing less depressed over the course of her lifetime. She finally found the inner peace she was looking for in her fifties, a time when she was past menopause.

To the degree that her depressive episodes may have been exacerbated by the hormonal fluctuation of her menstrual cycle, menopause itself may have contributed to relief from depression. Psychologically, this biological transition would have also signaled the end of any hope for children, no matter how unrealistic these hopes had become given the existence of blocked fallopian tubes. In her later years, Benedict experienced what Margaret Mead subsequently called "post-menopausal zest."[76] Some have speculated, in fact, that Mead conceived the term from having observed Benedict in that period of her life.

By 1931, Franz Boas, seeing that Benedict was now living on her own as well as making important contributions to the field of anthropology and to the university, finally obtained for her a tenured position in the department as assistant professor. Two days before her forty-fourth birthday, she accepted an assistant professorship from the administration at Columbia for $3,600 a year, the equivalent of perhaps ten times that amount today. At this point, she also began taking over an ever-growing number of responsibilities in the graduate anthropology program such as directing theses and handling additional administrative matters as Boas approached retirement age.

Not long afterward Ruth Benedict published *Patterns of Culture* (1934), which became one of the most important books in anthropology in the first half of the twentieth century. In this work Benedict defined the concept of culture for the non-anthropologist, and placed great emphasis on the then controversial idea of cultural relativity. What was normal, she believed, was not absolute. Benedict argued that the ethnocentrism of Western cultures is based on a lack of perspective of the outsider, so that we identify "our own socialized habits with Human Nature."[77] She made a plea for the emergence of "culture-conscious" individuals, meaning those who could take the outsider's perspective and maintain objectivity toward other peoples. Culture-consciousness was contrasted with the notion of racial purity, increasing popular in Germany in the 1930s, which she criticized as "merely another version of the in- and the out-group" and not referring "to the actual biological homogeneity of the group."[78] To illustrate the plasticity of cultural behavior, Benedict proposed the study of "primitive cultures" as a laboratory in diversity. Her hypothesis was that many cultures, including our own, were particularly suited for a single type of personality style. She selected three cultures for discussion: the Kwakiutl, a Northwest Native American group between Puget Sound and southwestern Alaska previously examined by Franz Boas; the Zuni and the Hopi, American southwest groups studied by Benedict and her colleague Ruth Bunzel; and the Dobu, an island group off eastern New Guinea that had been recently analyzed by Reo Fortune, a New Zealand anthropologist who at the time was the colleague and spouse of Margaret Mead.

Benedict described in her book how cultures have particular patterns, similar to the ways in which individuals have particular personality styles (hence the term culture as "personality writ large"). A major theme for Benedict was that individual behaviors within a culture can be understood only when seen in relationship to the whole, when behaviors and customs are integrated into a meaningful pattern. She focused on the differences between the Pueblo Indians who pursued an "Appolonian" style (a term borrowed from Nietzsche), embodying a very orderly existence, as opposed to the Plains Indians who followed a "Dionysian" style, which was more frenzied and disordered. Meanwhile, the Dobu was portrayed by her as having a paranoid, self-aggrandizing style that valued aggressive behaviors. Reading between the lines in her discussions of the three cultures, one can see Benedict was commenting, either directly or indirectly through contrast, on American culture as well.

In the book, Benedict integrated her descriptions of cultural patterns with her previous work on abnormality in psychology, using personality traits, trance phenomena, and male homosexuality as her chief examples. In "Anthropology and the Abnormal," an article in the *Journal of General Psychology* (1934) that became the essence of the

275

last chapter of *Patterns of Culture,* Benedict used homosexuality as an illustration of "culturally discarded traits . . . selected for elaboration in different societies."[79] She put forth the hypothesis that the psychological consequences of conflict between a homosexual individual and his culture are apt to become mistakenly identified with homosexuality itself. Using the Native American institution of the *berdache* as an illustration, she demonstrated how in a different culture men could perform women's roles and sometimes marry other men and at the same time occupy a recognized place in society. Just as any one language only uses some of all the possible sounds available to human beings, each culture values and elaborates only some aspects of the entire range of human behavior. As she wrote, "individuals whose characteristics are not congenial to the selected type of human behavior in that community are the deviants, no matter how valued their personality traits may be in a contrasted civilization."[80] She went on to outline a program of therapeutic intervention, based on teaching tolerance of diversity and developing self-reliance on the part of the patient. Benedict stated, "If he can be brought to realize that what has thrust him into his misery is despair at his lack of social backing he may be able to achieve a more independent and less tortured attitude and lay the foundation for an adequately functioning mode of existence."[81] When the American Psychiatric Association removed homosexuality as a category of mental disorder in 1973, largely in response to pressure from the gay rights movement, a factor used in their rationale was quite similar to Benedict's reasoning back in 1934, namely that homosexuality is not "a disadvantage in all cultures or subcultures."[82] By this time, however, Benedict's work on the subject was no longer referenced, either by the APA or by the anthropologists cited by the APA in their report.[83]

While *Patterns of Culture* was well received in academic circles and gradually accepted within the public at large, it was not without its critics. Some pointed out that Benedict's depiction of cultures tended to emphasize an "ideal" as opposed to "real" behavior, and that she ignored certain data that did not support her hypothesis. Others questioned her unwavering belief in relativism. Nevertheless, the book became a significant point of departure for further debate and future research in the field of anthropology. Later released in an inexpensive paperback format, *Patterns of Culture* was translated into fourteen languages and read by countless thousands of students and general readers over the next several decades. Her anthropological work contributed to a paradigm shift in psychiatry and psychology in subsequent generations, in which homosexuality was eventually removed from the category of mental illness and previously acceptable behaviors such as domestic violence against women achieved more public scrutiny and condemnation.

Not only did she make an impact through her written work, Benedict also influenced the fields of psychiatry and psychology by her personal involvement and interaction with the leaders in each of these disciplines. For example, she collaborated with psychiatrist Harry Stack Sullivan and contributed to the journal he founded, *Psychiatry*. She became part of the Hanover Seminar of Human Relations in New Hampshire in the summer of 1934 (when psychiatrist Erik Erikson formulated his theory of stages of development), meeting regularly with a group that included such noted figures as Erich Fromm, John Dollard, Margaret Mead, and Karen Horney. Benedict supported Horney's modification of Freudian ideas and encouraged the redefinition of normal and abnormal in many areas, pointing out how cultural factors affect mental health. Horney later published *The Neurotic Personality of Our Time*, which emphasized the relative nature of normality within any given cultural context.[84] In the mid-1930s Benedict joined a New York Psychoanalytic Institute seminar led by psychiatrist and psychoanalyst Abram Kardiner and, two years later, began participating in a small class led by Rorschach expert Bruno Klopfer. This same kind of interaction on her part continued during the Second World War as Benedict was invited to become a Fellow in the Washington School of Psychiatry, where her colleagues included Frieda Fromm-Reichmann, Harry Stack Sullivan, Erich Fromm, and Janet Rioch.

Benedict also served as one of the prime models for psychologist Abraham Maslow's concept of self-actualization, which became popular during the next two decades. As a young research associate in psychology and later as a college professor, Maslow participated in a number of classes and seminars with Benedict and other anthropologists and psychologists. According to his later writings, he developed his ideas about self-actualization based on his admiration for Benedict and for the Gestalt psychologist Max Wertheimer: "the effort of a young intellectual to try to understand two of his teachers whom he loved, adored, and admired and who were very, very wonderful people."[85] Self-actualizing people, according to Maslow, have a need to fulfill their potential; they are "focused on problems outside themselves that called on their energies, usually some responsibility or duty to humankind," and live "in the widest possible frame of reference." According to Maslow, "They saw 'concealed or confused realities more swiftly and more correctly than others,' in areas from art and science to public affairs."[86]

Maslow proceeded to expand on Benedict's concept of "synergy," based on lecture notes she prepared as a visiting scholar at Bryn Mawr College in the spring of 1941.[87] Developed as a way to compare cultures, synergy was defined as social arrangements that permit the individual to serve his or her own interests and the interests of the group simultaneously. Benedict described high-synergy cultures as high in morale, secure, and low in aggression, whereas low-synergy cultures were low in morale, insecure, and high in aggression. High-synergy cultures were also characterized by the siphoning of wealth to meet the needs of the whole society. Benedict's concept of synergy could be applied to the individual as well, wherein a high-synergy person would be someone who transcends the polarity between self-interest and altruism.

Despite Benedict's emergence as a major figure in the field of anthropology, when Franz Boas officially retired as chairperson of the department at Columbia in the late 1930s, she did not become his permanent replacement. The all-male governing board of the University, steeped in tradition, stood firm, unwilling to break with the past and designate a woman as department head. Instead, Ralph Linton, brought in from the University of Chicago, was made the new chairperson in 1937, and his relationship with Benedict immediately became antagonistic. Linton, who would be described today as an extreme male chauvinist, did not appreciate her presence and did everything he could to disparage her and diminish her influence. (Benedict's student Sidney Mintz later wrote that Linton boasted after Benedict's death that he had killed her by using the occult powers of a leather pouch from the Tanala.)[88] Privately Benedict referred to Linton as "a swine" and tried to avoid him. When he joined Kardiner's seminar, which then moved to Columbia and became known as the Linton-Kardiner seminar, she decreased her participation and began moving in other directions.

Not feeling very comfortable in the new climate of the Columbia anthropology department, Benedict took a sabbatical leave in 1939-1940 in order to write, living for a time with her sister's family in southern California. Besides working hard on a number of major projects during this period, she found time to establish a close relationship with a woman named Ruth Valentine, a clinical psychologist and fellow Vassar alumna four years her junior. (Benedict was fifty-two and Valentine forty-eight when they met.) As it turned out, the two stayed together for the remainder of Benedict's life, sharing a residence on Central Park West in New York and living in Washington, D.C., when Benedict was employed there during World War II. Valentine also served as the executive secretary for Benedict's major research projects in the immediate postwar period.

Although she had strong opinions on many subjects, Benedict had never been politically active earlier in her life, either in the woman suffrage movement before 1920 or in other reform efforts later on. As a scholar and social scientist she always worried about compromising her objectivity regarding sensitive issues, and sought to avoid public controversies through much of her career. In the late 1930s, however, as the emergence of Hitler and his extreme racial views appeared to threaten the world order, Benedict felt moved to take an open stand. As Margaret Mead wrote: "she became committed to an absorbing moral purpose—better racial relations."[89] Over the next few years, she published several magazine articles on the subject of race, and her book, *Race: Science and Politics*, which contained a fervent plea for racial tolerance in the world—and also at home in America, was published in 1940.[90] Later, during the Second World War, she collaborated with a younger anthropologist, Gene Weltfish, to produce an easy-to-read, low-priced pamphlet, *The Races of Mankind* (1943), which contained essentially the same message but, given its form, exerted much greater impact.[91] Though a few Southern politicians vigorously objected to the material included, it eventually sold nearly a million copies. The United Auto Workers of the CIO created a cartoon film carrying the same theme, and Benedict and Weltfish put together a children's book based on the film, called *In Henry's Backyard*.[92] In a subsequent interview on the issue of race, Benedict stated, "Variety among peoples is a thing to be cherished."[93]

As an indication of her strong commitment to democratic values and to the Allied war effort in the mid-1940s, Benedict went to work for the United States government in Washington, D.C., in the Office of War Information. Given her field of expertise, she was put in charge of the preparation of studies analyzing foreign cultures. Though based largely on secondary sources rather than primary research, the information gathered was very useful to government officials. These studies examined the cultures of certain allied nations but the most important project undertaken by Benedict's group was an analysis of Japan, the major U.S. adversary in the Pacific, whose ways were little known in the Western world. Such assessments of national character, applying anthropological methods to analyze complex modern societies at a distance, marked a major departure from previous works of anthropology. Out of this endeavor to understand Japan and its people came Benedict's last book, *The Chrysanthemum and the Sword* (1946). An in-depth survey of the behavioral patterns of the Japanese, our "most alien enemy," the study proved helpful in shaping postwar attitudes toward the proud but defeated nation. The author's advocacy of a culturally respectful style of governing the country during the U.S. occupation clearly influenced American policy makers' decisions and led to retaining the Emperor of Japan in his place after the war. Even many readers among the Japanese recognized the perceptive analysis presented in the volume. Still in print, it is generally considered her most well-written book.

In the following year, 1947, partly in response to the success of her wartime work, the U.S. government provided Benedict with a considerable grant to direct a program of broad research in contemporary cultures. This was perhaps the most ambitious anthropological research project ever undertaken up to that time. In this project a strong emphasis was put on the study of child-rearing practices, something that Benedict had always viewed as important predictors of adult behavior. She had first written a separate article on the subject in the late 1930s, and delivered a paper "Child Rearing in Certain European Countries" early in 1948. In recognition of her growing stature both at home and abroad, Benedict was selected to be president of the American Anthropological Association for 1947-1948, and in the latter year was finally made a full professor at Columbia University. Unfortunately, during that same period, recurring illnesses, including hypertension, began to take their toll. She had traveled over the summer of 1948 to attend and lecture at UNESCO meetings in Czechoslovakia, and friends noted her fatigue and asked her to slow down her schedule. But not long after her return home and inauguration as full professor, Benedict died at the age of sixty-one following a coronary thrombosis that September. She remained alive at the end for five days, with Margaret Mead at her side. Benedict's partner Ruth Valentine, in California at the time, traveled to join her and was with her when she died.

Although Benedict passed on before completing all the projects she had recently undertaken, she had accomplished a great deal professionally and personally over the previous quarter of a century, and had come to embrace a more positive attitude toward life. As Benedict's sister Margery wrote to Margaret Mead upon learning of her death:

> I'm so thankful that in the last years she developed a true love
> of life; -- that her blue devils vanished, and she could relax in
> peace. She commented to me only this summer on how strange
> it was, that in her early days she had been completely out of
> step with her generation, unable to feel that instinctive joy of
> life that seemed well-nigh universal in youth, -- but that now in
> late middle age, when so many of her generation had become
> disillusioned and cynical and bored with life, -- she was out of
> step with her generation by far outstripping most of them in her
> keen interest in living![94]

As she had located her devils outside of herself, Benedict located emotional distress within the relationship between an individual and society rather than within the individual. For these reasons she disliked and avoided psychoanalysis, and she influenced the field of psychiatry to consider the conflicts posed by culture for the individual. Clarifying and understanding the emotional distress that accompanies marginality was at the core of her concerns in anthropology and psychology. Benedict herself had an unusual capacity for empathy, and particularly for putting herself in the place of other marginalized persons and imagining their experience. An unpublished essay, titled "If I were a Negro," for example, expressed her feelings about what it was like to face racial discrimination on a daily basis.[95] While she used her outward status as a white Protestant and *Mayflower* descendant to have her message heard, she used her internal experience of marginality to guide her thinking and research. As a teacher, she urged her students to project themselves into the cultures they read about and "to imagine what that life must be like."[96] As Lapsley has pointed out, she was careful never to discuss lesbianism, and her written examples always related to male homosexuality, but one can guess that her developing sexual orientation as well as her failed attempts at marriage and childbearing contributed to her ability to empathize with other marginalized individuals.[97]

In discussing Benedict's legacy, Carolyn Heilbrun targeted two areas of her generativity by stating that she "was a writer and professional teacher of great importance, both as a model for younger anthropologists and in her crusade against racism."[98] Benedict's expression of generativity over the course of her lifetime was multi-dimensional, ranging from warm concern for her nieces and nephews, friends' children, students, and colleagues, to efforts on a global scale to end discrimination and promote international cooperation. In addition to her many supportive relationships with individuals, she worked on a more abstract level to end racism and cultural bias against homosexuals by educating the public through her articles and books. She hoped to communicate to the public that deviancy is not absolute and that we can step outside of our own culture and observe our behavior and values from a new perspective. After World War II, she participated in UNESCO programs designed to study national differences with the goal of bringing about a more cooperative world. As a feminist, she was an acute observer of the limitations of society and of childbearing for women's identity development, advocating "one's own individual world of effort and creation." In that her work gave her life meaning and provided connectedness with others, she was successful in helping herself and helping others as well, over time becoming an example of her own concept of the high-synergy individual.

NOTES

[1] Margaret Mead, *Blackberry Winter: My Early Years* (New York: William Morrow, 1972), 246.

[2] Margaret M. Caffrey, *Ruth Benedict: Stranger in This Land* (Austin, TX: University of Texas Press, 1989).

[3] Abram Kardiner and Edward Preble, *They Studied Man* (Cleveland, OH: The World Publishing Company, 1961), 204.

[4] According to Hilary Lapsley, *Margaret Mead and Ruth Benedict: The Kinship of Women* (Amherst, MA: University of Massachusetts Press, 1999), 285, the original title of her book *Race: Science and Politics* (1940) had been "Race and Racism," but the publisher requested the alternative title be used since the word "racism" was not yet well known in the United States.

[5] Personal details of her childhood come mainly from an autobiographical essay written in the 1930s and published after her death in Margaret Mead, *An Anthropologist at Work: Writings of Ruth Benedict* (Boston: Houghton Mifflin, 1959), 97-112. The quotation is found on page 99. (Hereafter cited as AW)

[6] AW, 109.

[7] AW, 100.

[8] AW, 103.

[9] Letter from Margery Fulton Freeman to Margaret Mead, September 18, 1948, Folder 117.2, Ruth Fulton Benedict Papers, Vassar College, Poughkeepsie, New York. Hereafter cited as RFB Papers.

[10] AW, 100.

[11] AW, 108.

[12] Judith S. Modell, *Ruth Benedict: Patterns of a Life* (Philadelphia: University of Pennsylvania Press, 1983), 37-41.

[13] AW, 105; Modell, *Ruth Benedict*, 41-42.

[14] AW, 105.

[15] AW, 111.

[16] Caffrey, *Ruth Benedict*, 59.

[17] The Orton School for Girls was founded and directed by Anna B. Orton, an 1880s graduate of Vassar College.

[18] AW, 121.

[19] AW, 120.

[20] AW, 122.

[21] AW, 130.

[22] AW, 141.

[23] AW, 141.

[24] AW, 133.

[25] Benedict, "The Woman-Christ," Folders 48.35 and 120.1, RFB Papers.

[26] Alice Miller, *The Drama of the Gifted Child: The Search for the True Self*, 3rd ed. (New York: Basic Books, 1997).

[27] AW, 133, 136; Caffrey, *Ruth Benedict*, 82.

[28] AW, 136.

[29] AW, 138.

[30] Modell, *Ruth Benedict*, 164.

[31] AW, 132.

[32] Modell, *Ruth Benedict*, 107.

[33] Houghton Mifflin later published the best-selling *Patterns of Culture*, and interestingly, published the Wollstonecraft essay after her death as part of her collected works.

[34] AW, 7.

[35] AW, 142.

[36] AW, 142.

[37] AW, 143.

[38] AW, 65.

[39] Kardner and Preble, *They Studied Man*, 206.

[40] Margaret Mead, "Ruth Fulton Benedict 1887-1948," *American Anthropologist* 51 (1949): 459.

[41] Esther Goldfrank, *Notes on an Undirected Life*, 36, quoted in Caffrey, *Ruth Benedict*, 84.

[42] Quoted in Modell, *Ruth Benedict*, 97.

[43] AW, 91.

[44] Margaret Mead, *Blackberry Winter*, 269.

[45] Benedict, Journal Entry, June 9, 1934, in AW, 154.

[46] Margaret M. Caffrey and Patricia A. Francis, eds., *To Cherish the Life of the World: Select Letters of Margaret Mead* (New York: Basic Books, 2006), 170-71.

[47] Jane Howard, *Margaret Mead: A Life* (New York: Simon and Schuster, 1984), 244.

[48] "Diary: 1923," AW, 58.

[49] Regna Darnell, *Edward Sapir: Linguist, Anthropologist, Humanist* (Berkeley, CA: University of California Press, 1990), 177.

[50] Benedict taught the course as a teaching assistant for Boas. She did not have a regular appointment at Barnard, which was affiliated with Columbia University. See Barbara A. Babcock, "Not in the Absolute Singular: Rereading Ruth Benedict," in Ruth Behar and Deborah A. Gordon, eds., *Women Writing Culture* (Berkeley, CA: University of California Press, 1995), 109-10.

[51] Mary Catherine Bateson, *With a Daughter's Eye* (New York: William Morrow, 1984), chap. 8.

[52] On the multi-faceted relationship between the two women, see Lapsley, *Margaret Mead and Ruth Benedict*, and Lois W. Banner, *Intertwined Lives: Margaret Mead, Ruth Benedict and Their Circle* (New York: Alfred Knopf, 2003).

[53] Lapsley, *Margaret Mead and Ruth Benedict*, 211.

[54] Quoted in Lapsley, *Margaret Mead and Ruth Benedict*, 72.

[55] Babcock, "Not in the Absolute Singular," 113.

[56] AW, 9.

[57] Interview, Folder 117.3, RFB Papers.

[58] AW, 344.

[59] Howard, *Margaret Mead*, 272.

[60] Letter from Zora Neale Hurston to RFB [1934?], Folder 30.4, RFB Papers.

[61] Letter to RFB, December 24, 1926, Folder 1.2, RFB Papers.

[62] Jessie Bernard, *Academic Women* (University Park, PA: Pennsylvania State University Press, 1964), 141-43.

[63] Benedict, Published Book Reviews, Folder 57.10, RFB Papers.

[64] Letter from Robinson Jeffers to Anne Singleton, January 13, 1929, Folder 1.5, RFB Papers.

[65] Caffrey, *Ruth Benedict*, 266.

[66] AW, 74.

[67] AW, 5.

[68] Raymond had previously had some connection with Robert Oppenheimer, later known as the "father of the bomb." See Lapsley, *Margaret Mead and Ruth Benedict*, 203.

[69] Benedict, Diary Fragment, June 15, 1934, Folder 36.1, RFB Papers.

[70] AW, 491.

[71] Letter from Abraham Maslow to RFB, March 6, 1940, Folder 32.8, RFB Papers.

[72] Mihaly Czikszentmihalyi, *Flow: The Psychology of Optimal Experience* (New York: Harper & Row, 1990).

[73] Benedict, Journal, Folder 36.1, RFB Papers.

[74] Benedict, Undated Journal Fragment, Folder 36.1, RFB Papers.

[75] Benedict, Folder 37.4, RFB Papers.

[76] Lapsley, *Margaret Mead and Ruth Benedict*, 261.

[77] Benedict, *Patterns of Culture*, 2nd ed. (Boston: Houghton Mifflin, 1959), 7. Later, Benedict would seek to explore the parameters of relativism. See Virginia H. Young, *Ruth Benedict: Beyond Patterns, Beyond Relativism* (Lincoln, NE: University of Nebraska Press, 2005).

[78] Benedict, *Patterns of Culture*, 16.

[79] Ruth Benedict, "Anthropology and the Abnormal," *Journal of General Psychology* 10 (1934): 59-82.

[80] Benedict, *Patterns of Culture*, 277.

[81] Benedict, *Patterns of Culture*, 279.

[82] American Psychiatric Association, *Diagnostic and Statistical Manual of Mental Disorders*, 3rd ed. (Washington, DC: APA, 1980), 380.

[83] In addition to the DSM-III cited above, see Ronald Bayer, *Homosexuality and American Psychiatry: The Politics of Diagnosis* (New York: Basic Books, 1981), and "Symposium: Should Homosexuality Be in the APA Nomenclature?" *American Journal of Psychiatry*, 130 (1973): 1207-16.

[84] Karen Horney, *The Neurotic Personality of Our Time* (New York: W.W. Norton, 1937).

[85] Richard J. Lowry, *A. H. Maslow: An Intellectual Portrait* (Monterey, CA: Brooks/Cole Publishing Company, 1973), argues that Maslow's ideas on the self-actualizing person developed over a decade and not in a moment of insight as Maslow described in 1971.

[86] Quoted in Caffrey, *Ruth Benedict*, 256. Interestingly, Maslow's description of the self-actualizing individual has similarities to Benedict's

description of Mary Wollstonecraft. See "Mary Wollstonecraft," in AW, 491.

[87] Abraham H. Maslow and John J. Honigmann, "Synergy: Some Notes of Ruth Benedict," *American Anthropologist* 72 (1970): 320-32.

[88] Lapsley, *Margaret Mead and Ruth Benedict*, 302.

[89] AW, 96.

[90] Ruth Benedict, *Race: Science and Politics* (New York: Viking Press, 1940).

[91] Ruth Benedict and Gene Weltfish, *The Races of Mankind* (Washington, DC: Public Affairs Committee, Pamphlet No. 85, 1943).

[92] Ruth Benedict and Gene Weltfish, *In Henry's Backyard: The Races of Mankind* (New York: Henry Schuman, 1948).

[93] Benedict, Interview, Folder 52.9, RFB Papers.

[94] Letter from Margery Fulton Freeman to Margaret Mead, September 18, 1948, RFB Papers.

[95] Benedict, "If I Were a Negro," Folder 120.8, RFB Papers.

[96] Barnouw, "Ruth Benedict," *American Scholar* 49 (1980): 506.

[97] Lapsley, *Margaret Mead and Ruth Benedict*, 211.

[98] Carolyn G. Heilbrun, "Pioneering Partnership," *Women's Review of Books* 17 (1999): 13.

Marilyn Monroe, Photo 20th Century Fox/Collection Sunset Boulevard/Corbis.

Chapter 8
Sexuality and Sadness:
"Her Womb Was Weeping"
Marilyn Monroe (1926-1962)

Hollywood actress Marilyn Monroe was one of the most celebrated figures of the mid-twentieth century, and though long departed is still among the most recognized women in the world. Through her looks, talent, and driving ambition, Monroe rose to fame in the early to mid-1950s, with a stream of hit movies and magazine photo spreads that turned her into a mega-star and sexual icon. Combining powerful allure with sweet innocence, she altered perceptions of women's sexuality, making its open display more acceptable on the big screen and in real life as well. For a while Monroe seemed to have it all—money, celebrity, and being courted by some of the most prominent men of the time. Yet by the end of the decade her life seemed to be moving on a downward slope and a couple years later, at age thirty-six, she was dead. Now, more than four decades afterward, many questions about the late performer remain unanswered, most notably the reasons behind her sad decline and whether or not her death was a deliberate suicide. Much of what has been said or written about her tragic fall has focused on her difficult childhood, her failed marriages, her stagnating career, her deteriorating health, and her relationships with the Kennedys. Yet among her personal problems, one that has not received sufficient attention was the great trouble she had in dealing with her childlessness. Although not well known by the public today, this failure to bring a pregnancy to term was a central part of her growing unhappiness in the years before her death. A good friend, poet Norman Rosten, later wrote that "her inability to have a child was to loom as a crucial disappointment. . . . The love goddess, the woman supreme, unable to have a baby; it was a dagger at her ego. . . . There was something wrong with her, inside her, a defect, an evil. . . . She yearned to be a mother, even if it meant temporarily putting films aside. She desperately wanted fulfillment."[1] One of her biographers, Anthony Summers, would call her unending quest for motherhood "the saddest preoccupation in her life." "Year after year as the fifties unwound, a vast public would wait and watch as Marilyn tried to have babies," Summers writes. "As marriage followed marriage the headlines would tell of repeated gynecological surgery or miscarriage after miscarriage. Time after time, Marilyn would speak of her longing for children, would make a point of favoring children's charities and funds for orphans. At her funeral, instead of flowers, donations were directed to children's hospitals."[2] While Summers may exaggerate to some degree the frequency of these reproductive failures, the essence of what he writes here is accurate. Monroe's preoccupation with becoming a mother and then being unable to do so clearly contributed to a decline in her creativity and a decline in her physical and mental health. Summers also mentions a possible connection between her infertility and the ending of her life on August 5, 1962; this date marked the fifth anniversary of an ectopic pregnancy loss during her marriage to playwright Arthur Miller.[3] There is no evidence to confirm that Monroe was aware of the anniversary, but she did know that Miller's new wife, photographer Inge Morath, was pregnant at that time and it is possible that Monroe's learning of the pregnancy may have affected her emotionally.

Although childless, Monroe was strongly committed to helping the younger generation and engaging in other forms of nurturance. As noted in the paragraph above, as she became a public figure, she took great interest in the lives of young people, visiting various children's hospitals, appearing at numerous charitable events and donating money to help other child-related causes. One of the organizations to which she contributed a substantial sum was WAIF, established by fellow film star Jane Russell, who was also infertile, to find homes in America for orphaned and abandoned youths from abroad. Today, funds from Monroe's estate continue to support a child center in London, which still bears her name. In addition, the actress developed positive relationships with her stepchildren and with the children of her mentors, playing games with the younger ones and serving as a close confidant to the older ones. She always kept pictures of them in her bedroom and frequently spoke to them on the telephone. In fact, one of the last phone conversations she had the night of her death was with Joe DiMaggio, Jr., the struggling son of her former husband. But while she derived pleasure from these relationships she never stopped wanting a child of her own.

Besides aiding and nurturing children, she was interested in protecting animals; it was a major theme of her last completed movie, *The Misfits* (1961), where Monroe's character Roslyn Tabor pleads for the salvation of wild mustangs. Her husband Arthur Miller had created the character based on a story he had written, "Please Don't Kill Anything," after having watched his wife throw dead fish back into the sea, push stems of cut flowers back into the earth, and become hysterical over a dead animal lying by the roadside. And while Monroe was too consumed by her career and her personal problems to be much of a political activist, she was profoundly interested in several humanitarian causes such as civil rights and the promotion of world peace. In her very last extended interview, in the summer of 1962,[4] she told the reporter: "What the world needs now is a greater feeling of kinship. We are all brothers, after all—and that includes movie stars, laborers, Negroes, Jews, Arabs—everyone. That's what I'm working on, working to understand."

Marilyn Monroe's life experience had, along with her fame and fortune, many aspects of marginality in addition to her infertility. Childhood was an especially difficult time as she grew up excluded from any semblance of a traditional family life with two parents and siblings. Her sense of exclusion and lack of belonging persisted until the end of her life, when she was still expressing her longings to be part of a nuclear family. Born in Los Angeles in June 1926, Norma Jeane Mortensen, as she was listed on her birth certificate, or Norma Jeane Baker, as she was known while growing up, never met her father and did not know with any certainty who he was. Later attempts to locate and meet with him proved unsuccessful. Moreover, she was not very close to her mother, Gladys Baker, and resided with her only for brief periods. Twice divorced and not always emotionally stable, her mother worked long hours as a film cutter in the movie industry as she struggled to make a living for her daughter and herself. Since Gladys felt unable to provide full-time care for her daughter, Norma Jeane lived mostly in foster homes and with relatives, and even for a time in the Los Angeles orphanage. This was especially the case after Gladys Baker was diagnosed as paranoid schizophrenic and committed to a state mental institution when Norma Jeane was eight and a half. After this point Monroe had little involvement with her mother, who remained confined for many years. While she would later make financial provision for Gladys and sometimes visited with her, she rarely talked about her with friends or associates. Evidently, the subject was always a source of great pain and embarrassment.[5]

It is difficult to know how Norma Jeane fared in her stays with various foster families or in the Los Angeles Orphans Home. Those involved in her upbringing later asserted that she was well cared for considering the circumstances but she strongly denied it. Monroe later charged that she was often treated shabbily and alleged that on at least one occasion she was sexually abused. In recalling the incident, she claimed that a male boarder where she lived coaxed her into his room and attempted to assault her. Much worse, she remembered, was the response of her foster mother who, when informed about what had just occurred, refused to believe the young girl and slapped her across the face for telling such a lie. As Monroe described the aftermath in her posthumously published autobiography:

> I was so hurt, I began to stammer. She didn't believe me! I cried that night in bed all night, I just wanted to die. . . . This was the first time I can remember stammering. . . . Once after when I was in the orphanage, I started to stutter out of the clear blue.[6]

The problem of stammering and stuttering, she said, would reappear at other times in her life, particularly at those moments when she was under severe stress. Most of her recollections of childhood focus on the negative aspects of her existence—the lack of love, the unpleasant surroundings, the absence of material things, the burdensome chores she had to perform, and incidents of mistreatment and abuse. Even though abuse is not uncommon in foster families, some biographers, however, have been skeptical regarding the legitimacy of the charges of abuse since she sometimes changed the details of her stories in retelling them to reporters.

Amid the deprivation and probable abuse that characterized Monroe's childhood, a former co-worker to Gladys, named Grace McKee, became Norma Jeane's legal guardian. "Aunt" Grace, as she was sometimes called, did not usually serve as a full-time parent, but she did look after her on a regular basis and helped direct Norma Jeane's future. It was she who more than anyone encouraged the young girl to think about becoming a movie star. During the hard times of the 1930s, Aunt Grace gave her a measure of hope. "Don't worry, Norma Jeane," she once said, "You're going to be a beautiful girl when you grow up. I can feel it in my bones."[7] Also childless and possibly infertile, Grace devoted a good deal of attention to Norma Jeane, especially trying to improve her appearance, buying her clothes and makeup, and molding her in the image of her favorite actress, Jean Harlow. Curiously, Harlow's life foreshadowed Marilyn Monroe's in many respects—rising from poverty to become a Hollywood star, going through a series of failed and childless marriages, and then dying young.

By early adolescence Norma Jeane was indeed developing into an attractive young woman and getting a great deal of male attention. Yet if she thought about being in the movies, she did little during these years toward actually pursuing such a goal. Although she may have in private uttered the lines of some of her favorite movie performers, she seemed too shy and introverted to act in school plays. Nor did she read much literature or show much interest in academics in general. Eventually she dropped out of high school in 1942 at age sixteen to marry Jim Dougherty, a neighbor and blue-collar worker roughly five years her senior. It was essentially an arranged marriage—organized by Grace McKee, who was moving out of state with her husband, in order to keep Norman Jeane from having to return to the Los Angeles orphanage. Monroe said later that she liked Jim, whom she had dated briefly beforehand, but was never really in love with him. Interestingly, she often referred to him as "daddy," and throughout her life generally sought out older men for companionship or marriage, and used similar words like "papa" or "pa" as terms of endearment when addressing them, perhaps reflecting the absence of a real father in her youth.

The marriage to Jim Dougherty did provide a home and a certain degree of stability for Norma Jeane in her late adolescence, but from the outset their relationship did not function smoothly. On the one hand, they were sexually compatible, and, according to Dougherty, Norma Jeane "thoroughly enjoyed sexual union." Her needs for security and acceptance, however, were not easily satisfied. The sixteen-year-old bride had trouble adjusting to her new role as housewife with its continuous cycle of cooking and cleaning. She had few friends and tended to rely on her husband for major decision making and handling complex household tasks. Dougherty in turn had trouble responding to her wants and needs, as he later wrote:

> She was so sensitive and insecure, and I realized I wasn't prepared to handle her. . . . Her feelings were very easily hurt. She thought I was mad at her if I didn't kiss her good-bye every time I left the house. When we had an argument—and there were plenty—I'd often say, 'Just shut up!' and go out and sleep on the couch. . . . I thought I knew what she wanted, but what I thought was never what she wanted.[8]

From the way Dougherty described his young wife during their marriage, it would seem that Norma Jeane sometimes experienced significant shifts in mood and behavior. Much of the time, he said, she would be quiet and withdrawn. This is corroborated by Dougherty's co-worker and later film star Robert Mitchum, who met her at the time and said she was "very shy and sweet, but not very comfortable around people."[9] But on certain occasions her demeanor changed and she became rather wild and extroverted. This more outgoing behavior occurred especially when she and her husband went dancing and Norma Jeane got caught up in the rhythms of the music and enjoyed the attention of other men.[10] One can see in this pattern a hint of Marilyn Monroe's future episodes of unrestrained exuberance, for example, the time she entertained American soldiers on stage in Korea and felt transformed by all their cheering. There is also the memorable scene from her movie *The Seven Year Itch*, where she becomes ecstatic while standing over a subway grate as her skirt rose up from the breeze. Another such moment occurred on the set of her last uncompleted picture *Something's Got to Give*, when she suddenly removed her flesh-colored bathing suit and swam naked around the pool with a shining glow on her face.

The issue of the young couple having children naturally arose not long into the marriage, although some elements of the story remain in dispute. In Monroe's version, she claimed that her husband wanted a child right away, but stated that the idea "terrified" her. "The thought of having a baby stood my hair on end. I could see it only as myself, another Norma Jean in an orphanage. Something would happen to me. Jim would wander off. And there would be this little girl in the blue dress and white blouse living in her 'aunt's' home, washing dishes, being the last in the bath water on Saturday night."[11] She said she couldn't explain her feelings about this outcome to Jim very well and at night would sometimes "lie awake crying." This didn't mean she was opposed to motherhood per se; indeed, she delighted in taking temporary care of Jim's young nephews and nieces. But she seemed to indicate that becoming a full-time mother was something which should be postponed until sometime in the future. In Dougherty's version, however, it is she who wished to have a child and he the one who stood opposed. According to his recollections, after he joined the Merchant Marine and was about to be shipped abroad at the height of World War II in 1944, she "begged to have a baby." A child, she said to him, would be her way of "having me with her." Dougherty rejected her pleas, insisting that raising a child alone would be very hard for her both emotionally and financially. "She really wasn't up to being a mother. I said we would have children after the war," he added.[12] Interestingly, Monroe never alluded to this exchange in any of her subsequent remarks on the subject of children.

If his side of the story was true and Dougherty had acquiesced, Norma Jeane may have conceived and born a child, and the rest of her life might have followed a different, more conventional course as a full-time housewife and mother. But, while her husband remained overseas during the war, she went to work at a local defense plant that made parachutes, and at one point was photographed for an armed forces newspaper. The response to the publication of her picture was totally unprecedented. Her combination of natural beauty and charming innocence apparently struck a huge chord with the paper's largely male readers. Soon other photographers came calling and pictures of her began appearing in all sorts of publications as well as on many posters and billboards. Not long afterward, she quit her factory job and started working full time as a photographer's model. Norma Jeane was helped along by Emmeline Snively, who ran the Blue Book modeling agency in Los Angeles and gave her important advice on makeup, grooming, dressing, and posture. Snively also recommended that she dye her hair blond—"a blonde could be photographed in any wardrobe and in any light," she said.[13] By mid-1946, the twenty-year old Norma Jeane, having achieved some success as a model, then decided to try breaking into the film industry. As these activities were incompatible with Jim Dougherty's traditional view of what a wife should be doing when he returned home after the war, the two quarreled and Norma Jeane, desiring to be more independent, chose to dissolve the marriage. A divorce was granted in Nevada in September 1946, and for her in particular there was no turning back.

Subsequently, Norma Jeane Baker Dougherty, or Marilyn Monroe, as she was renamed when she entered the motion picture business, focused on building her career. (The new name was given to her by Twentieth Century-Fox casting director Ben Lyon, who combined the last name of her maternal grandmother, Della Monroe, with the first name of former stage actress Marilyn Miller.) Although she once told another budding starlet, Clarice Evans, that she hoped to have four children, two of her own and two adopted, Monroe was obviously not talking about the present time. Once she had emerged as an aspiring Hollywood performer and signed a movie contract, she put aside any thought about children since she knew that a pregnancy would get her fired and destroy any chance of achieving stardom. When the subject had come up near the end of her marriage to Jim Dougherty, she showed no interest and allegedly told him that becoming pregnant would ruin her figure.

Some individuals in more recent times have challenged the idea that Monroe had always been childless as a young woman. There is the claim by a woman that she is Marilyn Monroe's long lost daughter, born in 1948, and another who said she was born in the spring of 1952, during the actress's hospital stay for an appendectomy, but these allegations have been quickly dismissed.[14] Less easy to cast aside is the account put forth by Monroe's former housemaid, Lena Pepitone, who stated that Marilyn once told her she actually had a child as an adolescent but had to give it away. In the narrative, Monroe claims that she was raped at one of the foster homes, became pregnant, delivered a child at the local hospital, and immediately thereafter her "Aunt" Grace forced her to turn over the baby to the authorities.[15] A few other friends from the 1950s such as Amy Greene, wife of Monroe's business partner at that point, have said they heard similar tales, though they thought it most likely that this was Marilyn's fantasy at a time she feared she might never give birth.[16] It is interesting that she seems to have told these stories only to female confidants and never to either of her later husbands. In fact, no really convincing evidence exists to support any story about her having born a child either in adolescence or in her early twenties during the immediate postwar years.

One related point on which full agreement does exist among chroniclers of her life is that Monroe had long-term gynecological problems and suffered early on from severe menstrual pain. Her first husband, Jim Dougherty, stated that "Norma Jeane had so much trouble during her menstrual periods, the pain would just about knock her out."[17] Down to the end of her days, Monroe would face heavy cramping and take large quantities of analgesic medications to deal with the problem. Many boxes of such painkillers from the famed Hollywood establishment, Schwab's Drugstore, could always be found in her studio dressing room. By the early 1950s she was diagnosed with endometriosis, a condition in which the uterine lining grows outside of the uterus, frequently causing scarring, adhesion of abdominal organs, and severe pain. Over the next decade she underwent surgery several times to obtain relief, including once just two weeks or so before her death. Many biographers assert that all her gynecological difficulties, and indeed her infertility, stemmed from having gone through several abortions as a young woman and as many as seven to fourteen during her lifetime. While she told others, including her later drama coach Paula Strasberg, that she did have numerous abortions and that her reproductive struggles were a punishment, it is possible that this was another made-up story, like that of having born a child as an adolescent. In fact, her longtime Los Angeles-based gynecologist, Dr. Leon Krohn, believed the rumors about her having had multiple abortions were grossly exaggerated.[18] It is true, of course, that Monroe did have many sexual partners over the years, and may have acquired sexually transmitted infections that contributed to the fallopian tube scarring. Whatever the cause, her gynecological problems did not go away and only worsened over time, despite all the surgeries and other attempts to ameliorate her condition.

There is, of course, an irony in the fact that the future sex goddess had severe gynecological problems and would be unable to produce a living child, and that a woman famous for her body would by her mid-thirties be afflicted by a number of ailments and need to undergo several surgical procedures. But it was not from a lifelong indifference to her physical condition that this situation emerged. Although in the last years of her life Monroe would often abuse her system with pills and alcohol, and sometimes gain too much weight, early in her career she took immense care of her body and face. She knew that her looks were her greatest asset and did what she could to maintain and even improve upon what nature had given her. As a starlet she had dental work to straighten her teeth and corrective surgery done on her jaw. In her small apartment, she had her own weight bench and dumbbells, which she used regularly to keep in shape. "I'm fighting gravity," she told one photographer. "If you don't fight gravity, you sag." She also liked to run and swim, and worked for hours learning dance routines when appearing in musicals. In addition, the budding star paid a good deal of attention to her diet. Once she could afford it, she started the day consuming cold oatmeal with milk, followed by two eggs, and washed it down with orange juice fortified by gelatin. Later on Monroe sometimes ate steak for breakfast—in fact, her choices seem not far different from the high-protein diets popular in more recent years. Throughout most of her career, the five-foot, five-and-a-half-inch curvaceous star kept her weight between 115 and 120 pounds, and never failed to attract admiring gazes from the public wherever she went.[19]

During the late 1940s to the early 1950s, Marilyn Monroe rose from being a barely known West Coast model to an internationally celebrated movie queen. But success did not come quickly or easily, and, in fact, at times she was minimally employed and had difficulty paying the rent. To support her quest for stardom, Monroe continued posing for magazine photographers and on at least one occasion posed nude, a portrait from the session later appearing on a popular calendar and then as the first *Playboy* centerfold after she became famous. When Marilyn Monroe was first identified as the nude calendar model some believed that her career might be in great jeopardy. But a scandal was averted by her candid admission of the deed, which she claimed had been necessary to help her survive through hard times. In fact, many people sympathized with her Cinderella-like story, which became a part of her mystique.

As part of her strong desire to succeed, Monroe was also alleged to have had sexual relations with a number of movie studio executives who she thought might advance her career. Even if the allegations are true, such actions did not seem to have achieved their purpose. When it came to being cast in films, she was at first only able to obtain a few bit parts. Both at Twentieth Century-Fox and Columbia Pictures, where she worked briefly, her on-screen appearances were usually of short duration and sometimes cut entirely from the final product. Many other Hollywood hopefuls in her situation gave up after a while and chose different, less competitive, pursuits. But Monroe was ambitious to be a movie star and refused to quit. She worked persistently to improve her talents, studying all phases of performing—including singing and dancing—and hiring European-trained acting coach Natasha Lytess to help her learn her craft. Lytess served as an adviser on the set of many of her early pictures, and later on, Michael Chekhov, nephew of the famed Russian playwright, offered her acting lessons as well. The aspiring actress also attended informal classes at the Actors Lab, where she learned the latest dramas and stage techniques. Through the efforts of her hard-working agent Johnny Hyde, Monroe eventually landed small but pivotal roles in two widely acclaimed films, *Asphalt Jungle* and *All About Eve*, which when released in 1950, brought her increased recognition and a long-term contract with Fox. In each of these pictures she played an inexperienced young woman who was the protégé and girlfriend of an older worldly man, but it was she who got the viewer's attention.[20]

After the appearance of these two films, Monroe's career started to blossom. Aided by an immense publicity campaign by Fox studios, her work on screen became more frequent and more substantive. She had parts in nine movies in 1951 and 1952, mostly light comedies such as *As Young as You Feel*, *Love Nest*, *We're Not Married*, and *Monkey Business*, but also the serious dramas *Clash by Night* and *Don't Bother to Knock*. In *Clash by Night*, despite playing a secondary character, several critics praised Monroe's performance; New York newspaper reviewer Alton Cook called her "a forceful actress [and] a gifted new star, worthy of all that fantastic press agency."[21] By early 1953, when Monroe appeared as a "femme fatale" opposite veteran actor Joseph Cotten in the suspense film *Niagara*, she was given star billing. Then, after playing featured roles in the big-budget musical *Gentlemen Prefer Blondes* (1953) and the popular romantic comedy *How to Marry a Millionaire* (1954), Marilyn Monroe became more than just a star—she was a major Hollywood sensation, pursued by fans and reporters wherever she went, and receiving thousands of fan letters each week. In the latter two films and in *The Seven Year Itch*, co-starring Tom Ewell and directed by Billy Wilder, which was released the following year,

1955, Monroe affirmed her image as a sweet but vulnerable love goddess and started to be recognized by some film critics as a talented comedienne in bringing self-parody to her recent sexy screen roles. She started receiving awards from the film industry for her performances and was frequently featured on the cover of the nation's most popular magazines such as *Life* and *Look.*[22]

Yet despite her meteoric rise and all the accolades she received, Monroe apparently did not derive much pleasure from her career successes or her personal life at the time. While she recognized that she was materially better off than in the past, what she had accomplished so far evidently did not bring her lasting satisfaction. In a statement later included in her autobiography, she described her conflicting emotions. The actress admitted that she was making "more money a week than I had once been able to make in six months. I had clothes, fame, money, a future, all the publicity I could dream of. I even had a few friends. And there was always a romance in the air. But instead of being happy over all these fairy tale things that had happened to me, I grew depressed and finally desperate. My life suddenly seemed as wrong and unbearable to me as it had in the days of my early despairs."[23] Monroe did not fully explain why she felt this way but apparently she had trouble reconciling the good things that were happening with her sense of inadequacy and lack of deserving. Feelings of depression and desperation continued to be with her to the end of her life, and, as will be seen, the inability to bear children clearly contributed to her growing unhappiness in the years to come.

At the time, of course, Monroe had no idea about her inability to bear children and the reproductive difficulties that awaited her. Indeed, despite her continuing gynecological problems and active movie career, the famous star began to think seriously about having children in the not too distant future. Unlike some actresses who in the days before the birth control pill accepted tubal ligation as the price of success in Hollywood, Monroe rejected such a course. Her desire to become a mother may have been influenced by the fact that her increasing celebrity did not satisfy all her personal needs. In addition, Monroe came of age with the postwar generation of the late 1940s and the 1950s when the "baby boom" was in full swing and motherhood was highly prized in American society. Women shown in newspaper and magazine ads or in television commercials were generally depicted as happy homemakers and mothers—not strivers in the workplace. Childless women were frequently looked down upon in the pro-natalist climate of that period. Perhaps like many other women of her era she thought bearing a child would, in the parlance of the times, make her a "complete woman." Perhaps too she hoped that by having a child of her own she could in part relive her childhood in a more positive way than the one she herself had experienced in various foster homes and in the Los Angeles orphanage. Whenever she talked about raising potential children she always mentioned that she would provide them with much better care than she had ever received. In contrast to what she claimed she felt in the past about being terrified of becoming a mother, she now looked at the idea in a truly favorable manner. "It's one of the things I dream of," she insisted.[24]

Monroe's strong wish for children is well illustrated by an incident that occurred in April 1952, even before she reached full stardom, when she entered Cedars of Lebanon Hospital in Los Angeles in order to have her appendix removed. The attending physician, Dr. Marcus Rabwin, found the following handwritten note taped to her abdomen as she lay there in the operating room awaiting surgery:

Dear Dr. Rabwin,

Cut as little as possible. I know it seems vain but that doesn't really enter into it. The fact that I'm a woman is important and means much to me.

Save please (I can't ask you enough) what you can. I'm in your hands. You have children and you must know what it means, please Dr. Rabwin, I know somehow you will! Thank you—thank you—thank you. For God's sake Dear Doctor. No ovaries removed please, again do whatever you can to prevent large scars.

Thanking you with all my heart.

Marilyn Monroe[25]

Wanting children in the days when unwed motherhood was severely frowned upon probably increased Monroe's desire to get married again. She had had a number of intimate relationships in the previous few years, most notably with a Hollywood voice coach and music director named Fred Karger, and afterwards with her agent Johnny Hyde, but none had succeeded over the long term. Karger, a handsome young man, whom she worked with and seemed to care for a great deal, did not want to marry her, while Hyde, a short and balding man thirty years her senior, who eagerly proposed wedlock, was viewed by her as being too old and unattractive. Moreover, though she liked Hyde and appreciated what he had done for her career, she didn't really love him. Also, in terms of her public image she did not want to be looked upon as a "gold-digger," which might have happened had she become his rich wife and then (since he had a heart condition) his rich widow. As she approached her late twenties Monroe joked about marrying the next available man who asked her.

However, she didn't have to wait long for in late 1952 she started dating former baseball great Joe DiMaggio, and after an extended fourteen-month courtship she agreed to marry the famed "Yankee Clipper" early in 1954. About him she said, "I was surprised to be so crazy about Joe. I expected a flashy New York sports type, and instead I met this reserved guy who didn't make a pass at me right away. . . . He treated me like something special."[26] His strength, stability, business acumen, and large Italian family apparently appealed to her as well. When asked by reporters following the wedding ceremony in San Francisco how many children she wanted, her reply was six (DiMaggio, who had not been an attentive father to his son Joe Jr. in his first marriage, said one). Over the next several months, Monroe received many more queries on the subject of children and always answered in an optimistic manner, saying she wished to start having them soon, so as to give Joe a little "bambino." There would, however, be no child or even a pregnancy during the short period of their stormy marriage, which ended after ten months.

While Monroe and DiMaggio had much in common, especially overcoming poverty and reaching celebrity status in their respective fields, conflicting attitudes about their future together made it difficult for them to remain married. DiMaggio apparently wanted an old-fashioned stay-at-home wife whereas Monroe held different ideas. Though she wished to become a mother and be part of a family, she had no desire to give up her career at this point, as her husband urged her to do. Very traditional in his views about women, the ex-ballplayer had great difficulty accepting Monroe's wish to remain a Hollywood actress. He was ill at ease among the movie people he met, seeing most of them as phonies who were exploiting his wife's talents. DiMaggio was also extremely uncomfortable with the manner in which she sometimes displayed herself in public in revealing attire. Two incidents in particular stand out. He became severely upset with her on their post-wedding trip to the Far East, after she had volunteered to entertain thousands of American soldiers on an outdoor stage in Korea wearing a provocative, low-cut dress. Then, some months later, they quarreled in a very heated fashion after the filming of the famous skirt-blowing scene in *The Seven Year Itch.* (Some reports claim he physically abused her that night.) Shortly thereafter the couple separated and then divorced. While in the early 1960s the two would resume a close friendship and talk seriously about remarriage, that outcome never came to pass.[27]

In the period after leaving DiMaggio, Monroe's gynecological problems continued to worsen, as she suffered increasingly severe pain from endometriosis. She is said to have feared periodic visits to the gynecologist and on occasion asked her friend Amy Greene to accompany her. Describing Monroe's reactions to one of these examinations, Greene declared: "Her whole womb was weeping." After the physician analyzed the actress's condition, he recommended that Monroe consider a hysterectomy. But she recoiled at the idea, summarily rejecting such a drastic alternative. "Marilyn was emphatic," says Greene. "She said, 'I can't do that. I want to have a child. I'm going to have a son.' She always talked of having a son."[28] Interestingly, when she went on shopping trips with Greene and sought to disguise herself to keep away potential crowds, she sometimes wore a large dress with a pillow inserted in order to look pregnant.[29]

At this point Monroe was faced not only with personal problems but had grown increasingly dissatisfied with the progress of her screen career, wanting more complex roles and higher pay. She felt the studio heads at Twentieth Century-Fox were taking advantage of her, casting her in stereotyped parts—as sexy, sweet but not too bright young women—bringing large profits to them and the company stockholders but doing little to adequately compensate her or further develop her acting ability. In response she sought to break her contract with Fox and form an independent film company in partnership with photographer Milton Greene (Amy Greene's husband), with whom she had collaborated on a number of magazine photo shoots. She also moved from Hollywood to New York City, intent on becoming a more serious and respected actress. In New York she began studying acting with noted drama coach, Lee Strasberg and his wife Paula, and attending the Actors Studio, famous for producing new "method" actors such as Marlon Brando and James Dean. In fact, Lee Strasberg later claimed that, other than Brando, Marilyn Monroe possessed the greatest amount of raw talent of any of the young performers he had ever worked with, and, in an unusual step for him, offered to give her private lessons.

In addition to acting classes, Monroe, seeking to better understand herself and cope with the still troubling personal issues she faced, also entered psychoanalysis, first with Dr. Margaret Hohenberg and then with Dr. Marianne Kris, who, along with her late husband Ernst Kris, had been disciples of Sigmund Freud. However, it is not clear that she benefited from the lengthy experience on the couch with either analyst as their focus was primarily on her painful childhood memories—subject matter that she did not want to think about much less talk about. During this time, Monroe returned to Hollywood only briefly in order to make one picture, having negotiated a more favorable contract with Fox, limiting her film appearances and allowing her to have approval over the studio's choice of directors. The movie she made was *Bus Stop* (1956), co-starring Don Murray and directed by Joshua Logan, in which she played another variation of the "dumb blonde," though this time with a poignancy and emotional depth that went beyond her previous roles and won her even greater critical acclaim. In this film especially, she very worked hard to develop her character.[30]

Monroe's desire for perfection and wish to be taken seriously was one of the main reasons for her astounding success as a movie star, but at the same time possibly one of the major causes of her eventual decline. According to screenwriter Ben Hecht, who collaborated with Monroe in the mid-1950s on her never finished autobiography: "her critical taste exceeded her creative abilities. That happens to lots of people out here [in Hollywood]," he wrote. "Writers worship Shakespeare and turn out [television] scripts for *Dr. Kildare*. Actors who admire John Gielgud end up as bit players. But these people usually come to terms with their lives."[31] Marilyn Monroe apparently could not. She pushed herself so hard she got into trouble, often taking on projects that were bound to be stressful. Fights with directors over particular scenes and studio heads over contract provisions eventually took their toll. Perhaps if she could have been more flexible about her goals as a performer she might have been less dissatisfied.

And if she had not been so persistent in the same way about her need to bear a child she might have fared better. But no change in either pattern occurred.

While seeking to become a more serious actress in New York, Monroe developed an intimate relationship with prize-winning playwright Arthur Miller. She hoped to find in him a man who would support and encourage her career aspirations but also serve as a protector and start a family with her. Like her previous husband, he was a decade older than she was, but much more serious and scholarly. Miller, in fact, had emerged as one of the nation's leading public intellectuals and a noted social critic. He was the author of such provocative plays as *Death of a Salesman*, *The Crucible*, and *View from the Bridge*. The press sometimes referred to the couple as "the Egghead and the Hourglass," or, as writer Norman Mailer put it, the union of "the Great American Brain" and "the Great American Body."[32] Miller, who had recently become divorced from his first wife, was truly enchanted by the now famous screen star. "She was simply overwhelming. She had so much promise. It seemed to me that she could really be a great kind of phenomenon, a terrific artist. She was endlessly fascinating, full of original observations, [and] there wasn't a conventional bone in her body."[33] Despite the criticism of some who said they were clearly unsuited for each other, the two were wedded at a friend's house outside New York City in June 1956.

It was during the early stages of her marriage to Miller that Monroe became most encouraged about childbearing. She appears to have conceived for the first time shortly after the wedding in the summer of 1956, but lost the pregnancy a few weeks later upon arriving in England to film *The Prince and the Showgirl* with the celebrated British actor and director Laurence Olivier.[34] Whether the miscarriage was related to the stresses of travel and the preparations for making the movie is unknown. Despite this initial setback, she remained optimistic about her chances for motherhood. When she conceived again in June 1957, about a year after the wedding, she was thrilled and apparently certain that it would all work out well this time. She told an interviewer, "A man and a woman need something of their own. A baby makes a marriage. It makes a marriage perfect."[35] Seeing her pregnant, Arthur Miller noticed that she had acquired "a new kind of confidence, a quietness of spirit [he] had never seen before."[36] Some years later, Monroe showed a friend a picture of herself taken that month and told her, "It was the happiest point of my entire life."[37] Unfortunately, this second pregnancy was also not successful. Within two months, while staying with Miller at a beach bungalow on Long Island, she began to experience excruciating pelvic pain and had to be rushed to a hospital in New York City. She was diagnosed with an ectopic pregnancy (a life-threatening emergency in which the embryo develops inside the fallopian tube) and underwent surgery at the beginning of August to remove the embryo. (A friend, James Haspiel, claimed that Monroe subsequently told him the lost child would have been a boy.[38]) The impact of the loss was naturally devastating. Monroe probably never entirely recovered from this traumatic episode, and, as mentioned earlier, she would die the night before the fifth anniversary of this event. As one biographer, Graham McCann, put it, "Monroe's ectopic pregnancy sent her into a series of self-recriminations; was it her fault or was it fate? There was 'something wrong with her,' something . . . which no promises nor prayers nor pills could correct. The sense of failure cut deep into Monroe's consciousness, and Miller was unable to help her overcome it. . . ."[39]

Despite the painful loss, Marilyn Monroe, after a short period of recovery, was evidently still trying to conceive a child, though it is not clear whether she was successful. Later that year, she wrote the following note to Norman Rosten and his wife Hedda, who had become her close friends, describing her condition:

> I think I've been pregnant for about three weeks or may be
> two. My breast(s) have been too sore to even touch—I've never
> had that in my life before also they ache—also I've been having

cramps and slight staining since Monday—now the staining is increasing and pain is increasing by the minute.

I did not eat all day yesterday—also last night I took 4 whole amutal sleeping pills—which was by actual count really 8 little amutal sleeping pills.

Could I have killed it by taking all the amutal on an empty stomach? (except I took some sherry wine also)

What shall I do?

If it is still alive I want to keep it.[40]

Yet it is somewhat questionable whether Monroe was actually pregnant on this occasion, or just hoping that it was true. This was not the only instance where she may have imagined herself being with child, according to some of those who knew her. "She wanted a baby so much," said dress manufacturer Henry Rosenfeld, a longtime acquaintance, "that she'd convince herself of it every two or three months. She'd gain, maybe fourteen or fifteen pounds. She was forever having false pregnancies."[41]

The actress was also in a quandary about the future of her film career and less happy in the relationship with her husband Arthur Miller. Her maid, Lena Pepitone, described this period of Monroe's existence as being dominated by many hours spent in bed, needing increasing numbers of sleeping pills to fall asleep, and calling for a drink as soon as she woke up. In an attempt to improve her health and overall outlook, the Millers, using mostly Marilyn's funds, bought a three-hundred-acre farm in Connecticut. They built a new wing on the eighteenth-century farmhouse, which she christened "the nursery." Monroe showed a fondness for animals as she took care of her basset hound, adopted a mongrel who wandered into the backyard, built a feeding station for birds, and acquired two talking parakeets. But if she enjoyed some phases of their life in the country, the out-of-work actress continued to be depressed. On one occasion, when back at their apartment in New York City, she took a barbiturate overdose and was found in a coma by Miller and had to be resuscitated by medical personnel. By this time, the marriage was becoming increasingly strained. Miller was growing more and more aloof; he was having difficulty writing and felt exhausted coping with the demands of Monroe's unhealthy state.[42]

Regardless of the status of her marriage and the possible hazards to her well being, Monroe's desire for children remained intense and she continued trying to get pregnant again. By having a baby, her body, she believed, according to biographer Graham McCann, "would at last be her own, since she felt it would exist for the child who belonged to her, a physical exclamation of blood, spirit, and soft, warm flesh. As a mother she hoped to have her existence justified by the wants she would supply."[43] She was someone who loved being with kids and naturally wanted her own child to raise. Arthur Miller once remarked, "To understand Marilyn best, you have to see her around children. They love her; her whole approach to life has their kind of simplicity and directness."[44] Miller's son Robert later echoed his father, saying: "Marilyn was very comfortable about kids. She didn't feel threatened or competitive around them. She was somebody who could get on the floor and play Parcheesi, and we would go bike-riding together."[45]

Norman Rosten also commented on Monroe's great affinity for young people. "Marilyn had enough of the child within her to be acutely conscious of the needs of children. She knew when they were happy or withdrawn; her own childhood taught her that. She was generous with them, especially so with our daughter Patricia. She was always giving her little gifts. The nicest of these was a dog named Cindy. Marilyn had found the animal in the country, starved and barely able to walk. She nursed the dog back to health with the aid of a local veterinarian and gave her to Pat on her birthday."[46] On one visit with the Millers, Patricia discovered the screen star's make-up kit in the family bedroom. Noticing this, Monroe cheerfully responded by offering to apply cosmetics to make the child look much older. "It was an invitation young girls of ten or eleven must dream of then and now and forever. Pat was transfixed," her father wrote.[47] The happy relationship with Patricia and the poems Rosten wrote about his daughter made Monroe, in her thoughts about children, more open to having a girl. (The friendship also influenced Monroe to provide money in her will for Patricia's education.)

The intensity of Marilyn Monroe's longing for children at this point can perhaps best be seen in the following anecdote. Near the Millers' apartment on the Upper East Side of New York City, Monroe developed a friendship with a young Israeli immigrant woman, Dalia Leeds, who brought her baby son to a neighborhood park each day. Leeds later recalled how the famous star dressed in a long coat and dark glasses sometimes sat with her on a bench and "talked mainly about children. She was very curious about being pregnant, about what you fed a child, how you diapered it—everything. . . . We laughed about having six children. She never confided in me about what difficulties she was having, but she very much wanted to have a child. . . . She would play with the kids, hold them in her lap, and they adored having her."[48] The fact that the famed actress asked the woman what it was like being pregnant would seem to cast doubt on the stories of her having born a child as an adolescent.

Another story of Monroe's desire to be a mother at this time comes from her maid Lena Pepitone, who tells of the actress's fondness for her two sons and how she frequently spent part of her afternoons playing with them. Acceding to her request for their company, Pepitone writes: "soon I was picking up Joey and Johnny each day after school, often with Marilyn's chauffeur, to take them to [Monroe's apartment on] Fifty-seventh Street. . . . The boys would stay until five thirty. . . . My boys had a wonderful time at Marilyn's. They would eat in the kitchen, bang on the piano, hide in all the closets, and, most important, play with her. . . . A favorite game for Joey and Johnny was using Marilyn's bed as a trampoline, while she sang them Broadway songs like 'I Get a Kick Out of You.'"[49] Occasionally, on a Sunday, Monroe would accompany the Pepitone family, with husband Joe driving, on automobile rides around the Connecticut countryside. On these trips, the movie star would usually hold little Johnny on her lap and would sometimes say to him as she nuzzled close: "I wish you could be mine." "Me, too," Johnny said, "but I already got a mommy!" "Marilyn hugged him even closer, and smiled bravely," wrote Pepitone, "But I could see that the tears were beginning to flow." She was always reluctant to give up the children and cried at the end of the day as the boys departed, Pepitone added. "Marilyn called both my sons her 'little dolls' and was forever thanking me for 'sharing them' with her. 'It's as close to a mother as I'll ever be now,' she wept."[50]

Obviously Monroe had strong maternal desires. But along with her genuine desire to be a mother, her longing for children may have had a strong component of fantasy, according to Susan Strasberg, daughter of the acting coach. In her account of her relationship with the famed actress in the mid- to late 1950s, *Marilyn and Me: Sisters, Rivals, Friends*, Strasberg wrote: "When Marilyn said she wanted children more than anything, I wondered if it was children or the *idea* of children she loved. She responded to young people, but babies were something else. She'd seemed frightened holding a friend's infant, as if reality intruded on her fantasy. Having a child would validate her as a complete woman in her mind." Strasberg also raises the question as to what kind of mother Monroe would have made, asking whether she would have lived up to the ideal that she created for herself. "Of course she was going to do all the things for her child that had not been done for her. She'd pay attention to it, never send it away, never lock it in a closet. It was strange to hear her talk about being a mother when she seemed such a child herself, but she swore fervently, 'I'd love it to death.'"[51]

During this period, Marilyn Monroe at times debated whether she should live quietly at home and focus all her attention on trying to achieve motherhood rather than returning to Hollywood and the strenuous process of making films. When her maid Lena Pepitone once asked her what she would do about her acting career if she had a child, Monroe smiled broadly and said: "Nothing! If I have kids—a kid—that'll be my life. Maybe later, in a long time, when she grows up, then maybe I might act."[52] The situation became less hypothetical in the second half of 1958, when she was preparing to work on *Some Like It Hot*, and suddenly became pregnant. She wrote to Norman Rosten, "Should I do my next picture or stay home and try to have a baby again? That's what I want most of all, the baby, I guess, but maybe God is trying to tell me something, I mean with my pregnancy." She also admitted, "I'd probably make a kooky mother, I'd love my child to death. I want it, yet I'm scared. Arthur says he wants it, but he's losing his enthusiasm."[53]

In fact, Monroe did proceed with the filming of *Some Like It Hot* in the fall of 1958 while she was pregnant and, unlike the way she handled the situation during *The Prince and the Showgirl*, did not try to keep it a secret. Naturally, she was happy to be in the pregnant state again, and enjoyed performing in some of the film's beach scenes (shot in San Diego) since she thought the sunshine and fresh air would be "great for the baby." Of course, she tried to take special precautions to avoid unnecessary movement and retire early each evening. However, the stress involved in the movie's production seemed at times to overwhelm her. Although she sparkled in her role as Sugar Kane, a struggling singer with an all-girl musical group in this splendid spoof of the gangster era of the 1920s, the actress often arrived on the set hours late and had difficulty remembering her lines. Upsetting clashes with director Billy Wilder and others apparently contributed to her need to consume too much alcohol and take heavy doses of barbiturates to fall asleep. Her gynecologist, Dr. Leon Krohn, who was in attendance much of the time, worried about her condition. As he said afterward: "She often told me how she longed for a child, but I cautioned her that she would kill a baby with the drink and the pills—the effects of those barbiturates accumulated, I told her, and it would be impossible to predict when just one drink will then precipitate a spontaneous abortion."[54] Whatever the reason for it, in December, shortly after the film's completion she suffered another miscarriage.

Although she continued to want children and had surgery six months later to try to improve her chances for motherhood, she would never become pregnant again. Indeed, the strain of successive pregnancy failures was beginning to take its toll on her and on her marriage to Miller, especially in conjunction with the other sources of her distress. The critical and box-office success of *Some Like It Hot*—the most memorable movie of her career—apparently did little to raise her spirits when it was released in the spring of the following year (1959). Nor did an intimate affair with the French actor Yves Montand, her co-star during the production of their less than successful film *Let's Make Love* in the first part of 1960, help much either. As one writer described her personal deterioration by this time: "Her insomnia and addiction to sleeping drugs, her reliance on psychiatric support, and her tardiness on the set were the outward signs of deep problems probably caused by her childhood years of loneliness, the pressures put upon her by the studios and the press, and the way she was exploited by her close associates. Her insatiable ambition also contributed to her decline."[55]

Monroe's growing unhappiness and lack of vitality became most evident in the summer of 1960 throughout the filming of *The Misfits*, the screenplay for which had been written by Arthur Miller with her in mind for the leading role.[56] Although Miller thought he was creating a sympathetic character based on a story he had published showing her love for all living things, Monroe disliked the way she was being portrayed. As in several of her previous films she felt her character (Roslyn) was too shallow and unrealistic. She was also upset that in the script Miller had used her actual words to reveal unflattering details of her private life, and after a while they were hardly speaking to one another. Beyond that, her fragile health was pushed to the limit by working in the heat of the Nevada desert, and on one occasion she was so ill she had to be flown by helicopter to Los Angeles to be hospitalized. Completion of the picture was severely delayed by her absences, her lateness, and her frequent inability to remember her lines before the camera. Director John Huston often had to plead and cajole to get her through her scenes. W. J. Weatherby, feature writer for England's *Manchester Guardian*, visited the Reno film set around the end of September and described the experience as "like standing in a minefield among all those manic-depressive people."[57] *The Misfits* was finally finished a few weeks later though it did not live up to expectations, receiving only lukewarm reviews when it was released the following winter. It also caused tremendous strain on Monroe's fellow actors, one of whom, Clark Gable, suffered a heart attack and died shortly after the filming ended, creating terrible feelings of guilt and a sense of responsibility on her part. Some claim she even considered suicide when she heard what had happened to him. Another casualty was Monroe's marriage to Miller, which officially ended early in 1961. While there were many reasons involved, the fact that she remained childless clearly contributed to the couple's inability to remain together. As Lena Pepitone later wrote: "She did love Mr. Miller, at least at first, but her pregnancy failures seemed to be the ruin of their relationship. They needed a child to hold them together."[58]

During 1961 Monroe did not make any additional films, spending much of her time trying to cope with continuing physical and emotional problems. Early in the year, when the actress was feeling seriously distraught after her divorce, her psychiatrist, Dr. Marianne Kris hospitalized her at the Payne Whitney Psychiatric Clinic in New York City. There, Monroe found herself virtually isolated within a unit meant for psychotic patients and soon seemed on the verge of decompensating. Through the intervention of her former husband, Joe DiMaggio, who threatened to tear down the building brick by brick if he could not secure her release, she was moved to

Columbia-Presbyterian Hospital, where she received better care. Following this second hospitalization, the two then spent much of the early spring together in Florida, as DiMaggio tried to help her regain her equilibrium. But ultimately they parted with Monroe still not in the best of health. In May 1961, after suffering from severe uterine bleeding, she underwent gynecological surgery in Los Angeles, which revealed blocked fallopian tubes. A few weeks later, on June 1, her thirty-fifth birthday, Monroe had gall bladder surgery at the Polyclinic Hospital in New York, her fifth hospital admission in ten months. Afterwards she returned to Los Angeles, seeking to live a quieter existence, and made arrangements to be treated for her emotional problems by psychoanalyst Ralph Greenson, M.D., whom she had seen sporadically over the previous couple of years, and now would see on a regular basis until the time of her death.

Indeed, Dr. Greenson would be the man most deeply involved in Monroe's day-to-day existence during her last year of life. Throughout this period she often saw him for therapy five or six times a week, hoping he could reverse her downward spiral and restore her health and dwindling self-esteem. A founding member of the Los Angeles Psychoanalytic Society and a colleague of Anna Freud, Greenson had dealt professionally with many Hollywood celebrities over the years. A popular lecturer as well as a therapist, Greenson believed in emotional involvement with patients as a way of establishing a reliable therapeutic relationship. He also thought that Monroe was not a candidate for psychoanalysis, given the severity of her psychological problems. To give Monroe, who had no family, a sense of stability, Greenson believed it would be beneficial to bring her into his home and make her one of his family. As a result, Monroe frequently had dinner at the Greensons after her therapy sessions, and befriended the doctor's wife and adolescent children. (Greenson's daughter Joan sometimes served as chauffeur for the star, who in return gave her presents and once threw her a big birthday party.) It was Dr. Greenson, too, who influenced Monroe to buy a house for herself, partly as a means to keep her occupied, seeing it in a way as providing a substitute for children. He also recommended a housekeeper for her, Eunice Murray, whom it is said, kept Greenson informed of the actress's activities on days he didn't see her for therapy. Greenson wrote to his colleague and friend Anna Freud on December 4, 1961:

> I took over the treatment of a patient that Marianne Kris had been treating for several years, and she has turned out to be a very sick borderline paranoid addict, as well as an actress. You can imagine how terribly difficult it is to treat someone with such severe problems and who is also a great celebrity and completely alone in the world. Psychoanalysis is out of the question and I improvise, often wondering where I am going, and yet have nowhere else to turn. If I succeed, I will have learned something, but it takes a tremendous amount of time and also emotion.[59]

At the outset, Monroe seems to have liked Greenson's personal style of treatment and at one point told him that after she was cured "maybe he could adopt her—to be the father she had always wanted. And his wife Hildi, would be her mother, and the Greenson children would be her brother and sister."[60] While his treatment plan would have appealed to her lifelong unmet needs for family and belonging, it is not clear that in taking this ultra-personal approach Greenson was very effective in improving Monroe's overall stability and confidence in the long run. Her friend and masseur, Ralph Roberts, said that she soon came to resent the psychiatrist's controlling manner, especially his trying to isolate her from almost everyone else in her life. In fact, some later critics claim that rather than helping her become better able to operate on her own, his efforts made her more dependent than ever. There are also assertions that the drugs he prescribed for her may have contributed to her death.[61]

Although warned by Dr. Greenson about her intimate involvement with powerful men who would simply use her, Monroe at some point in

1961 started an ongoing affair with President John F. Kennedy, whom she met briefly thereafter from time to time. It culminated in her controversial public appearance at Madison Square Garden in New York the following year, where in a revealing gauzy dress she sang "Happy Birthday" to the President in an overtly sexual manner. She also allegedly had a brief relationship with the President's brother Robert Kennedy, the Attorney General, in the last months of her life, though certain recent biographers deny they were ever intimate. Some conspiracy theorists, on the other hand, are convinced that the affair was intense and passionate. They speculate that she and Robert Kennedy were together at her home on the day she died and had a bitter argument just hours before her death. A few even claim his associates gave her a lethal injection, in order to prevent her from exposing her secret relationship with the Kennedy brothers and revealing classified information. Invariably, critics of the various conspiracy theories reject the idea that RFK was even in Los Angeles that day and believe that any government plot to have her murdered is completely absurd.[62] Regardless of the extent of her intimacy with the Kennedy brothers, these associations were probably one-sided on her part, and ultimately had a harmful emotional effect.

Interestingly, even around some of the Kennedys, Monroe's thoughts appear to have drifted to the subject of children. Through her connection with the Kennedy family on the West Coast, she spent a good deal of time in the company of their brother-in-law Peter Lawford and his wife Patricia Kennedy Lawford on visits to their Santa Monica beach house. Mrs. Lawford later confided that "Marilyn seemed haunted by her childlessness, asking endless questions about my children and all the Kennedy children." She seemed particularly interested in Jacqueline Kennedy's childbearing experiences, which had included a number of miscarriages. Peter Lawford sometimes found Monroe looking around the playroom, "silently admiring my children's toys and books."[63] (Lawford was apparently one of the last persons to speak to her the night she died, with her communicating to him on the telephone in a fading voice: "Say goodbye to Pat, say goodbye to the president, say goodbye to yourself, because you're a nice guy.")[64]

Children were evidently still on her mind in other ways in what turned out to be the last months of her life in mid-1962. In an interview with a reporter from *Redbook* magazine, she talked about being in close touch with her stepchildren, Joe DiMaggio, Jr., and Robert and Jane Miller, and how important they were to her. "I take a lot of pride in them. Because they're from broken homes too, and I think I can understand them. I've always said to them that I didn't want to be their mother or stepmother and such . . . I just wanted to be their friend. . . . I can't explain it, but I think I love them more than I love anyone."[65] In her last published interview in the early summer of 1962, one of the questions asked was what she wished for more than anything else in life. "I want to have children," she replied enthusiastically. "I used to feel for every child I had I would adopt another," she added, sounding something like the African-American entertainer Josephine Baker, who adopted twelve. "But," she went on, "I don't think a single person should adopt children. There's no Ma or Pa there, and I know what that can be like."[66] The reference to adoption would seem to imply that the actress was seriously thinking about the possibility of proceeding in that direction. In fact, sometime earlier that year, Monroe had visited an orphanage in Mexico, perhaps looking at potential adoptees. While observing the facility, apparently she became distressed with the conditions in which the children were living. In response, she wrote out a check to the overseers for a thousand dollars, then tore it up and instead made a contribution of ten thousand dollars.

While thinking about children and trying to cope with her personal problems, Monroe, in the early spring of 1962, also went back to work in Hollywood at Fox studios starring in a film to be called, ironically, *Something's Got to Give*. This was the first film of her career in which she played the role of a mother, and one of the bright spots for the actress was being around the two young children in the cast. But the making of the picture would be marred by her health-related absences and her lack of cooperation on the set. Her behavioral difficulties even led her psychiatrist Dr. Greenson to cut short a family vacation abroad in order to try to resolve the situation.[67] For their part, the bosses at Fox were not very enthusiastic about this particular film project, which was hampered by delays and not expected to be very profitable. After her trip to New York for President Kennedy's birthday party in May, Monroe was dismissed by the studio for having appeared on the set only twelve days during the first month of shooting. Although after some weeks of negotiations she was subsequently reinstated to finish the picture, there would be no happy ending. Monroe was found dead of a drug overdose in her Brentwood home in the early morning hours of Sunday August 5th before the filming had actually resumed.[68]

The immediate reaction of the American people to the news of Monroe's death was one of shock. How could the celebrated movie star, who seemed to have everything to live for, be dead of an apparent suicide? How could one of the most desired women in the world die alone on a Saturday night? Few knew much about her recent personal difficulties, but the public felt a profound sadness. Her funeral was a small, private affair hurriedly arranged by former husband Joe DiMaggio, with most of the press and people associated with the film industry barred. They, along with the Kennedys, were seen by DiMaggio as being primarily responsible for her demise, and only a limited number of friends and relatives were invited to attend. In his eulogy, Lee Strasberg, Monroe's friend and mentor, after dwelling on the tragedy of her early death, declared: "She had a luminous quality—a combination of wistfulness, radiance, yearning, that set her apart and yet made everyone wish to be part of it, to share in the childlike naiveté which was at once so shy and yet so vibrant."[69]

There has, of course, been a great deal of debate about how Marilyn Monroe felt in the last months, weeks, and days of her life. Was she truly on a downward spiral, feeling increasingly unhappy, and drifting irrevocably toward suicide? Or, was she at last moving ahead and taking control of her existence, but somehow died accidentally from a drug overdose, improperly administered? The authors of many of the early books written about the actress generally take the first approach. They see only a step-by-step decline resulting from her anxiety-filled experiences making movies, along with her troubled relationships with men, leading to greater drug dependence and depression, and ultimately to a self-inflicted death. More recently, biographer Donald Spoto, after interviewing many of her former friends, has argued the second position, claiming that her life was actually improving, and that far from being depressed and hopeless, she was starting to have a more positive outlook. She was, he said, looking forward not only to completing *Something's Got to Give*, but thinking about future projects. She had, in fact, recently traveled to Palm Springs together with Hollywood columnist Sidney Skolsky to talk with Jean Harlow's mother about the idea of making a film based on the life of the late actress. In addition, according to Spoto's sources, she was planning to remarry Joe DiMaggio. In the last weeks of her life, said her makeup man, Whitey Snyder, she radiated charm and good health. She had lost fifteen pounds and ordered a fancy new dress, allegedly for the wedding, just three days before she died. Even Dr. Greenson wrote that she was "feeling fine" in those final weeks and thought her death was caused by an accidental overdose.[70]

On August 20, 1962 Dr. Greenson wrote the following to Anna Freud in response to a note of sympathy she had written him regarding Monroe's death:

> It was so nice of you to write me with such understanding. This
> has been a terrible blow in many ways. I cared about her and
> she was my patient. She was so pathetic and she had had such a
> terrible life. I had hopes for her and I thought we were making
> progress. And now she died and I realize that all my knowledge
> and my desire and my strength was not enough. God knows I

tried and mightily so, but I could not defeat all the destructive forces that had been stirred up in her by the terrible experiences of her past life, and even of her present life. Sometimes I feel the world wanted her to die, or at least many people in the world, particularly those who after her death so conspicuously grieved and mourned. It makes me angry. But above all I feel sad and also disappointed. It is not just a blow to my pride, although I am sure that is present, but also a blow to my science of which I consider myself a good representative. . . .[71]

But even if one accepts the idea that Monroe was making progress and about to change her life for the better, one wonders whether she could have altered her long-standing behavioral patterns, given her history of strained relationships with men and dependence on alcohol, analgesics, and sleeping medications. There is the question about whether she could ever have been at ease with her career and the process of making movies; practically every film she made, especially in her last years, caused her deep personal stress and anxiety. Rarely did she see eye-to-eye with any of her directors, and the degree of conflict seemed to be getting worse with each new production. At the same time, she had little desire to walk away from the spotlight. Even though Monroe sometimes talked about leaving Hollywood permanently and living with a strong male protector and being just a housewife, part of her loved being a star and at the center of public attention. "I have too much fantasy to be only a housewife," she reflected toward the end of her life. As an actress she had a strong desire to prove herself and show she could play other roles besides being "a dumb blonde." She had, in fact, at times left the limelight and lived out in the country with Arthur Miller but was not especially content during those times either. One can also ask whether having a child in her life would have made a difference. If she had followed through and adopted a child would that have changed her life? Would she have recovered from drug dependency and improved her overall health if she had taken on the responsibility of providing day-to-day child care? Would she have kept her composure in dealing with the multiple problems that child rearing entails? Would the kinds of conflicts she always had with men have diminished in a broader family situation? Unfortunately, we can never know the answers to these questions.

Although Marilyn Monroe died more than four decades ago in 1962, she has remained a strong presence in our culture. Never really disappearing from sight, she is better known than most current movie stars and more recognizable than virtually any woman in history. Her movies have been the subject of many retrospectives. *Some Like It Hot* was recently voted the greatest film comedy ever made by a panel of movie experts, and Monroe was chosen as the most notable female entertainer of the second half of the twentieth century. There is a constant flow of books and documentary films about her, and Marilyn Monroe memorabilia continue to bring high prices at auctions. The fact that she died so young and under mysterious conditions is only part of the reason for her ongoing fame. She made a major impression on the American psyche with her combination of sexuality, innocence, and vulnerability. One wonders whether she would have had such a mystique if she lived a longer life and if she had at last become a mother.

Monroe, clearly the most famous of all our subjects, was the only who died well before menopause. As such, she had the least opportunity during her lifetime to integrate her talents with her wishes for nurturing and to find a broader expression for her generativity. Her concern for the next generation is clear from her relationships with the young people in her life and her generosity to children's welfare causes in general. Monroe's face, prominent around the globe today, is frozen in time, forever young, smiling, and alluring. The sexual presence she is remembered for is disconnected from what she repeatedly verbalized was most important to her, having a child. Praised for her body and her talent, she felt a sense of failure in both creating a family and living up to her own standards of performance. Her sexuality attracted attention and fame but never brought the long-term sense of belonging that she craved her entire life. As she stated in her last interview, a "sex symbol becomes a thing. I just hate to be a thing."[72]

NOTES

[1] Norman Rosten, *Marilyn: An Untold Story* (New York: NAL/Signet, 1973), 46-47.

[2] Anthony Summers, *Goddess: The Secret Lives of Marilyn Monroe* (New York: Macmillan, 1985), 21.

[3] Summers, *Goddess*, 172. Some writers point out that she took the medication causing her demise on the previous night, August 4th, and may have actually died before midnight though she was not officially pronounced dead until the early morning hours of August 5th.

[4] Quoted in Donald Spoto, *Marilyn Monroe: The Biography* (New York: HarperCollins, 1993), 544. For a list of the charitable causes Monroe contributed to, see Adam Victor, *The Marilyn Encyclopedia* (Woodstock, NY: The Overlook Press, 1999), 52.

[5] On her childhood, see Marilyn Monroe, *My Story* (New York: Stein & Day, 1974), chap. 1-3; Fred Lawrence Guiles, *Norma Jeane: The Life of Marilyn Monroe* (New York: McGraw-Hill, 1969), part 1; Spoto, *Marilyn Monroe*, chap. 2-4, and J. Randy Taraborelli, *The Secret Life of Marilyn Monroe* (New York: Grand Central Publishing, 2009).

[6] Regarding child abuse, see George Barris, *Marilyn: Her Life in Her Own Words* (New York: Birch Lane Press, 1995), 23-24; Monroe, *My Story*, 20-21; Sarah Churchwell, *The Many Lives of Marilyn Monroe* (New York: Henry Holt, 2004), 156-63.

[7] Monroe, *My Story*, 15.

[8] On her first marriage, see Monroe, *My Story*, 30-31; James Dougherty, *The Secret Happiness of Marilyn Monroe* (Chicago: Playboy Press, 1976); Spoto, *Marilyn Monroe*, chap. 5. The quotations come from the Spoto book and are found on 78, 79, 81.

[9] Quoted in Spoto, *Marilyn Monroe*, 82.

[10] On her mood swings, see Spoto, *Marilyn Monroe*, 82-83.

[11] Monroe, *My Story*, 30-31.

[12] Quoted in Spoto, *Marilyn Monroe*, 86.

[13] Spoto, *Marilyn Monroe*, 96.

[14] Crank stories about individuals claiming to be Monroe's child are recorded in Victor, *Marilyn Encyclopedia*, 54. Perhaps the most absurd tale connected to this subject is put forth by Donald H. Wolfe, *The Last Days of Marilyn Monroe* (New York: William Morrow, 1998), 204-5, where the author implies that the father of the alleged child born in 1948 was John F. Kennedy, a man she seems not to have met before 1960.

[15] Lena Pepitone, *Marilyn Monroe Confidential: An Intimate Personal Account* (New York: Simon and Schuster, 1979), 85-87.

[16] Summers, *Goddess*, 23.

[17] On her gynecological problems, see Summers, *Goddess*, 23; Spoto, *Marilyn Monroe*, 297,401.

[18] Spoto, *Marilyn Monroe*, 146.

[19] Cari Beauchamp, "The Secret Life of Marilyn Monroe," *Women's Sports and Fitness* 1 (July-August 1998): 118-23.

[20] On her early movie career and quest for success, see Spoto, *Marilyn Monroe*, 110-201.

[21] Spoto, *Marilyn Monroe*, 195.

[22] On her reaching stardom, see Spoto, *Marilyn Monroe*, chap. 12.

[23] Monroe, *My Story*, 116.

[24] Monroe, *My Story*, 31.

[25] Quoted in Spoto, *Marilyn Monroe*, 218-19.

[26] Quoted in Victor, *Marilyn Encyclopedia*, 77. For a fuller version of their meeting, see Monroe, *My Story*, 126-31.

[27] For the relationship between DiMaggio and Monroe, see Roger Kahn, *Joe and Marilyn: A Memory of Love* (New York: William Morrow, 1986), and Richard Ben Cramer, *Joe DiMaggio: The Hero's Life* (New York: Simon and Schuster, 2000).

[28] Summers, *Goddess*, 123.

[29] Norman Mailer, *Marilyn: A Biography* (New York: Grosset and Dunlap, 1973), 133.

[30] On her move to New York and new relationship she arranged with Fox studios in the mid-1950s, see Spoto, *Marilyn Monroe*, chap. 14-15.

[31] Quoted in Kahn, *Joe and Marilyn*, 235. On the theme of her perfectionism, see Barbara Leaming, *Marilyn Monroe* (New York: Crown Publishers, Inc., 1998).

[32] Mailer, *Marilyn*, 157.

[33] Spoto, *Marilyn Monroe*, 319.

[34] On this first pregnancy, see Spoto, *Marilyn Monroe*, 375-76, though some sources dismiss this as just a rumor.

[35] Quoted in Summers, *Goddess*, 172.

³⁶ Arthur Miller, *Timebends: A Life* (New York: Grove Press, 1987), 457.

³⁷ Quoted in Summers, *Goddess*, 172.

³⁸ Summers, *Goddess*, 172.

³⁹ Graham McCann, *Marilyn Monroe* (New Brunswick, NJ: Rutgers University Press, 1988), 151.

⁴⁰ Rosten, *Marilyn*, 72.

⁴¹ Quoted in Summers, *Goddess*, 23.

⁴² On this period, see Summers, *Goddess*, 173-75; Spoto, *Marilyn Monroe*, 393-96.

⁴³ McCann, *Marilyn Monroe*, 148.

⁴⁴ Quoted in McCann, *Marilyn Monroe*, 149.

⁴⁵ Deborah Solomon, "Goodbye (Again), Norma Jean," *New York Times Magazine*, September 19, 2004, 65.

⁴⁶ Rosten, *Marilyn*, 47.

⁴⁷ Rosten, *Marilyn*, 47-48.

⁴⁸ Quoted in Gloria Steinem, *Marilyn* (New York: Henry Holt, 1986), 86-87.

⁴⁹ Pepitone, *Marilyn Monroe Confidential*, 121.

⁵⁰ Pepitone, *Marilyn Monroe Confidential*, 122.

⁵¹ Susan Strasberg, *Marilyn and Me: Sisters, Rivals, Friends* (New York: Warner Books, 1992), 125.

⁵² Pepitone, *Marilyn Monroe Confidential*, 109.

[53] Quoted in Summers, *Goddess*, 180.

[54] Quoted in Spoto, *Marilyn Monroe*, 401.

[55] Albert F. McLean, "Marilyn Monroe," *Dictionary of American Biography*, Supplement 7 (New York: Charles Scribner's Sons, 1981), 546.

[56] On the filming of *The Misfits*, see Spoto, *Marilyn Monroe*, 429-47.

[57] Quoted in Summers, *Goddess*, 195.

[58] Pepitone, *Marilyn Monroe Confidential*, 123.

[59] Letter from Ralph Greenson to Anna Freud, December 4, 1969, Anna Freud Papers, Box 37, Folder 10, Library of Congress, Washington, D.C.

[60] Cramer, *Joe DiMaggio*, 405.

[61] On Greenson, see Spoto, *Marilyn Monroe*, 421-29.

[62] On Monroe and the Kennedys, see Summers, *Goddess*, 209-97, which claims that both the President and Attorney-General had ongoing intimate relations with the actress, and Spoto, *Marilyn Monroe*, 486-93, 560-63, 599-611, which minimizes her personal involvement with each of them. A recent biography, Evan Thomas, *Robert Kennedy* (New York: Simon and Schuster, 2000), 191-93, 428-29, also questions whether the Attorney-General was ever sexually intimate with Monroe, stating that there is nothing in the FBI files on the matter. But Cramer, *Joe DiMaggio*, 405, prints the transcript of Monroe's session with her psychiatrist where she talks about a personal relationship.

[63] On Monroe's visits to the Lawford home, see Peter H. Brown and Patte B. Barham, *Marilyn: The Last Take* (New York: Dutton, 1992), 105.

[64] Quoted in Spoto, *Marilyn Monroe*, 571.

[65] Interview in *Redbook*, quoted in Victor, *Marilyn Encyclopedia*, 54.

[66] Quoted in Steinem, *Marilyn*, 42.

[67] Letter from Ralph Greenson to Anna Freud, June 11, 1962, Box 37, Folder 10, Anna Freud Papers, Library of Congress.

[68] Spoto, *Marilyn Monroe*, chap. 21-23.

[69] Quoted in Strasberg, *Marilyn and Me*, 260.

[70] On her alleged plan to remarry DiMaggio, see Spoto, *Marilyn Monroe*, 549, 555.

[71] Letter from Ralph Greenson to Anna Freud, August 20, 1962, Box 37, Folder 10, Anna Freud Papers, Library of Congress.

[72] Richard Meryman, "Marilyn Monroe: The Last Interview," *Life*, August 17, 1962, 72.

INDEX

CPSIA information can be obtained at www.ICGtesting.com
Printed in the USA
243747LV00003B/1/P